THE PLANNING GAME

THE
PLANNING GAME
LESSONS FROM GREAT CITIES

ALEXANDER GARVIN

W. W. Norton & Company

NEW YORK · LONDON

For information about permission to reproduce selections from this book, write to
Permissions, W. W. Norton & Company, Inc., 500 Fifth Avenue, New York, NY 10110

For information about special discounts for bulk purchases, please contact W. W. Norton
Special Sales at specialsales@wwnorton.com or 800-233-4830

Manufacturing by KHL Printing Co.Pte Ltd
Book design by Jonathan D. Lippincott

Library of Congress Cataloging-in-Publication Data
Garvin, Alexander.
    The planning game : lessons from great cities / Alexander Garvin. — First Edition.
        pages   cm
    Includes bibliographical references and index.
    ISBN 978-0-393-73344-0 (hardcover)
1. City planning—Case studies. I. Title.
    HT167.G37 2012
    307.1'216--dc23

                                                                                2012013068

ISBN: 978-0-393-73344-0

W. W. Norton & Company, Inc., 500 Fifth Avenue, New York, N.Y. 10110
www.wwnorton.com
W. W. Norton & Company Ltd., Castle House, 75/76 Wells Street, London W1T 3QT

2 4 6 8 0 9 7 5 3 1

CONTENTS

Market Street, Philadelphia (2010).

ACKNOWLEDGMENTS

I met Edmund Bacon, the primary player in chapter 7, in the fall of 1996. I knew right away that I wanted to write about him and his extraordinary role as the planner of modern Philadelphia. For the next nine years I traveled four or five times a year to spend the day with Ed, walk around Philadelphia while discussing his work, and soak up his insights into the planning process. His influence on my work as a planner and my writings about planning cannot be overstated.

Other individuals who have contributed to this book include thousands of students who played simulated planning games of my invention during the more than four decades I have taught at Yale. Thousands more have been involved in real-life planning in New York, Georgia, Tennessee, Texas, Florida, Nebraska, and Maryland. I thank them for what they taught me about planning neighborhoods, cities, suburbs, and metropolitan regions. It is their cumulative wisdom that is the backbone of this book.

Bob Bruegmann and Rick Rubens, two friends with very different views of planning, have provided me with the support, counsel, and criticism that every author needs. Bob told me to drop the "great players" approach; Rick encouraged me to make it more prominent: their contrary advice has helped me to place in proper perspective the contributions to planning of the four great figures featured in this book: Georges-Eugène Haussmann, Daniel Burnham, Robert Moses, and Edmund Bacon.

I am indebted to Joshua Price, who helped to create the many original maps, plans, and diagrams that explain the story that the text alone could not tell.

I discussed parts of this book with Matthew Goldstein, Lance and Carol Liebman, David McGregor, Joe Rose, Jim Schroder, Robert A. M. Stern, Ryan Salvatore, and all my teaching assistants at Yale. Among the individuals whom I consulted for chapter 2 are Charles Newman, Genie Birch, and mayor Joe Riley (Charleston, South Carolina), and former mayors William Hudnut (Indianapolis), Glenda Hood (Orlando, Florida), and Manny Diaz (Miami); for chapter 3: Bruce Alexander, Jane Thompson, Matt Jacobs, my brother George Garvin, John Alschuler, Arthur M. Coppola (chairman and CEO of the Macerich Company), and Randy Brant (executive vice president.); for chapter 5: Dennis McClendon; for chapter 6: Tim Mennel, Owen Gutfriend, Jack Bronston, and John T. Olds (Robert Moses's grandson); for chapter 7: Greg Heller, John Meigs, and Paul Levy; and Zak Snider for his work on the site plan of Society Hill. I thank all of them. Any mistakes, however, are entirely my own.

The book itself would not have come into being without Arthur Klebanoff, my long time agent, and Nancy Green, the best advisor-editor any author could ever hope for. The text itself has been immeasurably improved by editor Rachel Abram and copyeditor Fred Wiemer. The wonderful layout is by Jonathan Lippincott.

Public meeting, DeKalb County, Georgia (2007).

ONE

THE PLANNING GAME:
AN INTRODUCTION

Somebody is always trying to change things. Every day, city and state agencies, chambers of commerce, private developers, and local citizens propose ideas to improve our cities and suburbs. Not all of these ideas will result in change; it is the process we know as planning that determines, to a large extent, which projects succeed and which ones fail to change our communities. Planning brings together the forces of government, business, finance, politics, and public opinion (and all the individuals who represent them) in order to produce change.

I have been thinking about the planning process for as long as I can remember. In September 1967, I was preparing the second class of my teaching career. I intended to discuss how commercial development is shaped by a range of players: lenders, brokers, small tenants, anchor tenants, bureaucrats, community leaders, elected officials, developers, architects, engineers, lawyers, etc., and I wondered how I could possibly make this interesting to a room of Yale undergraduates. The answer lay in the characteristics of the planning process itself. I turned the class into a game in which students played the roles of people and institutions engaged in designing and financing a shopping center.

For two hours the classroom buzzed with

negotiations, strategy sessions, posturing, anger, and delight. By the end of the class the students had worked out a deal, a site plan, and even some leases. The better students anticipated that there would be opposition to the changes they were trying to make, and these students either adjusted their activities to avoid opposition or devised strategies to minimize or overcome their opponents. The students learned to consider very carefully possible consequences—including unfortunate ones—before deciding how to proceed. By the time the class was finished, they had learned not only how shopping centers are developed, but, more important, how competition, entrepreneurship, and skill operate at the very heart of our market-driven economy. Since then thousands of students have played planning games of my devising that deal with housing, zoning, neighborhood revitalization, and many other issues that involve planners. Every year a new group of students reinforces my initial observation that the planning process resembles a game.

Like chess, baseball, or any other game, the planning game has players who devise actions and strategies that culminate in tangible results; and, like other games, it has winners, losers, and also-rans. Unlike those games, however, the planning game has very serious long-range consequences. It affects people as individuals and also the larger environment in which they live. Planning often brings hardship; it can damage lives and hurt innocent bystanders. And, unlike other games, planning involves a huge number of people with different roles and objectives, for whom winning may mean very different things. At any one time the players may include community groups, civic organizations, elected and appointed public officials, bankers, lawyers, architects, engineers, dreamers, reformer-critics, developers, privately owned businesses and utility companies, cultural institutions, etc. The list is endless. Most of these participants do not call themselves, or even think of themselves, as planners. *But they are.*

Less than six months after I introduced the planning game to my classroom, I was asked to help devise a plan to preserve Bushwick, a poverty-stricken neighborhood in Brooklyn that was literally burning down. Advocacy planning was an idea sweeping the planning profession,[1] and I thought this was my chance to fight for a needy neighborhood. But my dreams of being an advocate planner soon hit a brick wall; I owned no property, was unable to finance anything personally, and had no authority to act on anybody's behalf. I was unable to get things done on my own. The reality in Bushwick was very different from the games I had invented for my students. In the real world, I was unable to assign roles to the necessary government players. Instead, I expected that government, vaguely conceived, would bring about the changes I thought were desirable.

In fact, government is always an active player in the planning game, regulating what and how things get done, offering inducements to other players to take actions that it considers desirable, and most important, making public investments. Public officials often prefer regulations and incentives to investments because they require no budget appropriations. But regulations simply bring certain present or future activities under government control; they do not necessarily generate action.

An example will make clear the limitations of government regulation. In 1931 the City of Charleston, South Carolina, enacted the nation's first regulations for "the preservation and protection of the old historic or architecturally worthy structures and quaint neighborhoods."[2] Despite these groundbreaking regulations, the charming antebellum structures in Charleston's Ansonborough neighborhood continued to deteriorate over the next four decades, until many of them had been abandoned. Regulation had failed to prevent the decay and abandonment of lovely old buildings that the citizens of Charleston believed merited preservation. Direct action was the best way to protect these properties—and that action did not come from the government.

In 1972 the Historic Charleston Founda-

Ansonborough, Charleston, South Carolina (1975 and 2011). The ongoing efforts of the Historic Charleston Foundation led to the revitalization of the Ansonborough neighborhood.

tion, a not-for-profit preservation organization, began a program that revitalized the Ansonborough neighborhood. The foundation took direct action in a number of ways. It acquired and demolished seven buildings that were incompatible with the rest of the neighborhood. It bought 58 other structures, of which it moved 4, rehabilitated 8, and sold the rest to new owners, who agreed to restore the buildings. It persuaded local banks to provide the mortgages, and by 1980 the neighborhood had been restored.[3]

As the experience of Charleston demonstrates, changing things is always easier by direct action. However, since no change-oriented entity, public or private, has enough money to pay for everything, effective players try to make what they believe are the most cost-effective expenditures. The desire for cost-effective spending provides the rationale for planning.

Cost effectiveness in planning is not only a matter of purchasing high-quality goods and services at low prices; it is also determined by the impact the expenditures make. In 1919, Walter Moody, the Chicago Plan Commission's first managing director, explained this better than anyone has done since. Planning, he said, is "a simple, common-sense procedure to make conditions more livable" by investing in "public improvements" with intelligence and "foresight," rather than in a "haphazard," uncoordinated manner.[4] Moody did not believe that every program of public improvements could be called planning. He pointed out that "a street widening unrelated to any other improvement or purpose" or a civic center created without reference to everything else in the city was not the result of planning. He called that sort of development "unplanning."[5]

The changes that result from planning must meet the demand for greater livability in the present. But if they are to be sustainable, they must accomplish other things as well. They must generate a private-market reaction, provide a framework for continuing changes in the future, and be adaptable so they can meet unexpected demands in the future. A century

ago Charles Wacker, the Chicago Plan Commission's first chairman, explained that genuine planning "fosters city growth by making it easier and cheaper to conduct all classes of business; increases and insures all property values by preventing many evils of haphazard building; makes every citizen a more efficient worker by saving time and money in transit of goods and people."[6]

This book presents a fresh look at planning, drawn from over forty years of practicing and teaching in the field. It reflects my current opinions on the planning game, and especially on the universality of the planning process. Chapter 2 surveys the wide array of players who participate in the planning game. Despite the serious nature of planning, affecting as it does people's communities, their daily lives, and their general well-being, most participants in the planning game—even those who are among its most successful players—own no property, finance nothing personally, and are not engaged in executing public works. They inspire, persuade, cajole, goad, and do whatever else is necessary to get others to bring their ideas to reality.

Chapter 3 considers the economic and political rules that govern the planning process. They provide the context within which the players operate, and the rules continually adjust to changes in supply and demand, shifting political objectives, and changes in the configuration of players. The chapter shows how the planning process is affected by those basic rules and by changes made to them.

While the first three chapters are illustrated with examples, some of them quite extensive, I devote four chapters, one chapter per city, to the elements of planning as seen through the experiences of Paris, Chicago, New York, and Philadelphia. Much has been written about these four cities. In revisiting them this book will demonstrate the universality of the planning process, and it will cast a different light on familiar stories.

The focus of most of the book is on the *public realm approach* to planning—an approach that emphasizes the importance of public invest-

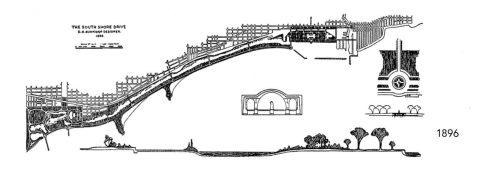

1896

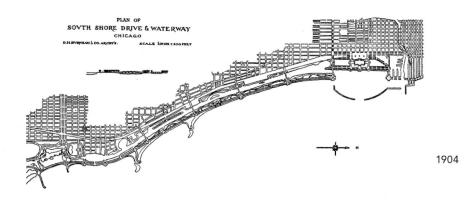

1904

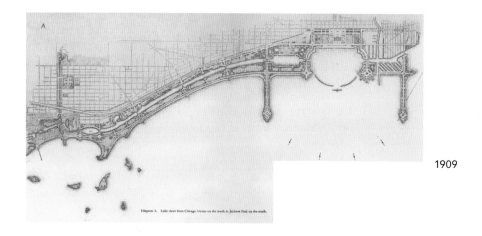

1909

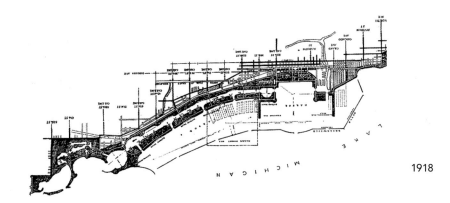

1918

1892

2010

OPPOSITE AND ABOVE: Chicago Lakefront. Daniel Burnham presented the city with a vision of its future lakefront. He and the Chicago Plan Commission kept adjusting the vision to better information and changing conditions until it was transformed into a splendid complex of parks, beaches, boat harbors, and drives.

ments in determining the future of what we own and control: our streets, squares, parks, infrastructure, and public buildings. This is our common property. It is the fundamental element in any community—the framework around which everything else grows. Cities that adopt the public realm approach to planning make it easier and cheaper to do business, make their citizens, in Wacker's words, "more efficient workers by saving time and money in transit of goods and people," and improve the quality of life of their residents. By combining public investments into a coherent agenda, they provide the leverage for capturing and guiding private investment to operate in the public interest while, in the process, improving whole neighborhoods, districts, cities, and even regions.

An agenda of this sort is not a wish list of things it might be nice to have, setting aside consideration of priorities or feasibility. It consists of actions that can and will be taken; otherwise there will be no change. This book argues that the only planning that matters is planning that is entirely implementation oriented.

Every chapter of this book discusses design. There are no commonly accepted rules that determine the design of neighborhoods, cities, or regions. Design is always subject to controversy. Important figures, such as Le Corbusier and Jane Jacobs, disagreed completely on matters of design. Philadelphia's foremost planner, Edmund Bacon, stopped working with the city's foremost architect, Louis Kahn, because he disagreed with Kahn's approach to design, which he dismissed as putting "a little tower here . . . a nice curving stairway there and a bunch of trees there."[7] Given such widespread disagreement, and despite the importance of design to successful planning, it is impossible to identify common rules of design that apply in every situation, at every time, in every location.

Chapters 4 through 7 discuss the public realm approach to planning, the planning process and its implementation, and the role of the planner. Each chapter is devoted to a different city (Paris, Chicago, New York, and Philadel-phia) and to the remarkably universal planning process that changed them fundamentally. In each case, planning met needs that were specific to the city. In nineteenth-century Paris and twentieth-century Chicago, planning helped the cities to meet the requirements of a modern commercial-industrial economy and the demands of their residents. The planning strategies chosen in New York between 1920 and 1960 assumed that the best way to continue to grow as an international economic powerhouse was to foster the suburbanization of a large portion of the labor force, while improving the quality of life within the city itself. Philadelphia adopted a strategy similar to New York's when it came to accommodating metropolitan growth: it built highways to promote the growth of suburbs. But while suburbanization depleted the labor force in both cities, New York's labor force was replenished by immigration from abroad and from other parts of the country. Philadelphia's was not, and it was, therefore, far more deeply affected by deindustrialization. But Philadelphia managed to save itself. Unlike many other American cities that experienced a similar combination of suburbanization of its middle class and deindustrialization of its economy, Philadelphia adopted planning strategies that transformed its central business district into one of the country's most successful center-city districts.

Readers may wonder about the contemporary relevance of planning in the nineteenth-century, or the turn-of-the-twentieth-century, or even the mid-twentieth-century. It is my contention that good planning in one place bears a strong resemblance to good planning in another, and the similarities can be seen in examples as disparate in time and place as Paris in the mid nineteenth century and New York in the mid twentieth. The issues that planners confront do not change with location or time: improving the functioning of entire metropolitan regions, improving the character of the physical environment, and improving everybody's daily life. The tasks undertaken by planners are also the same, everywhere and at all times: making capital investments that provide needed infrastructure and community facilities, improve public services, and encourage private development; altering land use and traffic patterns to improve the way cities and suburbs function; raising money to pay for those investments; and gaining and maintaining public support for those activities. Thus, an understanding of where, how, and why planning has succeeded in the past helps us succeed today.

Others may object to my choice of cities. When they think of planning, they think of entire design systems: Beaux-Arts proposals for symmetrical clusters of buildings and axial vistas; modernist oases of continuous, green, open spaces punctuated by occasional tall buildings; or New Urbanist images of quaint houses with picket fences and gabled roofs. As Jane Jacobs wrote more than a half century ago, these conceptions may explain "everything in a flash, like a good advertisement" but they say little about how cities work; nor do they explain how to change them for the better.[8]

Still others will be unhappy that I use the word "planning" without such modifiers as city, regional, suburban, or neighborhood. They assume that planning should take place on a neighborhood, city, suburban, or regional basis and that the techniques used for one are not the same techniques used in other types of planning. On the contrary, I believe that planning strategies are universally applicable, whether they are directed to relatively compact downtown Philadelphia or the sprawling New York metropolitan area.

Very little of this book is devoted to plans. Some plans are lovely but fanciful descriptions of what we want the world to be. They decorate coffee tables, collect dust on library shelves, and sometimes intrigue people who like to muse about what might have been. Dwight Eisenhower, an expert on the subject, once remarked, "Plans are worthless, but planning is everything."[9] Indeed, plans that change nothing *are* worthless. A small number of plans, however, like the 1909 *Plan of Chicago*, have helped change daily life for the better. Plans can be useful, but as Eisenhower understood very well, anyone who wants to change anything must do more than publish a document. They must engage in planning.

Finally, this book will attempt to answer two questions. The first was posed by Alexander Hamilton in the *Federalist Paper No. 1*: are we capable of establishing good government through "reflection and choice," or are we destined to make political decisions through "accident and force?" By the end of this book, the reader will understand that the answer is "both" and will have a clear sense of where and how they come into play in the planning process.

The second question addresses the skepticism of today's world about the possibility of effecting change. Is it true that intelligent planning is impossible today because times have changed? One of the major themes of this book is that times have not changed as much as we think they have. Nineteenth-century planners, like planners in the 1960s, a time when they thought government and private money were plentiful, faced the same difficulties experienced by planners today, who believe money is scarce. The idea that planning used to be easy but has become difficult is a myth. The notion has become conventional wisdom because there has never been a commonly accepted understanding of what planning is, what its players are engaged in, the rules that govern what they do, or why successful planners are able to change neighborhoods, cities, suburbs, and even entire metropolitan regions.

I hope these pages will inspire readers to enter the planning game themselves; to adapt its observations to their own time, political context, and place; and to become the heroes of future editions of *The Planning Game*.

Participants in the planning game in NYC (2009).

TWO

THE PLAYERS

In late 1967 a hundred residents of the Bushwick section of Brooklyn met with a professional planner to decide what government should do for the neighborhood. The planner began by asking, "What do you want in Bushwick?" As people in the room spoke up, he listed their desires on an enormous sheet of paper. Suddenly, a very angry woman took the floor. "We don't need a wish list," she said. "We want things to change, but we don't know what's realistic. You're the professional! You should be telling us what the alternatives are, how they can be paid for, and what you recommend. Then we'll decide." This woman articulated one of the key elements of the planning game, that different players have different roles to play.

The planning game has two types of players. Some play starring roles; these are the people who devise, initiate, implement, or prevent change. The others play supporting roles, providing the stars with the financial or political support and the design expertise they need to succeed.

The stars of the planning game tend to be well-known figures: community leaders, visionaries, reformer-critics, bankers, public officials, or private developers. They are often fascinating personalities, and their activities frequently, and unfairly, outshine the contributions of other participants. It is as if others had no role, or as if earlier and sometimes more important planning initiatives did not share the credit for changing cities and the quality of life in them. Fine actors know that a performance in a supporting role can be the difference between success and failure. This book is filled with people who played supporting roles, and it is important to recognize and treasure their achievements.

Nevertheless, the star players illustrate most effectively the way planning affects our lives and our communities. Colorful figures will dominate these pages, but it is my intention that some of the less spectacular players will be restored to view.

THE ROLE OF THE PUBLIC

The public is an important supporting actor in the planning game, but it is not always clear what "the public" means. Does it include chambers of commerce, national labor unions, political parties, neighborhood associations, or all of these? What is its role: giving vent to frustration, opposing or endorsing a proposed development, providing public testimony, advocating its likes and preferences, or proposing alternatives? Is the public a different entity from its elected representatives? The answers will vary, depending on who is responding, where they live, what they believe, and the role they are playing. Often, more than one of these groups will be asserting the primacy of their role and will often disagree with each other.

In the mid twentieth century, in reaction to decades of secret agreements, the public demanded an explicit role in the planning process. In those days high-handed redevelopment officials routinely obtained legislative approval for uprooting entire neighborhoods before residents were aware of what was happening. Community resistance brought a positive response from the Eisenhower administration, which altered the urban renewal program to require "citizen advisory committees." The Johnson administration went further; its Model Cities Program called for "widespread participation," and its poverty program required "maximum feasible participation." In all these instances there was an inherent problem in government sponsorship of public participation. It gave some people the illusion that they personally determined what other people could do with their property, their money, and their time. It certainly complicated the development process. But, as Churchill said: "Democracy is the worst form of government except all those other forms that have been tried."[1]

Public participation in planning is now widespread throughout the United States. New York was one of the earliest cities to institutionalize citizen participation when it established informal community boards in the early 1950s. Community boards became a formal part of the land-use review process in the 1961 revisions to the city charter. Today every land-use decision taken by the New York City Council is preceded by local public hearings and an advisory opinion from the relevant fifty-member community board, as well as by city-wide public hearings and a vote of the thirteen-member City Planning Commission.

Many other cities have established community boards, mandated by law, to vote on projects within their jurisdiction. Public officials

and private developers have learned that if they do not pay careful attention to the public, their projects will be stalled or defeated. Whatever the issues of the day, opposition to government action emerges whenever people are unhappy with proposed changes to their lives. Opposition quickly grows into demands for transparency, objectivity, open competition for government contracts, and participation in the decision-making process. Thus, projects are now routinely brought before the public for review, and, for better or worse, the public is a player in the planning game.

COMMUNITY ACTIVISTS

Whenever the public is aroused, community activists emerge. They identify objectives, propose activities, work together with all the groups that have similar concerns, and they negotiate with other players who represent alternative viewpoints.

When the Martin Luther King, Jr., National Historic Site and Preservation District was established in 1980, the surrounding neighborhood, once the home of prosperous African-American residents of Atlanta, was filled with dilapidated buildings and empty lots. Local

Atlanta (2004). Neighborhood leaders insisted on the rehabilitation of the old buildings around the birthplace of Martin Luther King, Jr.

leaders did not believe that preservation of one building, the birthplace of Martin Luther King, Jr., was enough to revive the neighborhood, so they formed the Historic District Development Corporation (HDDC) to reverse housing deterioration and revitalize the district. Progress was slow until 1993, when Mtamanika Youngblood became the HDDC's first paid executive director and, later, its board chair.[2]

The program Youngblood devised continues to this day. It has three goals: "retaining the historic and cultural character of the existing community, non-displacement [that maintains] neighborhood diversity by intervening and improving life opportunities for residents, and linking mixed-income, mixed-use development to sustainable economic growth, thereby creating an environment where families can be self-sufficient."[3] The HDDC proceeded on a block-by-block basis to build new houses on vacant lots, to rehabilitate existing buildings or help their resident owners obtain the financing that would allow them to restore their homes, and to develop larger mixed-use and residential complexes that were consistent in character

with the rest of the neighborhood. This successful community-based planning effort has revitalized the area and is now a model for other Atlanta neighborhoods.

Citizen activists who were attracted to the planning game in the sixties were usually well educated, sometimes disaffected, and often relatively affluent city residents who desired more responsive local government. That was the case in Seattle in 1963. Five years earlier the business and civic leaders had formed the Central Association to advocate the interests of downtown Seattle; it later became the Downtown Seattle Association. In 1963 the association proposed a complex of hotels, office buildings, apartment houses, and garages to replace what they thought of as the dilapidated and outmoded Pike Place Market.[4]

Pike Place Market is a complex of buildings on a steep hill along the Seattle waterfront. Begun in 1907 as a farmer's market, it was home by the 1920s to more than 400 produce stands, fishmongers, butchers, restaurants, and craftspeople.[5] In the 1940s, however, the market began a slow decline; as major producers began

Pike Place Market, Seattle (2007). Local activists were able to save this national landmark from being torn down.

to supply large stores by truck, refrigerated container, and air, the occupants of the market found it difficult to compete. By 1959 only 53 market stalls remained. Four years later, under pressure from the Central Association, the city administration decided to seek a federal grant for a Pike Plaza Redevelopment Project.[6]

Architect Victor Steinbrueck, attorney Robert Ashley, painter Mark Tobey, and leaders in the art and preservation communities formed Friends of the Market to prevent demolition of what Mayor Dorm Braman called "a decadent, somnolent firetrap."[7] The city reduced the size of the project, but not enough to please Friends of the Market. Steinbrueck eventually led a successful effort to have the State of Washington's Advisory Council on Historic Preservation approve designation of 17 acres as the Pike Place Market Historic District, pursuant to the recently passed National Historic Preservation Act of 1966. Nevertheless, in spite of the historic district designation, the Department of Housing and Urban Development (HUD) approved a grant for the redevelopment project in 1971.

Friends of the Market petitioned to place Pike Place Market on the ballot that fall. They won the vote: a referendum that stated clearly that Pike Place Market "played and continues to play a significant role in the development of Seattle" carried by more than 23,000 votes.[8] As a result, the Pike Place Market Preservation and Development Authority was established in 1973 to administer the market district. In 2010 the market covered twenty-two acres and was patronized by more than 10 million people each year.[9]

Friends of the Market and the Historic District Development Corporation are among the increasing number of effective neighborhood-based players in the planning game. Their effectiveness comes from the skill of their leaders, the responsiveness of other players, and their determination to succeed in changing things in their community. The Friends of the Market were successful because they mobilized the citizens of Seattle and produced a referendum vote that the political leaders of the city had to respect. The HDDC already had the support of political

leaders; they had to convince local, often poor, business owners and lending institutions to work with them. In addition to engaging other players, however, it was their determination to achieve results that led to their success. They knew how to get others to perform the roles that would allow everybody to win.

Many organizations promote their own agendas by entering the planning game. In the early twenty-first century, they include proponents of a greener environment, of landmark and historic preservation, low-rent housing, improved public transportation, better education, less public spending, lower taxes, pedestrian precincts, public art, the de-emphasis of private automobiles, etc. Broader, more traditional, civic organizations sometimes advocate for better government, improving the local economy, protecting the civil service, safeguarding property rights, and establishing regional government. Any one of these groups may play a crucial role at some point in the planning game.

It is most common, however, for community groups to enter the fray for negative reasons—to prevent a project from going forward. Great good can often follow, but these groups do not begin with a development agenda. For example, Barbara Mikulski, later a U.S. senator from Maryland, gained notoriety in 1968 when she organized community opposition to a proposed sixteen-lane section of Interstate Highway 95 that was to have passed through Fell's Point, the Polish-American neighborhood of Baltimore in which she lived. Her passion certainly contributed to her success; she said later that at a local meeting, "I jumped up on a table and I cried, 'The British couldn't take Fell's Point . . . and goddamn if we'll let the State Roads Commission take Fell's Point."[10] More important, Mikulski helped assemble a coalition that included residents of the predominantly African-American neighborhood of Rosemont, which also would have been dismembered by the highway. By coordinating their efforts, the residents of Fell's Point and Rosemont won the battle and kept I-95 from passing through their neighborhoods.

Community opposition to government action

Overton Park, Memphis (2006). Active community opposition stopped an interstate highway from cutting this park in half.

is very much part of the planning game, and battles are not always won by future stars like Senator Mikulski. During the 1960s, supporting actors prevented Interstate Highway 40 from destroying 24 acres of forested land in Memphis, Tennessee, which would have split 342-acre Overton Park into two pieces. This battle was started by residents of nearby communities and was won by attorneys who put together a lawsuit, *Citizens to Preserve Overton Park v. Volpe*.[11]

On one side were members of the city's business and political establishment, who were united in support of the highway because they felt it would improve the city's competitive position within its metropolitan region. On the other side were the lawyers hired by Citizens to Preserve Overton Park, who argued that the secretary of transportation could not, on technical grounds, approve the route. They asserted that property in Overton Park could not be taken for highway construction unless there was no "feasible and prudent alternative." If there were no such alternative, the proposed project should include all possible planning to minimize harm to the park.[12]

The case of Citizens to Preserve Overton

Park was defeated in two lower courts, but it was unanimously reversed by the Supreme Court in 1971 and returned to the district court for review. The district court sent the matter to Secretary of Transportation John Volpe for redecision. In 1972, Secretary Volpe requested that an environmental impact statement be prepared, pursuant to the National Environmental Policy Act. The Federal Highway Administration failed to investigate the alternatives fully and accurately, however, so the following year Secretary Volpe disapproved the route, stating that he could not make a finding that there were no "feasible and prudent alternatives" to acquiring a part of Overton Park.

VISIONARIES

As important as community activists may be, their opinions fade in importance with the passage of time. On the other hand, ideas launched by persuasive visionaries take on increasingly important, almost legendary, status. They inspire us and sometimes provoke us. Truly great visionaries provide ideas that other players will transform into a widespread approach for urbanization. At the same time, there are also visionaries whose ideas display ignorance about how cities work, and their recommendations change nothing.

The early plans for the rebuilding of the World Trade Center provide a good illustration. In the wake of September 11, virtually every well-known architect produced a scheme for redeveloping Lower Manhattan. A major art gallery commissioned the most imaginative of them "to do something positive and helpful" that would demonstrate "the symbolic, political, economic, and social importance of architecture." It exhibited sixty individual visions that were later published in a beautiful book.[13] In the absence of a client, property owners, a means of financing, or public approval, most of the exhibitors produced futuristic images without any indication of how they would be used or who would occupy them. They did not deal with the real issues of rebuilding. Visions of this sort are often forgotten within a few years. In rare cases they provide the pearl of an idea that lives on with growing insistency.

The literature of planning and architecture is filled with ideas of visionaries who people erroneously believe had a dramatic impact on the landscape. Frank Lloyd Wright (1867–1959), for example, promoted his vision of the future, Broadacre City, so successfully that people believe it affected development, when in fact it was an artful display of what was already happening in suburbs throughout America in the 1920s and 1930s.[14] In contrast, the carports and single-story residences that Wright actually designed and built had more impact on suburbia than all the books, models, and drawings of Broadacre City. Among the other designers who are mistakenly thought to have influenced the planning of cities and suburbs are Antonio Sant'Elia, Tony Garnier, Arturo Soria y Mata, Buckminster Fuller, Paolo Soleri, Rem Koolhaas, and advocates of plug-in megastructures.

Occasionally, a visionary will produce an idea that, for better or worse, will be widely adopted. The common open space in Clarence Stein's 1928 design for Radburn, a planned new community in Fairlawn, New Jersey, probably inspired the organization of numerous suburban condominium communities, both gated and open. Victor Gruen's design for Southdale, the world's first skylighted, air-conditioned shopping mall, opened in Edina, Minnesota,

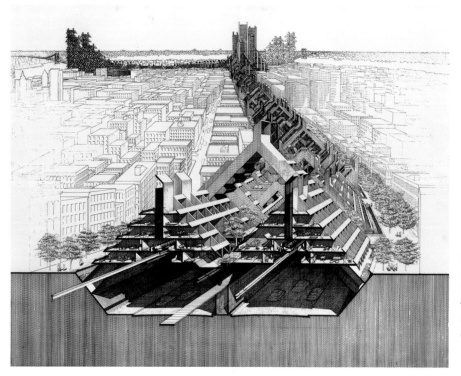

Lower Manhattan Expressway (1968–72). Megastructure proposed for construction over a never-built highway by architect Paul Rudolph.

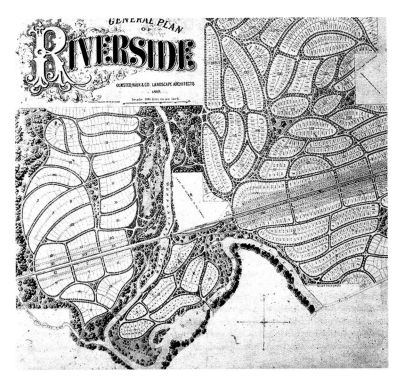

Plan of Riverside, Illinois (1869).

Riverside, Illinois (1997). Olmsted and Vaux established a common standard of houses set back from the street, with front lawns and an arch of trees at the property line, making the public realm the dominant element in the landscape.

in 1956. Similar climate-controlled shopping malls are now common throughout the world. More recently, Andrés Duany and Elizabeth Plater-Zyberk influenced countless developers and designers to create more humane suburban subdivisions. Among visionaries, however, it seems to me the influence of Frederick Law Olmsted, Ebenezer Howard, and Le Corbusier exceeds that of virtually everybody else.

Frederick Law Olmsted (1823–1903), working with architect Calvert Vaux, designed Manhattan's Central Park, America's first public park. Central Park provided a model for future park development everywhere. The same is true of Olmsted and Vaux's parkways for Brooklyn, Buffalo, and Chicago. In addition, Olmsted provided a formula for suburbanization that was adopted throughout the United States by devel-

opers and government officials, many of whom had never heard of him or had never thought of him in this context.

There had been subdivisions with curvilinear roadways long before 1869, the year that Olmsted and Vaux completed a plan for the new community of Riverside, nine miles outside Chicago. Unlike some English precedents, Riverside did not include walls separating private property from public streets. Instead, its front lawns provided a particularly American opportunity for neighborly community life, while back yards provided each family with whatever level of privacy it desired. The concepts launched at Riverside seem obvious: "good roads and walks, pleasant to the eye within themselves, and having at intervals pleasant openings and outlooks" with houses that pro-

Prairie Village, Kansas (2011). Many suburban subdivisions that were developed after World War II unconsciously adopted Olmsted's formula.

vided for "domestic life, secluded, but not far removed from the life of the community."[15]

Olmsted understood that there was no way to prevent people from building "ugly inappropriate houses." He solved this problem by devising a method for preventing buildings from forcing themselves "disagreeably upon our attention when we . . . pass along the road."[16] Houses were set back from the street, and large shade trees were planted at the property line. This insured that individual houses would recede into the background and an arch of street trees would dominate the public realm.

Many developers adopted Olmsted's formula without understanding the philosophy behind it. Too often, however, the trees have succumbed to budgetary considerations and the front lawns have been cut back to a few

St. Louis County, Missouri (2011). Curvilinear streets with houses set back from the street by front lawns have become commonplace.

feet. The result is a mass-produced formula that long ago lost its connection to Olmsted's vision. Furthermore, many people believe that the landscaped subdivisions produced by these developers were either organic outgrowths of local topography or had evolved naturally from daily use.

Ebenezer Howard (1850–1928) dreamed of a different way of shaping suburbanization. Where Olmsted's vision concentrated on individual subdivisions, Howard's vision encompassed an entire region. His ideas first appeared in print in his 1898 book, *To-morrow: A Peaceful Path to Real Reform* (revised and reissued in 1902 under its better-known title, *Garden Cities of Tomorrow*).[17] The vision it advocated would extend the best of city life into the territory around overpopulated cities by creating small, self-sufficient garden cities surrounded by agricultural greenbelts. The countryside would remain pristine, while people would benefit from both nature and community life.

In Howard's vision the beauty of nature would combine with social opportunity to create sustainable settlements without slums or smoke. There were not to be any commuters in the Garden City. The 30,000 people living in each 1,000-acre town would all work there. Their food would be supplied by 2,000 farmers who lived in the surrounding 5,000-acre greenbelt. In the twenty-first century, when the global economy provides inexpensive produce from large suppliers around the world, the notion that farmers with 2.5-acre farms could supply a wide selection of foods to urban areas at affordable prices seems at best naïve.

Howard advocated his garden city among social activists in Britain even before he published his book. In 1899 he founded the Garden City Association (whose name was later changed to the Town and Country Planning Association). Because his vision failed to materialize, he established a joint stock company in 1903 to purchase land and develop garden cities. Its first project was Letchworth Garden City, 35 miles north of London, designed by Raymond Unwin and Barry Parker. In 1919, Howard and his associates formed another company to create Welwyn Garden City, about 20 miles north of London. Neither city looks anything like Howard's geometric diagram, just as daily life there does not resemble his vision. While some residents live and work in the garden city, many more commute. Food comes from around the world, not just from their very real greenbelts.

It was Howard's vision, not his diagram or his Utopian ideas about the way people ought to live, that inspired generations of planners, designers, developers, and public officials throughout the world. Supporters everywhere wanted governments to promote planned new-community development as a way of preventing urban overcrowding and wasteful suburbanization. During the Great Depression, the Roosevelt administration initiated a program of building such communities. It hoped to create ninety-nine of them but only built three: Greenbelt, Maryland; Green Hills, Ohio; and Greendale, Wisconsin. After World War II, Britain enacted a New Towns Act that, over twenty-six years, produced twenty-two similar satellite new towns.[18] The Nixon administration created fifteen planned new communities under Title VII of the Housing and Urban Development Act of 1970.[19] Similar national programs were tried in France, Sweden, and Israel.

One other important vision shaped urbanization during the twentieth century. Visionaries who produced images of "the city of tomorrow" believed that existing forms of urbanization were obsolete and that cities required complete reconstruction. The often contentious advocates of this vision in Germany, France, Holland, Sweden, England, and the United States

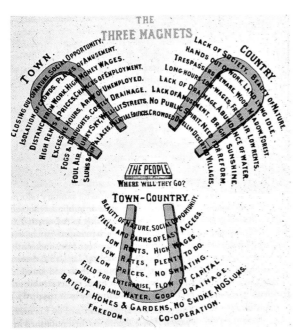

Ebenezer Howard sought "a joyous union" of the best of country life with the best of the city. In devising the concept of a garden city, he was also able to discard the worst aspects of both.

Radburn, New Jersey (2006). In designing their first "garden city," Howard's disciples, Clarence Stein and Henry Wright, grouped single-family houses around landscaped common open space that provided residents with a unique recreational resource.

imagined a properly functioning new world, in which efficient mass production and equitable distribution of goods and services would satisfy all the needs of the world's residents. They conceived their task to be that of devising a housing prototype that could be standardized, mass-produced, and erected in the same manner on open land anywhere in the world.[20]

Consequently, modernist architects and planners proposed new building types designed to meet minimum standards; they believed this would be a cost-effective way to supply modern housing to the entire world. The visionary who perhaps best exemplifies this approach was the French architect, painter, sculptor, and writer Charles-Édouard Jeanneret (1887–1965), better known as Le Corbusier.

At the Salon d'Automne in Paris in 1922, Le Corbusier exhibited powerful images of a contemporary city of 3 million inhabitants. It would be built on four fundamental principles: decongesting the center city, increasing housing density, increasing the means of circulation

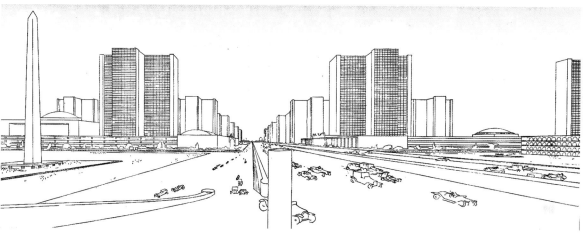

Le Corbusier's vision for a modern city of 3,000,000 (1922).

The idea of high-density living in high-rise towers in a park is beautifully illustrated in Le Corbusier's 1929 proposal for Buenos Aires.

and amount of land devoted it, and increasing the amount of land devoted to landscaped open space.[21] How does one decongest a city while increasing density and augmenting the amount of land devoted to transportation and parks? Le Corbusier's answer was to reduce the amount of land devoted to buildings, while making the buildings tall enough to accommodate a large number of people and activities.

While there were other adherents of this modernist proposition, Le Corbusier became its most ardent and effective proponent. In 1925 he exhibited the Plan Voisin, in which he demonstrated how the principles he had set forth earlier could be realized in Paris. He proposed that the government expropriate, demolish, and rebuild Paris district by district, retaining only exceptional monuments, like the Louvre or Notre-Dame Cathedral.[22]

In the United States, the Plan Voisin became the model for large-scale housing projects and for the federal urban renewal program that subsidized redevelopment between 1949 and 1973. Western Europe adopted it as the proper way to rebuild city districts that had been destroyed by the Nazis. In postwar Russia and Eastern Europe, Communist regimes employed the principles of the Plan Voisin to mass-produce whole residential neighborhoods.

Perhaps the most appealing and influential image of the city of tomorrow is Le Corbusier's drawing of what many people call "towers in the park," made for Buenos Aires in 1929.[23] Developers and government agencies elsewhere could rarely afford to spend the kind of money that would permit such a low percentage of land coverage. As a result, very few American or European redevelopment projects provide the ideal environment Le Corbusier envisioned. One of the rare exceptions was designed by Ludwig Mies van der Rohe and Ludwig Hilberseimer, who had dreamed of a modernist world quite similar to Le Corbusier's when they lived in Germany during the 1920s. Working with two Americans, landscape architect Alfred Caldwell and real estate developer Herbert Greenwald, they designed Lafayette Park, an urban renewal project in Detroit. In the years since Lafayette Park opened, Detroit has been plagued with a declining population, housing abandonment, and a myriad of social problems. Nevertheless, Lafayette Park has remained continuously well maintained and occupied by a population that is racially and economically integrated. It provides an important demonstration that, intelligently planned, the city of tomorrow can provide a satisfying living environment.[24]

Lafayette Park, Detroit (2008). The idea of "towers in the park" was executed with panache by Mies van der Rohe in a project that included low-rise buildings and gorgeous landscaping by Alfred Caldwell.

Robert F. Wagner Houses, Manhattan (2011). Throughout much of the 20th century the dream of "towers in the park" became a sadly misunderstood cliché.

Some of the most influential supporting players in the planning game propose no vision of their own, but their critique of the environment around them is so persuasive that they inspire others to change it. Much of our landscape is the product of their attempt to eliminate undesirable conditions or to oppose an unacceptable proposal, not of a desire to create something wonderful. When they are effective, reformer-critics set forth an agenda that others adopt and eventually bring to fruition. This usually happens when their critique explicitly reveals things that many people already believe or instinctively know to be correct. Because communication plays such an important role, it is not surprising that many of the most prominent reformer-critics have been writers. Among them, three people stand out: Jacob Riis, Lewis Mumford, and Jane Jacobs.

If the measure of success in the planning game is the degree to which one improves the lives of ordinary people, then Jacob Riis (1849–1914) wins hands down. This Danish-born photojournalist and muckraking writer-lecturer came to America from Denmark at the age of twenty-one. At first he lived among the poorest of the poor and took whatever jobs were available, but eventually he went into journalism; in 1877 he became a police reporter for the *New York Tribune*. Eleven years later, work-

ing for the *New York Sun*, he began to take the photographs that, had he done nothing else, would have been enough to obtain the constituency he needed to win his battle with the slums.[25]

In addition to his work as a journalist and photographer, Riis wrote sixteen books that were read throughout America and remain classics in the literature of cities. The first and most famous of them, *How the Other Half Lives*, describes the dreadful living conditions in the slums of New York and implicitly sets forth the agenda that would terminate the deplorable conditions Riis was determined to end.[26]

One sentence expresses perfectly the core belief of Riis and like-minded reformers of the period: "The bad environment becomes the heredity of the next generation."[27] They proposed to deal with the bad environment by ending construction of tenements, clearing them wherever possible, and providing recreational opportunities for the residents of slum neighborhoods. Riis was part of the coalition that forced the New York State legislature to enact the Small Parks Act of 1887 and the Tenement House Act of 1901, both of which advanced their antislum agenda.

The Small Parks Act enabled local governments to condemn privately owned property for the purpose of creating public playgrounds.[28] Following its passage, New York City (followed by cities across the country) initiated a program that created hundreds of playgrounds, beginning with with the clearance of Mulberry Bend, a notorious Lower East Side slum, and the creation in its place of Columbus Park (formerly Mulberry Bend Park). Riis described the impact of this transformation:

Mulberry Bend, Manhattan (pre-1887). This photograph by Jacob Riis portrays one of the notorious slums on the Lower East Side.

> I do not believe that there was a week in all the twenty years I had to do with . . . [Mulberry Bend] as a police reporter, in which I was not called to record there a stabbing or shooting. . . . It is now five years since the Bend became a park and the police reporter has not had business there during that time; not once has a shot been fired or a knife drawn.[29]

Riis's battle with slums culminated with passage of the Tenement House Act of 1901. Every new apartment would have to have at least one toilet, a kitchen sink with running water, and windows in every room that opened onto courts of a certain size.[30] At that time more than 2.4 million New Yorkers lived in nearly 642,000 apartments that did not meet these minimum standards.[31] A century later, in 2005, two-thirds of pre-1901 tenement apartments had been demolished and countless others had been remodeled, rewired, and air-conditioned.[32]

Lewis Mumford (1895–1990) was an even more prolific writer than Riis. He wrote nineteen books and a great many articles on subjects that ranged from technology and design to history and literature. Unlike Riis, he did not inspire legislation or redevelopment efforts, and he did not directly affect the growth and development of a single city. He was effective because he changed what people thought and did; in particular, he changed the assumptions and beliefs of other players in the planning game. The articles Mumford wrote as a regular columnist for the *New Yorker* magazine between 1931 and 1963 provided him with a platform for disseminating his opinions.[33] His books were even more influential.

Along with Clarence Stein, Mumford was one of the influential members of the Regional Planning Association of America, an informal group of Ebenezer Howard's American followers who were determined to influence suburban development. Many of them were also involved with the City Housing Corporation, a limited-dividend company established to build moderate-income housing that reflected garden city ideals. Mumford purchased and for many years lived in one of the 1,202 row houses in Sunnyside Gardens, Queens, the corporation's first project. Moreover, in numerous books and articles he promoted Radburn, the suburban planned community in New Jersey that best represented the ideals of the garden city movement.[34]

Where Riis favored outraged exposés, Mumford played a behind-the-scenes insider's role. Clarence Stein, who was on the Design Review Board of the 1939 New York World's Fair, convinced the leadership of the Fair to endorse daily presentation of a film that he produced for the American Planning Association.[35] The film, entitled *The City*, presented the designers' views of what urbanization should be. Stein asked Lewis Mumford to write the script and Aaron Copland to compose the musical score.

The movie presented a choice between the chaos, congestion, and misery of life in overcrowded old cities, and the sun, fresh air, safety, healthiness, and cleanliness of new green communities built into the countryside. Images of Radburn, New Jersey, and Greenbelt, Maryland, provided exemplars of healthy new communities. Jones Beach provided the model for public recreation, while broad, tree-lined parkways with landscaped medians illustrated the transportation of the future. The parkways, along with Jones Beach and public improvements that made the World's Fair possible, were the work of Robert Moses. Visitors to the Fair, many of whom were unaware of Mumford or Stein, came away believing that the ideas presented in *The City* provided the correct direction for future metropolitan development.[36] Mumford's many magazine articles and books were even more successful in promoting his ideas, as well as those of Howard and Stein.

For the three decades before Jane Jacobs became the primary reformer-critic in America, Lewis Mumford's writings provided the ideas that influenced our thinking about cities. Like Mumford, Jacobs (1916–2006) had a long career as a journalist and writer. But Jacobs was not an insider, and she was a bit like Riis in

Sunnyside Gardens, Queens (2011). The street where Lewis Mumford lived between 1927 and 1936.

Hudson Street, Manhattan (2010). Jane Jacobs based her opinions about what constituted a healthy neighborhood on the street where she lived: Hudson Street.

her vocal opposition to whatever she believed to be wrong. Her book, *The Death and Life of Great American Cities*, appeared in 1961, and it changed the way many people in the planning game, myself included, thought about cities. Jacobs believed that the modernist formula promoted by designers like Le Corbusier produced projects that were "marvels of dullness and regimentation, sealed against any buoyancy or vitality of city life."[37] Her critique of the suburban prescriptions advocated by Howard, Stein, and Mumford was that they "simply wrote off the intricate, many-faceted, cultural life of the metropolis."[38]

Jacobs argued that cities need "a most intricate and close-grained diversity of uses that give each other constant mutual support, both economically and socially . . . "[39] that "insure the presence of people who go outdoors on different schedules and are in the place for different purposes, but who are able to use many facilities in common."[40] Her prescription for achieving this was a pattern of short blocks occupied by a dense concentration of users, interrupted by as many streets as possible, with buildings that contained a variety of uses and had been built at a variety of times.

None of Jacobs's other books have had the

same impact, but the prescriptions she advocated in *The Death and Life of Great American Cities* have become the conventional wisdom for most people involved in urban development. Cities function well and their inhabitants are happier wherever Jacobs's prescription has been applied intelligently. But like most formulas, it has been applied by some people who do not understand where it is appropriate and where it is not.

Some public officials, for example, think they are following her recommendations by requiring ground-floor retail stores in all buildings. Jacobs would have explained that the population densities in some residential areas are too low to support widespread retail. Some preservationists, on the other hand, think they are applying her ideas by freezing development. Jacobs would have replied that, unless new activities are introduced that meet the changing desires of its residents, and unless affordable new buildings are introduced, a neighborhood will begin to lose its vitality.

The impact of Jacobs's ideas cannot be underestimated. Her admirers, however, have blown out of proportion her role as a community activist and have made her into the primary opponent of Robert Moses, who had already acquired plenty of opponents during the three decades before Jacobs came onto the scene.

Riis, Mumford, and Jacobs attracted constituencies for their critiques and saw their prescriptions adopted. The slums that Jacob Riis inveighed against disappeared. Low-density community development, of the sort Mumford advocated, is now routinely built by developers. Jane Jacobs remains a vivid presence in the public consciousness, although usually as leader of the opposition to "bad guy" Robert Moses. Jacobs may have profoundly disagreed with the ideas of Le Corbusier and Ebenezer Howard, but their ideas and hers continue to influence players who enter the planning game.

GOVERNMENT AGENCIES AND PUBLIC OFFICIALS

Sometimes the money that fuels the planning game comes from government. A discussion of the myriad agencies that have developed over the past century at the federal, state, and local level is far beyond the scope of this book. Nonetheless, it is important to demonstrate, if only briefly, how they perform their roles.

Most people think that government consists of operating agencies that deliver services, overhead agencies that determine priorities, and the elected officials to whom they are accountable. But local government in America is usually a mix of public and private entities, appointed and elected officials, and tenured civil servants and staff who serve at the pleasure of those officials. Each locality will have a combination that reflects its particular history, its politics, and its financing mechanisms.

Government agencies play a variety of roles. Some agencies tell other players what, how, and where they can play the game. The federal Department of Transportation, for example, establishes dimensions for various types of traffic arteries, the California Coastal Commission determines what can be built within the coastal area of the state, and the Philadelphia City Planning Commission manages the city's zoning, height, bulk, and use requirements. Other agencies are active players, either providing money

for development or executing projects themselves. The federal Department of Housing and Urban Development (HUD), for example, provides subsidies for low-income housing, the New York State Empire Development Corporation acquires property and finances its development, and the elected Minneapolis Park and Recreation Board owns and operates a 6,642-acre park system, consisting of 182 properties.[41]

These and thousands of other agencies operate in accordance with congressional statutes, state constitutions, and local laws. The roles they play, however, are determined as much by the source of their financing, the character of local politics, and the function they were established to serve. Similarly, the role of agency personnel depends on whether they have tenure and how they obtained their positions: by competitive civil service examinations, noncompetitive civil service appointment, union membership, response to advertisements, volunteering, political patronage, or a combination of these.

Like the members of neighborhood groups and civic organizations, people who work in government agencies believe they have the right to determine what others do with their property, money, and time. But that is in fact the role of a completely different set of public officials. In every city and state, we elect leaders whom we specifically entrust with that responsibility. Among them, governors, mayors, and senators are the most prominent, and even they do not have an unlimited right to tell others in the planning game what they may or should do.

Governors are rarely involved with public action at the local level. Occasionally, as discussed in Chapter 6, they are involved in planning for parks, highways, and other statewide investments affecting local communities. Sometimes governors are responsible for investments that have a major impact on their state's communities. At the urging of Governor Thomas E. Dewey of New York, the state legislature in 1946 established a Temporary Commission on the Need for a State University. This led to the creation of the SUNY system, which now includes the preexisting campuses in Albany and Buffalo as well as new facilities in Binghamton, Stony Brook, Purchase, and other communities. These state universities are magnets, attracting tens of thousands of students and teachers to communities throughout the state, where they generate thousands of jobs, as well as millions of dollars in private and public spending. Dewey was also responsible for the establishment of the New York State Thruway Authority in 1950. This independent public corporation built and manages a 570-mile system that predates the federal interstate highway system. Nevertheless, governors are only rarely major players in the planning game. Mayors are much more likely to be active participants.

Unlike most other players in the planning game, mayors are generalists. They have to know about and take part in all aspects of planning—providing vision, criticizing and changing what is wrong, negotiating transactions, finding and hiring talented personnel, balancing budgets, managing agencies, pleasing constituencies, defeating opponents, and so very much else. As generalists, they must speak the languages of law, finance, real estate, design, public administration, and sometimes foreign languages as well. New York City's Mayor Fiorello LaGuardia, for example, was as comfortable speaking Italian and Yiddish as he was speaking English.

Effective mayors are deeply involved in the affairs of their communities. Polling data indicate that Mayor LaGuardia (1934–45), Cleveland's Tom L. Johnson (1901–9), and Pittsburgh's David Lawrence (1946–59) were among America's most effective mayors.[42] We don't admire them because they fixed potholes, but because they articulated a vision for the future of their cities, promoted that vision with their constituents, attracted supporters who participated in its realization, and negotiated deals that allowed

Pittsburgh (1900 and 2002). Mayor Lawrence and banker Richard K. Mellon initiated the redevelopment of the Golden Triangle, which triggered the reinvention of Pittsburgh as a postindustrial city.

Chicago (2005). Mayor Daley was responsible for creating more than 70 miles of new planted medians.

them to win the planning game. The same is true of several more recent mayors, such as Richard M. Daley of Chicago (in office 1989–2011), Joseph P. Riley, Jr., of Charleston, South Carolina (elected in 1975 and still in office), Manuel Diaz of Miami (2001–9), and Glenda Hood of Orlando, Florida (1992–2003). These mayors faced a variety of issues and came up with different solutions.

Richard Daley, for example, left an indelible green stamp on the city of Chicago. He sponsored legislation to encourage green construction, he invested in public parks, and he started programs to improve the environment. The most unexpected and visible part of his green legacy, however, consists of small slivers of green space that are now prominent throughout the cityscape. These bits of property were already owned by the city, which, beginning in 1996, installed planters in the medians of city streets and along its sidewalks and planted new trees throughout the city. By 2006, Chicago had more than 70 miles of newly planted medians and 300,000 additional street trees. When Daley left office, Chicago's proliferation of flower beds, street trees, and planted medians were greatly admired by visitors to the city and were the subject of enthusiastic newspaper and magazine articles. The program is a vivid example of a public-realm investment strategy that requires no expenditure whatsoever on property acquisition.

Mayor Joe Riley's efforts in Charleston illustrate the less glamorous, but yet important, impact mayors can have. The small changes he has made to improve the day-to-day functioning of the city, to enhance its appeal as a tourist destination, and to maintain Charleston as a pleasant place to live all explain the city's growing popularity. Since Riley was elected in 1975, the city's population has grown by more than 50 percent, to a 2010 high of 120,000.

One of Mayor Riley's earliest accomplishments was the restoration of Charleston's historic waterfront. The city's role as a maritime center had been declining for years, and the retaining walls and piers along the Cooper River were crumbling. Riley began the restoration in 1979 by acquiring land along the waterfront. He raised $13 million to create the lovely, eight-acre Waterfront Park, which opened in 1990. This park, a half-mile long, is more than a recreational facility. By including the remnants of piers and old piles, the park provided a connection to Charleston's past. Equally important, it became part of a continuous waterfront walking experience that begins at the Battery, reaches the park, and continues along the Cooper River.

Waterfront Park was followed in 1991 by the creation of a Visitor Reception and Transportation Center (VRTC) in the northern part of downtown. The VRTC was created by adapting nineteenth-century warehouses for contemporary use. It includes an information center, a

Charleston, South Carolina (2011). Mayor Riley initiated improvement of the city's waterfront parks and promenades.

gift shop, a visitor planning counter, exhibition space, and a theater—all within an environment rich with reminders of the city's antebellum history. This array of services in an attractive setting quickly made the VRTC a favorite stopping point for tourists driving into the city.

Architect Jaquelin Robertson, who was involved in the design of both the VRTC and the Waterfront Park, believes that Mayor Riley's success results as much from his insistence on quality details as from cultivation of the city's heritage.[43] The mayor, for example, has made sure that sidewalks are made of bluestone or brick, rather than concrete; parking garages do not present blank walls to the street but are lined with stores at the sidewalk level; and all public buildings use the most appropriate, rather than the least expensive, materials. Riley's nurturing attention to details over nine mayoral terms may seem minor—but it has made all the difference to this charming city.

While Charleston's problem was decline, Miami's problem was rapid growth. When Manny Diaz was elected mayor, Miami was a rapidly growing city of 362,000 people in an equally rapidly growing county of 5.5 million. The city, however, was bankrupt and was sub-

ject to the supervision of a state financial oversight board. The mayor's first priority was to put the city on a sound administrative and financial footing.

But Diaz was as concerned about the future of the city as about its present. Ordinances enacted in 1934, 1960, 1982, and 1990 had shaped Miami's growth in the twentieth century.[44] Few of the buildings that people wished to build when Diaz took office complied with these ordinances. Planners had to go through numerous public hearings, and City Council members had to vote to adjust the zoning for each and every project.

Mayor Diaz chose to regulate Miami's growth decades into the future by launching a comprehensive rezoning initiative, which he placed under the guidance of the architecture and town-planning firm Duany Plater-Zyberk & Company.

In April 2005 the planning process began with five hundred public meetings, workshops, and discussions. The mayor's intention was to end a highly politicized development process that cost unnecessary time and money and that was producing a cityscape neither convenient nor satisfying. At the end of what turned out to be a four-year process, Miami enacted an easy-to-understand zoning framework, known as Miami 21.

Miami's new zoning encouraged creation of compact, easily walkable, mixed-use neighborhoods and urban centers, whose density and intensity of use were related to the amount of transit service. Under the old zoning, office buildings had to be built on top of multi-level parking garages, and this had a deadening effect on street life. Miami 21 required the exteriors of garages to be wrapped with residences that had windows looking out onto the city. The old zoning permitted commercial and residential towers to be built next door to bungalows, but under Miami 21 new towers would have to step down in a manner that respected the scale and character of their smaller neighbors. Most important, most construction could proceed as-of-right.

Metropolitan Orlando presented different challenges. It was neither a slowly deteriorating city, like Charleston, nor a concentration of skyscrapers servicing an international clientele, like Miami. It was, however, one of the nation's fastest expanding cities. Metropolitan Orlando, which had a population of 523,000 in 1970, grew to more than 1,645,000 before Mayor Hood left office in 2003.[45] Orlando's rapid growth had been the very essence of suburban sprawl, and the mayor was determined to transform it.

From the beginning of her term Mayor Hood demonstrated her ability to manage urbanization. In 1993, just after she came into office, the federal government announced the decommissioning of the 1,093-acre Orlando Naval Training Center, which had been in operation since 1968. Mayor Hood was intent on having it developed as a carefully planned new community, rather than the featureless tract housing that characterized most development in the city's outlying areas. She persuaded the Department of Defense to pay for a private consultant who would assist the city in deciding how to proceed, and she estab-

Miami, Florida (2005–9). After more than five hundred meetings the city adopted a new easy-to-understand zoning framework. Above, the old zoning. The revised zoning, below, requires transitional mid-rise buildings between the high-rise corner structures and the one-family houses on the rest of the block.

Baldwin Park, Orlando, Florida (2006).

lished a Base Reuse Commission to determine the property's future. In short, the process that Mayor Hood initiated led to the selection of a developer who would create a planned community, including two lakes, 200 acres of parkland, and a pedestrian-oriented village center surrounded by relatively high-density residential development.

The planning process took six years and involved over 250 public meetings. The citizens of Orlando achieved consensus and an award-winning development. Mayor Hood's problem was different from those that faced Mayors Riley and Diaz, but all three were hands-on mayors, who cared about the smallest details of the planning process.

If mayors are the public officials most likely to change the physical character and daily life of cities and suburbs, legislators are in general the least likely. Sometimes, however, a legislator makes a real difference. Senator Robert F. Wagner (1877–1953) is rarely mentioned in histories of American city planning, but he probably did more than any other U.S. senator to alter the face of the United States.

Wagner, an immigrant from Germany, became the youngest-ever leader of the New York State Senate. In 1926, after seven years on the New York State Supreme Court, he won election to the United States Senate, where he served until his resignation in 1949.[46]

The formative experience of Wagner's life was the investigation of the Triangle Shirtwaist Fire of March 1911. With Assembly Speaker Al Smith (later governor), Wagner co-chaired the New York State Factory Investigating Commission created by the legislature to look into the devastating fire. The commission's recommendations led to passage of fifty-six pieces of legislation regulating building construction and occupancy, fire safety, wages, and labor practices. Reformers had long sought many of these

Fire at the Triangle Shirtwaist Factory, Manhattan (1911).

Riverwalk, San Antonio, Texas (2007). The WPA helped to pay for the creation of one of Texas's major tourist attractions.

laws.[47] The investigation greatly enhanced the reputations of Wagner and Smith.

Wagner became one of the U.S. Senate's most active and influential figures. His accomplishments included federal collection of unemployment statistics, a system of public employment agencies, unemployment insurance, a guarantee of the right to form and belong to a union, and the establishment of the National Labor Relations Board. His impact on the planning game, however, derived from sponsorship of the Emergency Relief and Construction Act of 1932, which allowed President Roosevelt to establish the Civil Works Administration (CWA) in 1933 and the Works Progress Administration (WPA) in 1935; from Title II of the National Industrial Recovery Act of 1933, which established the Public Works Administration (PWA); and from the Housing Act of 1937 (the Wagner-Steagall Act), which produced public housing for families of low income in apartments built and managed by more than 3,000 local housing authorities.[48]

College Court, Louisville, Kentucky (2008), was one of fifty housing projects financed by the PWA.

Over 3,000 public housing units at the Gouverneur Morris, Borgia Butler, and Daniel Webster houses, Bronx (2006), were financed by the Wagner-Steagall Act of 1937.

The CWA and WPA put millions of unemployed people to work and changed cities all over the country. During its two-year existence, the CWA built or renovated 40,000 schools, 3,700 playgrounds and athletic fields, 998 airports, and countless other facilities.[49] And when the activities of the WPA were terminated in 1943, it had built, improved, or enlarged 650,000 miles of roads, 78,000 bridges, 125,000 civilian and military buildings, 800 airports, 7,000 miles of airport runways; operated 1,500 nursery schools; and presented 225,000 concerts, plays, and vaudeville acts, produced almost 475,000 works of art and at least 276 full-length books.[50]

The PWA, which closed down in 1939, spent $6.085 billion on 34,508 projects, which included rural electrification grants and the construction of "70 percent of all the educational buildings built in the country during the same period; 65 percent of all the sewage treatment plants; 65 percent of all the courthouses, city halls, and other nonresidential public buildings; ten percent of all the roads, streets, bridges, viaducts, subways, and other engineering structures, and 35 percent of all the hospitals and allied public-health facilities."[51]

The PWA's most controversial program involved federal condemnation of fifty sites in thirty-five cities to make way for the construction of 25,000 apartments.[52] In 1935 a property owner in Louisville, Kentucky, objected to having his property taken in order build rental housing, claiming that the Fifth Amendment required that the site be reused for a "public purpose," such as a post office, school, or police station. When the appeal reached the Supreme Court, the Roosevelt administration withdrew, fearing that the PWA would lose the case.

The Housing Act of 1937, sponsored by Senator Wagner and Representative Henry Steagall of Alabama, solved the problem. It provided subsidies to local housing authorities, which were authorized under state constitutions to condemn private property either to eliminate blight or to provide housing for persons of low income. Under the new act, the federal government subsidized debt service payments on local bonds, provided that the local authority only paid a nominal sum in lieu of real estate taxes. Thus, persons of low income, who were to be the occupants of public housing, essentially had to pay just enough rent to cover operating expenses. By 1987, when the program came to an end, it had created 1.45 million apartments.[53]

LENDING INSTITUTIONS

The ideas of visionaries and reformer-critics may inspire players in the planning game, but the players cannot achieve anything without money. The money that enables development may come from banks, insurance companies, investors, purchasers of securities, friends, or even the future occupants of a proposed project. Wherever the money comes from, backers always try to minimize the risk of unforeseen events causing adverse effects, to maximize protection from losses if something goes wrong—as it often does—and to obtain a reasonable return for the use of their money.

In America the role of lenders took on particular prominence during the savings and loan crisis in the early 1990s and again during the subprime mortgage crisis in the first decade of the twenty-first century. In both cases, for different reasons, financial institutions had been providing an almost endless supply of money on extremely favorable terms. When their loans began to go sour, they had to deal with huge losses. Some passed on their losses to others; some went out of business; most cut back their lending at least for a while. In both crises the problems of the lenders forced other players out of the planning game. The consequences were so serious in each case that the national government stepped in to bail the lenders out. But despite these two vivid crises, which underscore the damage lenders can cause, they continue to play positive roles in city development.

Most of the time, lenders are behind-the-scenes players, but occasionally a lending institution plays a primary role. Teachers Insurance & Annuity Association, Connecticut General Life Insurance Company, and Chase Manhattan Bank, for example, were virtual partners with the Rouse Company in bringing the planned community of Columbia, Maryland, into existence. Columbia was a 1960s effort to provide an alternative to sprawling suburban subdivisions. Of Columbia's 15,600 acres, 5,300 were set aside as public open space; this space included three lakes, nineteen ponds, and 83 miles of walking, jogging, and bicycling trails. Within this framework, individual villages centered around schools, recreational facilities, and stores.[54]

Since this initial investment in infrastructure and community facilities could not be repaid from initial projected sales revenues, the lenders deferred debt-service payments for ten years. By doing so, the Rouse Company and its lenders set a gold standard for suburban development throughout the United States, but ten years were not long enough to prevent serious financial difficulties. Although Teachers and Chase lost money on their investment in Columbia, they nonetheless provided a large part of the financing for the Rouse Company's redevelopment of Quincy Market in Boston, and they profited handsomely from that investment.

Chase Manhattan Bank played an important role in developing both Columbia, Maryland, and Quincy Market, but its contribution to New York was even greater. Chase was responsible for the first significant effort after World War II to improve business conditions in Lower Manhattan. The decline of Lower Manhattan relative to Midtown had been a growing

Columbia, Maryland (2001).

concern to many in the business community, especially to banks and insurance companies clustered around Wall Street. In the decade between 1947 and 1956, 15.1 million square feet of new office space was erected in Midtown, more than existed in the Loop in Chicago, the nation's second-largest office district. But during that time only 1.1 million square feet of space was added in Lower Manhattan, in three modest office structures and one six-story addition.[55] The situation was so serious that in 1952 the *Journal of Commerce* published articles predicting that businesses would soon be relocating from Downtown to Midtown.[56]

In November 1955 the Chase Manhattan Bank, under David Rockefeller, announced that it would consolidate its nine-building, 8,700-employee operations on the two blocks bounded by Nassau, Liberty, William, and Pine streets. The scheme that emerged was a superblock, designed by the firm of Skidmore, Owings & Merrill. A one-block section of Cedar Street was closed, creating a 2.5-acre site that would be shared by a 60-story, 1.7 million-square-foot office slab, along with the existing 38-story building that had housed Chase Manhattan's headquarters since 1928 and a spacious new pedestrian plaza. Chase's investment was substantial enough to convince developers to follow suit. Between 1960, when the new Chase Manhattan Bank Building was ready for occupancy, and 1975, when the World Trade Center was completed, forty-seven buildings opened in Lower Manhattan, offering 39.1 million square feet of office space.[57]

PRIVATE DEVELOPERS AND PUBLIC ENTREPRENEURS

The biggest stars in the planning game are private developers and public entrepreneurs. They are the people who discover or create opportunities, seize them, and make change. In this chapter and the next we will look mainly at private developers. The importance of public entrepreneurs in the planning game is so great that it will be the focus of much of the rest of this book.

There are a few not-for-profit organizations that play small but important roles in the planning game. The Trust for Public Land, for example, has been involved in more than 3,500 projects all over the United States, ranging from the creation of community gardens and small neighborhood playgrounds to land conservation covering a total of 2.5 million acres (1.01 million hectares).[58] Bridge Housing, a nonprofit development company based in California, has been involved in the development of affordable housing for more than 13,000 households.[59] Most developers, however, operate on a for-profit basis.

Entrepreneurs are major players in the planning game. Whether private or public, they differ from the other players we have considered in a number of respects. They cannot allot the time necessary to study a situation; they must act while an opportunity exists. And because they have limited time for studies, they must also act on limited information. Private developers and public entrepreneurs are like lenders (but unlike all other players) in that everything they do puts them at risk. The chief difference between developers and public entrepreneurs, on one hand, and all the other players, on the other, is that they have to live with a far higher level of uncertainty.

Private developers and public entrepreneurs transform innovations, often discovered by others, into new and frequently profitable projects. Their most important role, however, is orchestrating the activities of the other players. Private developers play the planning game largely to enrich themselves, while public entrepreneurs play the game on everybody's behalf, but their activities are in many respects similar. They both bring projects to fruition, but the public entrepreneur explicitly seeks to develop projects that benefit a neighborhood, city, or region. The community benefits of privately developed projects are happy byproducts of activities whose purpose is private gain.

Like other entrepreneurial personalities, private developers identify consumer demand, perceive opportunities to supply that demand, usually adopt tested (but sometimes novel)

Country Club Plaza, Kansas City (2011). Customers park in the split-level garage, walk past smaller retailers and make purchases on their way to and from their ultimate destination.

ideas, take risks, find money to pay for their projects, seek public support, find capable associates, and keep at it until they succeed. They are able to do all this because they know how to market their ideas, they have flexible deal-making personalities, and they persist until their projects are implemented. Henry Flagler, the Van Sweringen brothers, William and Alfred Levitt, Philip Klutznick, William Zeckendorf, Gerald Hines, and Trammell Crow are among the private developers who have altered the American landscape. A look at the activities of two other private developers, Jesse Clyde Nichols and Herbert Greenwald, will help us to understand the role developers play in the planning game.

J. C. Nichols (1880–1950) began his career in real estate at the beginning of the twentieth century with money he borrowed "from farmers around his home town of Olathe, Kansas."[60] He used the money to buy land and build small houses in Kansas City.

Nichols believed that Kansas City would spread out from downtown, and he therefore started acquiring property three and a half miles south of town. Like many real estate developers, he believed the future was in the suburbs, and he made money by buying there when land was cheap and selling at higher prices when the

market was ripe. Some developers, including Nichols, also put pressure on government to build roadways to bring their property within easier reach of the growing number of middle-class automobile owners.

Nichols had trouble marketing to homebuyers in the suburbs because there were no amenities there: no stores, no movie theaters, no place to play golf or go for a drink. So in 1913 he organized the first of what would be the area's several country clubs.[61] This, too, was similar to what other suburban developers were doing. Like them, Nichols understood that in order to attract customers, he had to provide recreational opportunities and community relationships that customers wanted. He differed from the other developers, however, in one respect: he explicitly named his project the Country Club District.

Nichol's important innovation came after World War I, when he went beyond recreation to providing the stores that home buyers insisted on seeing before moving to an area. Many urban and suburban locations included several stores within a single building, in single ownership, with a consistent architectural image. Nichols concluded, however, that his site needed to be big enough to fulfill all the retail requirements of the area, to be a major destination for shoppers who did not live nearby, and to be easily accessible to suburbanites who came by car, with a place to park when they arrived. The project also had to have room to accommodate the trucks that delivered the goods they were selling. Most important, the project had to be managed and marketed by a single entity, the J. C. Nichols Company. These observations led Nichols to create the Country Club Plaza, the world's first shopping center.

Nichols employed other techniques in the Country Club Plaza that are still used in shopping centers today. The architecture had a consistent look—Spanish colonial. Other shopping centers copied this iconic image as a way of creating a destination that shoppers could identify. But after a falling away from unified design in the 1950s and 1960s to cut costs, developers decided by the end of the twentieth century that pared-down projects did not do as well as those that were branded by their imagery.

Another technique the Nichols Company employed was percentage leasing. In the beginning, the Country Club Plaza had trouble persuading retailers to move to a residential location that was not fully occupied. The retailers needed enough customers to generate sufficient income to pay the rent. So Nichols proposed a base rent merchants could afford, to which he added an agreed-upon percentage of sales when sales rose above a defined minimum.

Nichols's most important technique was to manipulate the flow of customers by renting first to major (anchor) tenants to attract shoppers from great distances; then locating parking some distance from those destinations; and

finally, renting to merchants who offered goods that would tempt the shoppers as they walked between their parked cars and the anchor tenants. Nichols leased space to the anchor stores at low rents and made up more than the difference by charging higher rents to the smaller stores situated along the customer's path.[62]

By 1950, when Nichols died, the Country Club District covered more than 5,000 acres. Its primary shopping center had become a form of real estate development that was common in America and was spreading around the world. By the turn of the twenty-first century, there were 44,426 shopping centers in the United States, containing 5.5 billion square feet of leasable area, and doing $1.1 trillion in annual sales.[63]

Like Nichols, Herbert Greenwald (1915–1959) began his career in real estate without any money, although he held jobs in real estate while he was at the University of Chicago. After graduation he went into teaching, but he also worked part-time as a fund-raiser for a philanthropic organization. There he befriended Samuel Katzin, owner of a successful Chicago automobile dealership. Katzin agreed to provide the equity capital Greenwald needed to start his own business, the Herbert Construction Company.[64]

Greenwald was full of ambition and chutzpah; with little experience and borrowed money, he wanted to create the best apartment building in America. In 1946, together with Katzin, he purchased one of the choicest sites available on Chicago's Hyde Park lakeshore, where he intended to erect the city's finest apartment

Country Club Plaza, Kansas City (2011). America's first shopping center has become the nucleus of an entire regional subcenter.

building, designed by the world's finest architect. His initial choice was Frank Lloyd Wright; but Wright wanted $250,000 before he would start, and Greenwald did not have the cash. Walter Gropius and Eero Saarinen turned him down. Fortunately, Gropius suggested Ludwig Mies van der Rohe. At that time the only buildings Mies had completed in America were on the campus of the Illinois Institute of Technology, where he ran the architecture program.[65]

After the First World War, Mies, Le Corbusier, and other modernist architects had begun to propose the idea of glass apartment buildings. Now, thirty years later, Mies wanted the Promontory Apartments (5530 South Shore Drive) to be the first glass-and-steel curtain-wall apartment building erected in the United States. Steel, however, was scarce and expensive in post–World War II America, and the initial design had to be discarded. The second design Mies prepared for Greenwald was an ultramodern, 21-story concrete-and-glass slab containing 122 apartments of five and six rooms.[66] No apartment building like it had been built anywhere in America and, not surprisingly, institutional lenders in Chicago refused to provide a mortgage on a building design that had never been tested in the marketplace or make a loan to a company that had never built anything. But, in Mies's words, "Herb needed no hope to begin, and no success to persevere."[67]

As unique as Greenwald's commitment to fine architecture was, his approach to financing for the Promontory Apartments was equally unusual. At the time, there were few cooperative apartment buildings in the United States, and they were primarily in New York City. They provided the model for Greenwald, who proceeded to sell stock in a cooperative housing corporation (co-op), which owned Promontory Apartments. The stock entitled the purchaser to occupy an apartment. Proceeds from sales of the co-op apartments at 5530 South Shore Drive, plus the cash that had been invested by Greenwald and Katzin, provided the equity required by the lender, whose $1.35 million, twenty-five-year, 4.5 percent mortgage covered the rest of the development cost.[68]

The scaled-down development cost for the simple design that Mies proposed allowed Greenwald to ask reasonably low prices for the apartments, and he was able to sell half of them from plans before construction started. He sold the remaining apartments before the concrete frame had been completed. Besides the low purchase price of the shares (and thus of the co-op apartments) and an excellent mortgage on the entire building, the building offered particularly attractive apartments. Wall-to-wall glass provided views of the nearby lakeshore that were more than competitive with suburban views from a picture window.

Three years after Greenwald began his relationship with Katzin, the Promontory Apartments were finished. He went on to work

860–880 Lake Shore Drive, Chicago (2005).

with Mies van der Rohe on the iconic 860–880 Lake Shore Drive Apartments and six more major apartment buildings in Chicago, as well as redevelopment projects in Detroit, New York, and Newark, and a number of projects that did not work out.

Once Greenwald had an appealing product (the glass apartment building) and a proven development team (including Mies van der Rohe), he sought opportunities to mass-market the product without putting up much cash. Opportunities came with the Housing Act of 1954. Developers of government-approved redevelopment projects under Title I of the Housing Act of 1949 now found that institutional lenders were interested in what they were doing, because the lenders for those projects were now promised Federal Housing Administration mortgage insurance. In those urban renewal areas, land had already been cleared, and the necessary approvals were in place. Greenwald thus did not have to purchase the property or cover the costs of relocation, demolition, and site preparation. He did not have to pay taxes, insurance, or other expenses until financing was in place. Furthermore, the sales price of the property was based on the proportion of the total development cost of the housing that allowed the developer to charge market rents. The difference between the actual cost of providing a shovel-ready site and the sale price was government-subsidized (two-thirds from the federal government and one-third from local governments).

On July 30, 1956, Greenwald's company purchased its first urban renewal site, in Detroit's Lafayette Park–University City Urban Renewal Area (originally the Gratiot Redevelopment Area).[69] Construction began six months later, following a design prepared by Mies, landscape architect Alfred Caldwell, and planner Ludwig Hilberseimer. Working with Mies, Greenwald went on to develop two additional urban renewal projects with glass apartment buildings in Newark, New Jersey. Greenwald's career was cut short in 1959, when he was killed in a plane crash at LaGuardia Airport, at the age of forty-three.

The concept of building shopping centers around anchor tenants, pioneered at the Country Club Plaza, spread across the United States and abroad. Glass apartment buildings are now common, although few of them are as beautiful as those Greenwald and Mies created. These glass buildings and shopping facilities have changed our cities and suburbs and have altered living patterns. Among planning techniques and clichés, they have become as ordinary as garden cities, slum clearance, or towers in the park.

Private developers and public entrepreneurs understand that they are not the sole participants in planning. This is particularly true of developers, who depend on lenders, public officials, lawyers, engineers, architects, tenants, and contractors. Herbert Greenwald's work would have been impossible without Samuel Katzin, Mies van der Rohe, institutional lenders, contractors, and, in his later projects, government urban renewal officials.

More than any of the other players, however, it is the public entrepreneurs who depend most on the other participants in the planning game. They are charged by the public with improving our cities and suburbs, usually without the legal authority to change anything. In doing that, public entrepreneurs, like private developers, identify demand, perceive opportunities to supply that demand, adopt already-tested but novel ideas, take risks, raise the money to pay for their activities, obtain public support, find capable associates, and keep at it until their perseverance results in public acceptance and construction. Their activities are constrained by ongoing events, the presence of other players, politics, and the time available for getting things done. They rarely get a second chance if something goes wrong.

Unlike private developers, however, public entrepreneurs are not in the planning game for profit. They explicitly operate on everybody's behalf. But like private developers, they are constrained by the need to finance their projects. Public entrepreneurs also face an additional, particularly onerous problem. Like community leaders and public officials, if they are unable to maintain political support, their role will terminate. Thus, while they are dependent on the economic rules that govern planning, they are even more dependent on the political rules.

Before we turn our focus to public entrepreneurs, however, we will follow private developers through one more chapter. Chapter 3 examines three retail projects undertaken by the Rouse Company, which developed shopping centers and planned new communities between 1939 and 2004. The development of the Rouse Company's project for Quincy Market in Boston helps us to understand the economic rules that govern private development; its involvement with Harborplace in Baltimore helps us to understand how political rules affect the development process; and its participation in the changing retail scene along Third Street in Santa Monica allows us to see what happens when political and economic conditions change.

Santa Monica Place, Santa Monica, California (2011).

THREE

THE RULES OF THE GAME

The previous chapter presented visionaries and reformer-critics, community leaders and public officials, and private developers and public entrepreneurs as players in the planning game, but it did not distinguish the winners from the losers and the also-rans.

There are two sets of winners and losers in the planning game. There are *winning players*, who succeed because they are adept at playing by the rules, and there are *winning bystanders*, whose lives and businesses benefit from the results of the game. There are *losing players*, who make mistakes because they do not understand the rules or because they foolishly ignore them, and there are *losing bystanders*, whose lives and businesses are in some manner damaged by the results of the game.

The planning game is governed by economic and political rules. Winners are skilled at applying them to their own advantage. They sometimes bend the rules, but they never ignore them.

These economic and political rules do not operate perfectly or independently, but they do determine what happens to a planning project. Each set of rules involves a particular set of issues, entails its own considerations, and calls for a particular set of skills. Moreover, the planning game includes players with different objectives, who play different roles at different times, often pulling in very different directions.

The first section of this chapter considers the economic rules that affect planning and development. As an illustration, it describes the evolution of Quincy Market in Boston, examining how the Rouse Company was able to succeed where everyone else had failed. James Rouse understood both the economic rules and the concerns that lay behind them. He created a development plan for Quincy Market and Faneuil Hall that was striking and imaginative, and it was the only one that could have led to success at that time. Rouse's success made Boston a winning bystander.

The second section presents the political rules that affect planning and development. In this section we see the Rouse Company again, operating in its home territory of Baltimore. Rouse developed Baltimore's Harborplace by using all his hometown savvy and his excellent political skills. As a result of the development of Harborplace, the rest of Baltimore's Inner Harbor was a winning bystander, along with Baltimore's tourist industry and its economy. It should be noted, however, that there were retailers and property owners in other parts of downtown Baltimore who lost customers to the new Inner Harbor.

The third section of the chapter looks at the issue of flexibility in the face of shifting conditions and unexpected consequences. Once more we look at the Rouse Company, this time in Santa Monica, California, and study its role in two related projects, Santa Monica Place and the Third Street Promenade. These projects illustrate the core concept that good development must make winners of both the players and the bystanders. A developer's financial success may be the bystanders' loss, and in such a case, the project is judged unsuccessful. In Santa Monica, willingness to rethink mistaken assumptions ultimately produced a highly successful development.

THE ECONOMIC RULES

Planning is neither profit-motivated business nor lighthearted play. It calls for major expenditures by some public entity that will stimulate even greater expenditures by the private sector. When governments install a new transit line, create a park, or build a bridge, they engage in the same activities required of any participant in a market economy. They will be subject to the same dynamics and considerations as the other participants.

The first economic rule of planning is to ignore needs and concentrate instead on present or future market demand. Perceived needs are what some people say other people should have, whether or not they want them, are able to pay for them, or wish to spend their money on them. Needs do not necessarily generate expenditure—demand does. Planners make matters worse when they apply formulas to calculate how things ought to be—a technique commonly known as "needs analysis"—and then shake their heads in dismay when, invariably, the world doesn't behave as it ought.

The second rule is to maximize net operating income (cash revenue minus expenses). Nobody wants to lose money, and effective players work hard to maximize cash flow and minimize their expenses. This is relatively easy

to understand when it comes to private business; failure to match revenues with expenses eventually results in a company going out of business. Governments, however, are usually required to maintain balanced budgets. When they fail to do so, they have to curtail services, terminate employees, or increase taxes.

The third rule, whether applied to a private business or a public agency, is to calibrate risk of failure and the loss of the money and time invested against possible rewards *at every stage of development*. In the case of private business, this is relatively straightforward. Failure to calibrate risk leads to loss of money and property; success generates new operating income. Where failure in the private sector results in hardship for the developer, failure in the public sector results in financial hardship for the citizens affected, and sometimes it produces resignations from public office and changes of administration. Reward is much more difficult to calculate in the public than in the private sector, because the beneficiaries are citizens and businesses, not government agencies.

No government or private business will be able to borrow money for very long to cover ordinary operating expenses. Capital expenditures are a different matter; they tend to use up more money than can be generated from the revenues collected in any one year. Thus, the fourth rule, whether applied to government or private business, is to borrow as much money as possible to cover the costs of capital development.

Money comes at a price. The price governments pay for the money they borrow is determined by the amount of money available and the competition bidding for it, plus a risk premium. That premium reflects the degree of risk investors carry that government might not be able to repay the bondholders who would, as a result, lose their investments. In the case of public borrowings, risk is determined by credit-rating agencies, who analyze the economy of the area affected, the record of the government agency involved, and the likelihood that there will be a sufficient stream of revenue to cover debt service on the bonds. Thus, the price of money to a government agency varies with the assessment of risk by the rating agency.

Governments cannot put up a bridge, a highway, or a park as collateral should they be unable to pay the required debt service. Moreover, they have to borrow the full amount needed for any capital project. They can, however, isolate some revenue streams from all other revenues and pledge those specific revenues to pay bondholders. Thus, in some cases the government will pledge a stream of revenue (tolls from a bridge, tunnel, or highway, or tax payments from the affected district) and issue *revenue bonds*. In other instances a government will pledge its *"full faith and credit"* as well— meaning that the bondholder can depend on being paid out of any and all revenue the government has available, not just the revenue from one particular project.

Private real estate developers act in a very similar manner in amassing the money they need for a project. The money comes from institutional lenders (such as banks), equity investors (such as pension trust funds), and from the partners in the deal. Developers borrow money for their projects from institutional lenders in the form of mortgages, which they promise to repay with interest from net operating revenues. Developers usually pay the least for money provided by long-term institutional lenders, because those lenders carry the least risk should anything go wrong. They have the right to payment in full before any other entity involved in the project is paid, and they have recourse to the property pledged by the borrower as collateral. Nevertheless, most institutional lenders generally lend an amount less than the full value of the property being developed, with the expectation that if they have to foreclose on the mortgage and resell the property, they will recover most of what they have lent. Equity investors, on the other hand, have a claim only on what is left over after the mortgage lender has been paid. Consequently, developers have to promise them a return that is higher than the interest paid to the institutional lenders. The developer, in turn, gets what remains after the lenders and investors have been paid.

As a result, we can refer to cheap money (provided by the mortgage lender, who takes the least risk), expensive money (provided by the investor, who takes a greater risk), and priceless money (provided by the developer, whose time, work, and reputation are also at risk).

When private developers must obtain approvals from one or more agency of government, their risks are of two different types. First, they spend time and money going through the process to obtain necessary permits and approvals. This is the period of greatest risk, because they rarely share expenses with anybody except, possibly, the investors. If the project does not go forward, they have invested time and money for naught. Furthermore, most government officials are insensitive to the fact that the longer the approval process takes, the more money the developers will have at risk. Should the process take too long, developers will be discouraged from going forward. Once government has approved the project, however, the developers face the same conventional risks as developers who do not need government approval.

Most government agencies do not get involved in real estate development. Their expertise is in providing public services or regulating what individuals and businesses do. Therefore, local governments often rely on a special agency to supervise a real estate project. That agency, in turn, is likely to seek experienced developers who will plan, design, and develop the property, find the money to finance it, manage the contractors who erect it, attract tenants to occupy it, and employ the staff to maintain and operate it.

In 1960, Mayor John Collins decided that the city of Boston had to take a major role in reshaping a historically important section of its downtown. This was a section of waterfront once characterized by thriving piers and warehouses, which was now known for vacancy and decay. Collins requested preliminary studies from the Chamber of Commerce and from a specially created Waterfront Commission. He charged the Boston Redevelopment Authority (BRA) to devise a workable strategy to restore

Quincy Market, Boston (1966, 1965, 2010). Faneuil Hall and Quincy Market were obsolete, deteriorating structures when they were acquired by the Boston Redevelopment Authority. The BRA envisioned a charming historical district but for seventeen years was unable to find a developer able to finance renovation of Quincy Market.

economic vitality to the area. In 1964 the BRA applied for and obtained urban renewal subsidies from the U.S. Department of Housing and Urban Development (HUD) to redevelop the area. The subsidies covered two-thirds of the project cost (land acquisition, relocation of residents, demolition of old buildings, and site preparation, minus any revenue from property sales), but left the actual redevelopment to the private sector.

The BRA wanted to save a few of the area's particularly cherished old buildings. Loft conversion was not yet common outside of Manhattan's SoHo neighborhood,[1] and it took the BRA several years to find developers who could transform the area's nineteenth-century warehouses into housing. The developers who got involved with this first stage of waterfront renewal renovated the Mercantile, Lewis, and Commercial wharfs and in 1971 made them available for residential occupancy. Finding a way to renovate Faneuil Hall and Quincy Market took longer.

Faneuil Hall had originally opened in 1742 as a market house with a large assembly hall on the second floor. Charles Bulfinch rebuilt and enlarged it in 1805. The Quincy Market buildings across from Faneuil Hall had been designed by Alexander Parris and were built over a government landfill project. When they opened in 1826, the market consisted of three buildings, each 50 feet wide and 535 feet long, separated by similarly long and narrow open spaces.[2]

At the time the BRA redevelopment plan was approved, Faneuil Hall and Quincy Market were still being used as a wholesale market. Edward Logue, Boston Development Administrator between 1960 and 1967, and the BRA staff wanted to rehabilitate and replace "the existing fruit and produce market with a promenade, specialty shops, entertainment and cultural facilities, and restaurants that would make the historic Faneuil Hall/Quincy Market area a vital and enduring link between Government Center and the Waterfront," and, in addition, "provide valuable supporting activities for the adjacent State Street financial district."[3] But no developer or lender in Boston would risk a penny on an area that the BRA had described in writing as "blighted; deteriorating and obsolescent."[4]

At roughly the time that Logue was trying to devise a workable scheme for Quincy Market, architect Benjamin Thompson became interested in the buildings. Thompson began by assigning students in his class at Harvard to come up with proposals, and in 1965 he began to try different schemes himself. Working with Jane Thompson, his wife and partner in the architectural firm of Benjamin Thompson & Associates, he developed the idea of creating a marketplace for small merchants, artisans, purveyors of fresh food, and restaurants.[5] Although Logue was intrigued with the idea, he did not see how it could be financed.

Logue left Boston for New York in 1968; four years later the BRA decided the time was right to find a developer who could rehabilitate the buildings. By then it had solved a number of problems. It had relocated the market's occupants and obtained a $2.1 million federal grant to help subsidize historic restoration. The BRA issued a request for proposals (RFP) that was won by a local developer with a plan prepared by Thompson. It proposed eliminating motor vehicles from the site's 6.5 acres and renovating the three buildings' 370,000 square feet of space. Some interiors would be gutted and additional floor space would be inserted. The second floor would be devoted to offices and the ground floor to retail shops, and the whole was to be developed within a common architectural framework.

The renovation ran aground on financing. There were still no lenders willing to finance the project because the developer could not produce signed leases and long-term rental guarantees from major anchor tenants. Department stores and most national chains were too big to fit into fifty-foot-wide buildings. Small local retailers, who might have been interested in small spaces, did not have enough money to provide long-term rent guarantees. In the absence of long-term financing or reliable tenant leases, the BRA terminated the relationship and sought a new developer.

Ben Thompson was still convinced his scheme was feasible. He approached Robert E. Simon, developer of the planned community of Reston, Virginia, who was unable to take on the project. Simon in turn recommended James Rouse, a successful Baltimore shopping center developer, who was best known as the creator of Columbia, Maryland. Simon contacted Rouse and urged him to consider the project.[6]

At this point the renovation began to gain momentum. Not only did Rouse understand its potential, but he believed he could obtain the necessary financing and tenants. Department stores, most national retailers, and other anchor tenants all needed too much space. Rouse in the end succeeded because he found a way to do three things: to attract tenants who did not need large facilities; to reduce the amount of money at risk; and to divide that risk into small enough parcels to enable individual banks to participate in an initial mortgage.

It is surprising that Rouse wanted to get involved with the project, because at that time Columbia was having trouble meeting its debt-service obligations. Rouse did not have the equity or market studies that lenders routinely require. Furthermore, he refused to commission market analyses because he was certain that they would fail to demonstrate the probability of adequate tenant rental payments.[7]

To complicate matters further, Rouse had a competitor for the project. Rouse had to convince the BRA to enter into a deal with him rather than with a local developer who was prepared to guarantee the city an annual payment in lieu of taxes (PILOT) of $500,000. In exchange for a ninety-nine-year lease Rouse offered to pay an annual ground rent of $1 plus 20 percent of sales revenue, which his firm guaranteed would never be less than $600,000 per year, plus a contribution of $500,000 over two years for promotion of the bicentennial celebration.[8] The BRA was not convinced he could deliver. Rouse, on the other hand, sought and obtained the active support of the new mayor, Kevin White, by offering him a level of involvement that most developers would have done their best to avoid. Rouse promised to report progress directly to the mayor and to discuss the project with him on a weekly basis.[9]

Even though Rouse had the mayor's backing, it took a year to put the deal with the BRA together and to obtain the necessary financing, but Rouse raised $3 million in equity. Teachers Insurance & Annuity Association, which had financed other Rouse projects, agreed to provide a long-term permanent mortgage of $21 million once the project was completed and was producing an agreed-upon amount of revenue. The Chase Manhattan Bank agreed to provide a construction loan covering half that amount if local banks would cover the rest. Local banks, however, were not willing to be at risk for $10.5 million.[10]

Rouse's solution was to break the project into three phases, beginning with the Central Quincy Market Building. The final deal with the BRA reduced the initial rent payments to $200,000 upon completion of the first building, and another $200,000 for each of the other two buildings. It also increased the ultimate rent to 25 percent of gross rental income plus a portion of net income (after expenses) in excess of $3 million.[11]

Developing the buildings in sequence reduced local bank exposure to $3.75 million and allowed the lender to pull out if any phase failed. Even that proved too big a risk for any single institution and, to reduce risk still further, nine Boston banks formed a consortium to provide the money.[12]

The renovation of the Quincy Market buildings encountered all the surprises and difficulties that come with old structures. Their physical condition proved to be worse than expected, which required an additional million dollars. Consequently, the BRA reduced the rental guarantee for the first three years by $1.05 million. Thus, by the time the project was completed, the total public subsidy had increased to $15.5 million.

The real challenge, however, was to find tenants whose sales revenues would be enough to cover the rental payments. Rouse hoped that when the tenants' rent payments were bundled

Quincy Market, Boston (2009). Adding pushcarts, whose owners could afford a high rent per square foot, increased rental revenue.

together, they would cover operating expenses, mortgage payments, and a large enough payment to the city. Most interested retailers would not move to the narrow spaces without room for storage. One solution was to increase the space available for rent. The other was to find retailers who would use small quantities of space but pay high rents per square foot. This solution would only work if Rouse could create enough retail spaces to maximize the number of such businesses.

The amount of space for rent was increased by: (1) enclosing within a glass roof and walls a corridor of additional space on either side of the Central Market, and (2) by renting locations for pushcarts and kiosks inside and outside the building. Thompson explained that "small spaces with low overhead, benefiting from steady foot traffic" would attract young craftspeople, as well as merchants whose businesses could be adjusted to respond to evolving customer demand.[13] Since the small pushcarts and kiosks occupied a tiny area, they could pay a high rent per square foot. Jane Thompson and Rouse Company staff scoured New England for artists, craftspeople, and small entrepreneurs who offered fashionable clothing, accessories, jewelry, and gifts that were not already

Quincy Market, Boston (2010). Thousands of customers were attracted to the festival atmosphere created by the vendors who occupied the small spaces inside and outside the buildings.

available in Boston. These merchants were in place in time for the opening.

One hundred thousand people visited on the day the first building opened in 1976. Crowds continued to stream in day after day; half came from Boston, a quarter from the suburbs, and tourists made up the remainder. In its first year, sales reached $235 per square foot, dwarfing the $150 per square foot in Rouse's most successful shopping malls. The returns improved in 1977 when the second building opened, and again the following year when the project, which Rouse called a "festival marketplace," was complete.[14]

It took seventeen years for Faneuil Hall and Quincy Market to reach completion. The project survived because local government provided subsidies until it could identify a capable developer. That developer, Rouse, put together a deal that worked in a market economy. The federal government subsidized the cost of historic restoration and paid two-thirds of the cost of planning, relocation, demolition, and site preparation; the City of Boston covered the other third. For more than a decade the city

collected no real estate taxes from the site and paid all the costs of maintaining the area. The subsidies continued until the Rouse Company obtained the necessary development loans and permanent financing and closed the deal with the BRA. The project survived its initial years because the city bought and maintained the buildings and provided the needed subsidies. The city's role, however, does not explain how the buildings were transformed into what Rouse called a "festival marketplace." That happened only because the actors involved were highly skilled at playing the economics of the planning game.

THE POLITICAL RULES

Once developers and public officials believe they have an agreed-upon project, one that is workable within a market economy, they still have to obey the political rules that govern planning. They must gain approval in the court of public opinion, they must disarm opposition, and, frequently, they must obtain explicit public approval in the form of legislation or a referendum. No matter the political system, approval is never automatic. There are many interests and many people involved in or affected by any given project. A successful planner must obtain approval from the right mix of players.

The first political rule is to start with your base. This usually requires obtaining active support from stakeholders.

The second rule is to reduce negative perceptions. This requires taking action to diminish resistance from opponents.

The third rule is to actively cultivate general acceptance by everybody else. This usually requires creating a positive buzz "on the street" and within the media.

There is a fourth rule, which is not always followed, but which prevents later problems. This is to gain formal certification, either by legislative action, referendum, or both.

In practice, obeying these rules means:

- convincing an apathetic and skeptical public;
- ensuring support from property owners concerned about additional taxes;
- overcoming critics (especially those with parochial interests);
- avoiding or surmounting legal barriers put up by opponents;
- obtaining approvals from government agencies;
- preventing delays caused by conflicts among the other players (especially the government agencies whose approval is essential).

The development of Baltimore's Inner Harbor and especially of Harborplace, its festival market, provides an excellent example of how political rules affect planning and how important political skill is to the successful completion of a project. Baltimore's Inner Harbor suffered from many of the problems that had plagued the Boston waterfront: rundown wharfs, empty warehouses, and a produce market that no longer made sense in that location. Like Boston, Baltimore had once been an active international port, but by the mid twentieth century,

shipping had moved elsewhere, leaving behind empty and decaying buildings.

James Rouse knew the site well. A native of Baltimore, he had been involved in earlier citizen efforts to reverse the decline of downtown Baltimore, beginning in 1954, when a group of retailers, alarmed at the closing of a department store, organized the Committee for Downtown, and a group of young financiers and business leaders created the Greater Baltimore Committee. Rouse had been the first head of the Greater Baltimore Committee's executive board.[15] Working together, the two groups formed the Planning Council, a private, nonprofit organization established to come up with a strategy to reverse the decline of downtown. It hired a professional staff and in 1956 raised money to prepare a concept plan for all of downtown Baltimore.[16] The council's first project was the redevelopment of a 33-acre area in the middle of downtown, called Charles Center, which the City Council approved in 1958. Charles Center included 1.8 million square feet of new office space, 430,000 square feet of retailing space, 800 hotel rooms, an 1,800-seat legitimate theater, 367 apartments, and parking for 4,000 cars.[17]

With Charles Center underway and with the active support of Mayor Theodore McKeldin, the city's activist business leaders took on waterfront redevelopment. In 1964 they commissioned a plan from Wallace-McHarg Associates. It called for demolishing existing piers, rebuilding bulkheads, correcting pollution, flooding, and foundation problems, and relocating railroad and utility lines. Unlike Boston, however, very little was to be preserved. All the buildings along the waterfront were to be replaced by new office towers, new housing, and new hotel and convention facilities. Bringing all this to fruition required eight more planning studies and a series of bond issues, which received voter approval between 1966 and 1982.[18]

By 1977 the area had been cleared. A promenade encircled the harbor basin and linked the unrelated recreation areas, empty sites, and scattered office buildings. These included the

Inner Harbor, Baltimore (1972). The reconstruction of Baltimore Harbor began without any tenants on land along the waterfront.

Inner Harbor, Baltimore (2009). The Rouse Company built two glass market structures similar to those at Quincy Market.

32-story World Trade Center office tower, the 40-story U.S. Fidelity & Guarantee Company Building, the 320,000-square-foot branch of the IBM Corporation (including a 700-car garage), and a new federal courthouse. The nearby Baltimore Convention Center was under construction, and plans for hotels were underway. But all this new planning and construction contained a flaw. Most of the activity at Inner Harbor took place on weekdays, during the hours when people entered and left the new office buildings. After 6 P.M. and on weekends the Inner Harbor was virtually empty.

Rouse felt he had the answer. A major retail and tourist attraction like Quincy Market would be just the thing to enliven the Inner Harbor and keep it active on evenings and weekends. There was no need to test-market the idea; the city was already running entertainment-related retailing along the waterfront on "Sunny Sundays," including flea markets, free concerts, boat races, and parades. Every Labor Day weekend, there was the Baltimore City Fair, which drew more than a million people to the Inner Harbor.[19]

When Rouse decided to create a festival marketplace in Baltimore's Inner Harbor, he already knew that Quincy Market was going to be a huge success. The concept had proven itself on a smaller scale earlier: in 1967 at Ghirardelli Square in San Francisco, in the late 1960s at Old Market in Omaha, and in 1972 at Trolley Square in Salt Lake City. Unlike these projects, however, the Inner Harbor had no charming older buildings that could be reused to create the necessary festival atmosphere. Rouse therefore commissioned Ben Thompson & Associates to create long, narrow, contemporary structures that, like Quincy Market, could be used by local craftspeople, small retailers, and restaurateurs. They called the two new glass and concrete structures Harborplace.

Rouse needed the backing of Mayor William Donald Schaefer, and he knew just how to get it. Rouse invited Schaefer to Boston for the opening of the second Quincy Market building. When Mayor Schaefer saw the pushcarts, kiosks, and noisy crowds clamoring to spend money, his competitive fire ignited, and he bluntly declared, "Baltimore has got to have one of these."[20]

The Quincy Market financial deal was adapted to the Inner Harbor's 3.2-acre site. As in Boston, the city would receive $100,000 in ground rent (with escalators over time), 25 percent of the net cash flow after operating expenses, debt service on the mortgage, and a 10 percent return on the developer's cash investment.[21] In February 1978, at the mayor's urging, the city council approved the Rouse proposal for what would become Harborplace.

This was just the beginning. Rouse would have to continue to use his political skills and his knowledge of Baltimore if he was to come out a winner. He had been chairman of the Greater Baltimore Committee in 1965, at the

time it published its initial proposals for the harbor, and from that experience, he knew what form the opposition to the project would take. In fact, there would be two main focal points of opposition: opposition to commercialization of the waterfront in general, and opposition to an exclusive deal with the city's major developer of shopping centers in particular. Rouse's task would be to gain approval for this festival marketplace in spite of the lively politics that characterized Baltimore.

Rouse had a long commitment to public involvement in planning, going back to his participation in Baltimore's Citizens Planning and Housing Association in the 1940s. In 1953, President Eisenhower recognized Rouse's commitment to public involvement in planning when he appointed him chair of the urban redevelopment section of the President's Advisory Committee on Government Housing Policies and Programs.[22] Moreover, throughout his career Rouse had actively worked to prevent blockbusting and discriminatory sales practices in Baltimore and to insure that all his projects would be open to everybody.

Rouse was right when he predicted that there would be opposition to commercialization of the waterfront. But some of the project's opponents were also opponents of Mayor Schaefer. They wanted him to suffer a defeat, and they chose to make Harborplace their battleground. As their opening salvo, they proposed an amendment to the city charter forbidding any commercial development along the 22-acre waterfront.[23]

This proposal attracted support from a number of groups: from nearby merchants who feared competition; from Little Italy and other ethnic neighborhoods, worried that Harborplace might draw away tourists; from residents of nearby Fell's Point who worried about the noise and crowds that might overflow into their neighborhood; from open-space advocates who wanted to restrict the use of the Inner Harbor to recreation; and from ordinary citizens who objected to overcommercialization. One opponent explained that "a slick shopping mall in the Inner Harbor" could damage both the existing

Inner Harbor, Baltimore (2009). The festival atmosphere along the waterfront attracts thousands of tourists from the metropolitan area and beyond.

"ma and pa" retailers and the new small shops being opened by young people attracted to charming older buildings.[24] Others argued that "nothing could be more short-sighted or callous than to give away a precious open space for a high-powered, money-generating, thinly veiled shopping mall that will obscure what is beautiful and enduring at the waterfront."[25] Harborplace was becoming the year's hottest issue.

Bruce Alexander, then director of commercial development for the Rouse Corporation, decided that the best way to defeat the opposition was to introduce a second charter amendment confining retailing to 3.2 of the 22 acres. Working with other leaders of Baltimore's business establishment, he put together a coalition of four groups: proponents of good government; residents of the city's prosperous neighborhoods who wanted a downtown destination that was lively in itself and that would trigger further revitalization; political allies of Mayor Schaefer; and leaders of Baltimore's African-American neighborhoods.[26]

The Harborplace coalition printed leaflets and distributed T-shirts advocating the project. Alexander attended countless community meetings. The African-American commu-

nity, whose causes Rouse had supported long before passage of the equal opportunity legislation of the 1960s, distributed 60,000 pamphlets supporting Harborplace. Its Ministerial Alliance urged congregants to support the charter amendment that permitted Harborplace, rather than the one that forbade it.[27]

Harborplace won the referendum; in African-American precincts, 72 percent of the votes were favorable.[28] The festival marketplace did indeed prove to be what was needed; it broke the logjam that was holding up development of the Inner Harbor, and it triggered its transformation. The 18 million visitors who came during the first year of operation made Harborplace the Rouse Company's top-producing project, with average per-square-foot sales that exceeded those of Quincy Market.[29]

Like every developer, Rouse was successful wherever his projects followed the economic rules. In Baltimore, however, where politics were intense, the political rules were especially important. Here Rouse made a concerted effort (1) to gain general acceptance for the concept of a festival marketplace on the waterfront, (2) to galvanize powerful proponents, (3) to neutralize the opposition, and (4) to obtain voter sanction.

Because Rouse understood both the political rules and the Baltimore context so well, he was able to bring home a victory. The residents of Baltimore were its beneficiaries.

CONTINUALLY CHANGING CONDITIONS

While economic and political rules are constants in the planning game, most other conditions are variable. Skilled players adjust their strategies to changes in taste, technology, government, conventional wisdom, and every other aspect of contemporary life. Sometimes a player ignores a rule and loses the game. In such a case, other players may adjust their strategies successfully and snatch victory from defeat.

Unexpected outcomes are not the only variables in the planning game. Fashion, for example, is particularly subject to change, and clothing retailers are perhaps the players most sensitive to changes in taste. But all retailers continually reposition their businesses in response to changing patterns of consumption. The shift from mom-and-pop stores to big-box stores is a good example.

Changes in technology also affect patterns of consumption. Few vacationers went to Miami Beach before the extension of the railroad, but the real flood of visitors arrived when air travel became inexpensive. In the present century, as people have come to do much of their shopping on the Internet, the double click has replaced the trip to the store.

Legislation, too, can have an impact on the commercial landscape. The Eighteenth Amendment to the Constitution, adopted in 1919, outlawed the transportation and distribution of liquor across state lines. The era of speakeasies coincided exactly with the fourteen years of Prohibition; they appeared as soon as Prohibition was enacted, and they disappeared when it ended in 1933.

Conventional wisdom is another important element in the changing context of the planning game. Throughout the 1940s, most players believed that the cure for impoverished slums consisted of clearing old buildings, even

entire neighborhoods; maintaining carefully separated land uses; and constructing entire districts of modern high-rise apartments. After the publication of Jane Jacobs's book *The Death and Life of Great American Cities*, an increasing number of players rejected those remedies and instead recommended neighborhood preservation and high-density mixed land use.

The lesson here is that while effective players in the planning game must obey relatively stable economic and political rules, they will fail if they do not adjust their strategies to the changing context in which planning takes place. In the evolution of Third Street in Santa Monica, California, over the past half century, we can examine both unexpected outcomes and creative recoveries.

The origin of the Santa Monica story lies in the opening of a pedestrian mall in 1959 in Kalamazoo, Michigan. The innovation that the Kalamazoo Mall introduced to America was the removal of vehicular traffic from retail streets and their transformation into pedestrian-friendly precincts. Kalamazoo's mall was successful, and for many cities it became the model of how to revive fading commercial districts. [30]

One of the earliest projects to be modeled on the Kalamazoo Mall opened in 1965 on Third Street in Santa Monica, California, two blocks from Palisades Park, which runs along Ocean Avenue on a cliff overlooking Santa Monica Pier and beach. Although east-west traffic was allowed to cross Third Street at signalized intersections, three contiguous north-south blocks between Broadway and Wilshire Boulevard became pedestrian-only precincts. The changeover cost $703,000, 90 percent of which was raised by assessing local businesses; the city paid for only 10 percent. [31] In addition, the city built 2,600 parking spaces in six flanking garages that provided access to more than one hundred stores, restaurants, and movie theaters located on those three blocks of Third Street. [32] Like Kalamazoo, Santa Monica now had an open-air mall, defined by its pedestrian-friendly character and centered on the Third Street businesses.

But further change was in the air. By the time the Third Street pedestrian mall opened, air-conditioned shopping malls were making their first appearances around the country. Civic leaders concluded that if Santa Monica did not open one, Third Street would lose business to any air-conditioned malls that opened in the Los Angeles area. In 1972 the Santa Monica Redevelopment Agency selected a three-block redevelopment site for an air-conditioned shopping center at the south end of the mall, just off the Santa Monica Freeway. In addition to parking lots, the site held scattered buildings containing fourteen residences, thirty-five businesses, and the headquarters of United Western Newspapers, publisher of the *Santa Monica Evening Outlook*.[33] The redevelopment agency issued a request for proposals (RFP) for redevelopment of those three blocks.

Two companies responded: the Rouse Company and the Hahn Company. Both had experience developing shopping centers. Hahn proposed a conventional air-conditioned shopping center combined with parking structures. The Rouse proposal was designed by a Santa Monica resident who was not yet well known, the architect Frank Gehry. Gehry had designed the Rouse headquarters in Columbia, Maryland, but he devised a much more ambitious scheme for his hometown: 200 apartments, a 400-room hotel, garages, and an air-conditioned retail center anchored by two department stores.[34] In spite of substantial opposition at public hearings, the City Council voted unani-

Third Street Pedestrian Mall, Santa Monica (1979). Pedestrianizing Third Street initially made it an attractive destination for local shoppers.

mously to reject Hahn and to negotiate a better version with Rouse.

In its deal with Rouse the redevelopment agency agreed to finance the parking structures with bonds. It anticipated that property values would increase both at the site and in the area surrounding the project. The increased property values would generate increased tax revenues; those revenues would be used to service the debt on the bonds.

Naturally, there were lawsuits claiming that the area was not blighted, that taking private property to transfer it to a private developer was unconstitutional, and that $15 million in city-bond financing for parking was a subsidy to the developer that discriminated against other retail businesses that did not have subsidized parking. The courts, however, upheld the legality of the redevelopment project.

Meanwhile, one of the three blocks was deleted from the site, and everything but retail and parking were eliminated from the project. Since Rouse was headquartered on the East Coast and Hahn had considerable experience building and managing similar projects in California, the two developers entered into a partnership to develop Santa Monica Place, a three-level, 120-store, air-conditioned mall anchored by Macy's and Robinson's department stores.[35]

When it opened in 1980, Santa Monica Place was both a roaring success and a major planning failure. It was unquestionably a money-making machine for Rouse and Hahn. In its early years, Santa Monica Place attracted hundreds of thousands of visitors every week—people who drove in, parked their cars, and went shopping.[36]

In this pattern lay its failure. The planners only satisfied demand for an air-conditioned shopping mall; not only did they not increase retail demand on Third Street, they drew away many of its customers. Within a few years the disaster was evident to everyone. What had been since 1965 a healthy but unexceptional pedestrian precinct was transformed after 1980 into three blocks of vacant buildings, empty movie theaters, and bedraggled retail stores selling low-priced items. As a result of this, the

Santa Monica Place (1991). The distinctive supergraphics of Frank Gehry's façade for Santa Monica Place acted as a billboard attracting drivers from all over the region.

Santa Monica Place (1992). Three stories of air-conditioned shopping initially attracted shoppers from all over Los Angeles County.

homeless people who had always been present on Third Street now became more visible, in fact a major presence.

The planners who had brought an air-conditioned mall to the south end of Third Street thought that they were moving with the times and keeping Third Street commerce competitive. They expected an increase in retail activity on Third Street, bringing additional jobs and taxes to Santa Monica. Instead, the new shopping mall introduced competition that resulted in the decline of retailing on Third Street. In fact, Santa Monica Place all but destroyed Third Street. The big winner at this stage was the Rouse Company; local merchants and some nearby residents were the losers. But the game was far from over.

Now the planners, who had misunderstood the economic rules, faced an abrupt political turnaround. The shopkeepers and property owners who had footed the bill to turn Third Street into a pedestrian space, as well as many of the residents of Santa Monica, demanded that the City Council repair the damage it had caused to Third Street.

City manager John Alschuler was the principal player managing the government's

Third Street Pedestrian Mall (1985). Many customers who used to shop at the stores along the pedestrian mall deserted it and chose to go to Santa Monica Place instead.

response. He felt that the Third Street pedestrian mall needed more than a new design; the street itself needed a constituency and an entity that would be responsible for its maintenance and management. Alschuler first proposed a minor vehicular roadway down the middle of Third Street. But his major plan, whose success rendered the roadway unnecessary, was adopted by the City Council as the comprehensive Third Street Specific Plan.

The plan was a package of actions. It created the Bayside District Corporation to manage the revitalization of the six blocks between Second and Fourth Streets, north of Santa Monica Place. It brought about the redesign and reconstruction of the pedestrian areas (by the ROMA Design Group), and it included a special zoning district, which allowed property owners to build additional floor area in exchange for including entertainment-related uses, access through their property to off-street parking, and housing on their properties.[37]

New multiplex movie theaters and restaurants attracted customers to the rebuilt and renamed Third Street Promenade. A popular farmers' market began operations twice weekly. In the early 1990s, Urban Outfitters opened a store on the Promenade, bringing in teens and twenty-somethings. Urban Outfitters' success attracted additional fashion outlets and national retailers, like Barnes & Noble, Borders, and Pottery Barn.[38] The winners in this stage of the planning game were the big

national stores on Third Street and many residents of Los Angeles County. Once again, the smaller Third Street merchants were the losers.

The Third Street Promenade became a destination of choice for people from communities in western Los Angeles County and beyond, and especially for young people. Street entertainers and restaurants created the sort of festival atmosphere the Rouse Company had brought to Quincy Market and Harborplace. By the late 1990s the local and national retailers on the Third Street Promenade were making more sales per square foot than Santa Monica Place.

By the mid-1990s, moreover, the retail environment had changed once more. Big-box, discount, and Internet retailers absorbed a growing share of retail consumer spending. Many traditional department stores had trouble competing, and most of the ones that were not part of large national chains went out of business. These trends directly affected business at Santa Monica Place.

Back in 1980, Hahn's interest in Santa Monica Place had been transferred to TrizecHahn, a company created when the Trizec Corporation of Toronto acquired the Hahn Company. In 1998, TrizecHahn left the shopping center business, and Rouse acquired its share of the Santa Monica Place project, hoping to reverse the decline of shopping at the mall. The following year Macerich, a large Santa Monica-based owner of shopping centers, purchased Santa Monica Place from Rouse, convinced that they would do better than Rouse—and they did.

Macerich identified four groups of customers coming to shop in Santa Monica: the increasingly hip and wealthy residents on the west side of Los Angeles County; tourists coming to California from around the world; residents from the east side of Los Angeles, the San Fernando Valley, and further inland, seeking interesting things to do and the cooler temperatures along the Pacific Ocean; and the city's growing daytime workforce.[39] Santa Monica Place had been a conventional, middle-market center, but now it was losing customers to alternatives that shoppers found more appealing, especially the popular national retailers who were replacing

Third Street Promenade (2011). After renovation and the introduction of incentives for entertainment-related occupants, the pedestrian environment and benign climate became a destination of choice for tourists from the Los Angeles region and beyond.

local merchants on Third Street. By 2000 these national retailers were attracting throngs of shoppers and achieving record sales. Shoppers no longer had any compelling reason to venture into Santa Monica Place. Macerich decided to reposition Santa Monica Place to appeal to this growing market and to tie the shopping center more closely to the Third Street Promenade.

But once again the redevelopment agency had more ambitious plans. Like Macerich, it wanted to connect the project to the civic resources that surrounded it—not just to Third Street, but also to the Santa Monica Pier to the west and the civic center to the south. At the same time, it encouraged Macerich to add 450 apartments in three 21-story condo towers, plus an office complex.

There was ample opposition to the city's plan. Frank Gehry, who now believed that shopping malls were "placating the public or second guessing the public, in effect talking down to the public,"[40] avoided becoming involved with the project's redesign. Some opponents thought the project would create too much vehicular traffic. Others opposed altering the skyline. Macerich was accused of "capitalist oppres-

sion." After several years of controversy, during which council members kept shifting their positions and their votes, Macerich decided to proceed under the existing zoning and not to seek further government action.

When Santa Monica Place reopened in 2010 after two years of construction, it was no longer a self-contained, air-conditioned mall. The skylight had been removed; several floors of parking, which had blocked the view of the main shopping area from the promenade, had been cut away; and circulation spaces were now open to Santa Monica's benign climate. Shoppers coming from the Third Street Promenade could cross Broadway and walk directly to high-end stores without going down steps, opening doors, or passing through a dark passage and a food court before getting to the central retail space. Robinson's and Macy's had been replaced by Nordstrom and Bloomingdale's; new retailers included Burberry, Vuitton, Tiffany, and others catering to a very high-end market. The food court was moved from the entry to the mall up to the third level, where customers could catch a glimpse of the ocean.

Third Street and Santa Monica Place (2011). Continuing the pedestrian world of Third Street into a repositioned, open-air Santa Monica Place attracted customers back to its department stores.

The only remnant of Gehry's work was the distinctive chain-link fencing on the south façade, with supergraphics announcing Santa Monica Place. Macerich hired the Jerde Partnership and ROMA Design, whose work on the Promenade it admired, to provide Santa Monica Place a completely new look.

The pendulum had swung from one extreme to the other. First, a successful Santa Monica Place destroyed Third Street. Then the development of Third Street sucked the life out of Santa Monica Place. It was only when they were in balance and fully accessible to each other that the project was a success.

The next four chapters cover specific aspects of the planning game itself, distinct from questions of who plays it and what rules govern it. The chapters explore in some depth the topics of investing in the public realm, the planning process, implementing an agreed-upon agenda, and the role of the planner. We

do not totally abandon the rules of planning. In each of the four cities discussed, planning that had been going on for decades came to an end when it could not conform to the economic rules and pluralist politics of a later era.

In Chapters 2 and 3 we have followed the ways in which political and economic rules affect private entrepreneurs. The same rules affect public entrepreneurs, who can take us to the heart of the planning experience through a focus on the public realm. Public entrepreneurs are the major focus of the next part of this book, where we look at different aspects of the planning process through the experience of four of the greatest of them. By focusing on Georges-Eugène Haussmann (1809–1891), Daniel Burnham (1846–1912), Robert Moses (1888–1981), and Edmund Bacon (1910–2005), we see that the planning process and the skills it demands are largely the same in different times and different places.

Paris, 2010.

FOUR

THE PUBLIC REALM APPROACH: MAKING PARIS *PARIS*

Paris is one of the most beautiful cities in the world, yet few of its buildings rank among the world's most extraordinary examples of architecture. The city's overall look has, in fact, less to do with architecture than with the public realm framework that guided the nineteenth-century planners who rebuilt it into the city we know today. When a visitor thinks of Paris, he or she is likely to think of the public spaces of Paris, the public realm shared by all those who sojourn there for a week or stay for a lifetime.

Paris is defined both visually and in its culture by many things: the tree-lined avenues; the sidewalk cafés where one can meet a friend or linger over the newspaper and a coffee; the shallow, sensuous curve of the Boulevard Saint-Germain; and the serene beauty of the parks, large and small, which both enhance their surroundings and are enhanced by them. It is this public realm that defines Paris.

It should come as no surprise, therefore, that Paris became *Paris* through a *public realm approach* to planning. Beginning in the middle of the nineteenth century, the city's leaders pursued a program of *public investment in public property*—in Paris's streets and squares, its transportation systems, its infrastructure and

public buildings, and its parks. Remarkably, they invested in each project not only because of its utility. Each investment was intended to shape the experience of daily life for the residents of Paris and to provide a framework for the changes that would take place over the next century and beyond. The Paris we know today is the product of those strategic public investments made by many different governments over nearly two centuries.

The metamorphosis of Paris truly began in 1848. In that year a revolution overthrew Louis-Philippe and the plutocracy known as the July Monarchy. Louis-Napoléon Bonaparte, nephew of the great Napoléon, returned from exile and was elected president of the new Second Republic. Three years later he overthrew that republic and proclaimed the Second Empire, which lasted until 1870.

Louis-Napoléon had spent the last years of his exile in England. He came back to Paris with admiration for many things English, not least of them the parks and squares of London. He would draw on those memories in the years of rebuilding to come.

The city to which Louis-Napoléon returned was vastly overcrowded and was experiencing a crisis in public services. In 1848 a little

Paris (1848). When Napoleon III came to power, Paris consisted of the twelve arrondissements within the Farmers-General Wall. The Champs Élysées extended from the outskirts of the city to the Tuileries and continued eastward along an initial section of the Rue de Rivoli.

over a million people lived inside the walls of the world's third-largest city, after London and Peking.[1] Some of its 1848 landmarks remain prominent today: the Seine, Notre-Dame, the Champs-Élysées. But the Seine stank from the raw sewage flowing into it from open street gutters, and it flooded Paris ten times between 1800 and 1848.[2] The towers of Notre-Dame were barely visible above the tightly packed tenements that covered the Île de la Cité. The Champs-Élysées originated in the countryside west of the city. It continued past the Arc de Triomphe (built between 1806 and 1836), through the wall of the Farmers-General (built between 1784 and 1791), and terminated at the Place de la Concorde (built before the French Revolution, between 1755 and 1775).

Paris in 1848 was divided into twelve densely packed districts, or arrondissements, which covered 13.3 square miles. The original twelve arrondissements included residences of the wealthy, retail shops, businesses and manufacturing establishments that were mostly small, and slums.[3] Living conditions were dreadful. Many of the city streets were described at the time as "mere trenches, dirty, and always humid with infected water." People moved through them "foot in the gutter, nose in infection, and eye struck at each corner by the most repulsive filth."[4]

Parisian businesses were already a vital part of France's economy, generating a quarter of the country's exports. Of their 350,000 employees, about one-third were involved in the production and distribution of garments and textiles, one-ninth in construction, one-tenth in metals, and another tenth in furniture.[5] Many of these industries produced the luxury products for which France was famous: gold and silver, inlaid wood furniture, embroideries for luxury dresses, and hand-sewn flowers. More modern industries were growing up in Paris, too. But the city's narrow, congested streets could barely handle their traffic, not to mention the traffic generated by the other 700,000 occupants of the city. Simply distributing food to these 1,050,000 residents was a problem. People arriving at any of the city's six railroad terminals made their way through a tangled, narrow maze of arteries used daily by thousands of delivery vehicles, hundreds of thousands of residents, workers, visitors, and 37,000 horses, whose droppings were supposed to be removed once a day.[6]

Paris would soon be unable to sustain the flow of goods and services to the businesses that provided jobs for its population. It was now competing with cities like London, Liverpool, Manchester, and New York for global economic dominance, and while living conditions in those cities were not much better, local governments were making steady improvements.

While Napoléon III (the title Louis-Napoléon adopted in 1852, when he proclaimed the Second Empire) ruled France, an unprecedented amount of money was spent to create an infrastructure and community facilities for Paris. These expenditures were intended to make it easier for Parisian industry to compete for customers and for its residents to live healthier, more pleasant lives. *The strategy succeeded*. The government created an entirely new water supply and distribution system, and sewer, park, and transportation networks that serviced all of Paris. Government investment triggered similarly massive spending by private businesses and the construction of more than 102,000 new buildings by property owners. The scope of change is astonishing when one realizes that a virtually new Paris was created in less than twenty-two years. It was achieved, however, at huge cost to many of the residents and businesses in the city; more than 117,000 households and 350,000 industrial and commercial jobs were relocated, and more than 27,000 buildings were demolished.[7] Much historical memory was lost along with the filthy, convoluted streets of old Paris.

It is often said that the rebuilding of Paris was easy because it was backed by Louis-Napoléon. But in Paris, as in any public planning project, nothing was simple. The Second Empire was not an absolute monarchy, where the emperor ordered change and it was done. There were plenty of players in the planning game, and they all (Napoléon III included) had to play by its rules.

The Second Republic was described by Karl Marx as a "motley mix of crying contradictions: constitutionalists who conspire openly against the Constitution; revolutionists who are confessedly constitutional; a National Assembly that wants to be omnipotent and always remains parliamentary . . . [and] royalists who . . . keep the Republic, which they hate."[8] Later, during the eighteen years of the Second Empire, Paris was ruled by a similarly shifting combination of entities that included Napoléon III and his ministers, three national legislative bodies (the National Assembly, the Senate, and an appointed Council of State), the prefect of the Seine, the Paris Municipal Council, the Seine departmental commission, the courts, twelve (and later twenty) arrondissement councils, and much of the same "motley mix" of constitutionalists, revolutionists, and royalists as under the Second Republic.[9] Nevertheless, the single most important figure in this "motley mix" of players was Georges-Eugène Haussmann, who was prefect of the Seine from 1853 to 1870.

Rue de la Colombe in nineteenth-century Paris.

THE TEAM THAT TRANSFORMED PARIS

Haussmann was a Protestant of Alsatian descent. He grew up in a middle-class family in Paris, where he attended the best schools and went on to study law. At the age of twenty-two he began his administrative career in Poitiers, working for two decades in a series of provincial subprefect and prefect positions.[10] In 1853, Napoléon III and his minister of the interior, the extraordinary Duc de Persigny, chose him to be prefect of the Seine.

Haussmann used his family connections—and even a school chum who was the son of King Louis-Philippe—to advance his career at every opportunity, but it was evident from the time of his first position, in Nérac in southwestern France, that he got things done. In Nérac, where the streets were unpaved, Haussmann found ways to finance road improvements. By the age of twenty-eight he had received the *Légion d'honneur* for building more schools than any other subprefect. In Saint-Girons he successfully terminated smuggling to and from Spain. It did not hurt, of course, that Haussmann's two grandfathers had been generals under Napoleon I. That provided him with an excellent Bonapartist pedigree and stood him in good stead when Napoleon's nephew became president in 1848 and emperor in 1852. But his brilliance was beyond doubt.

Georges-Eugène Haussmann.

As prefect of the Seine, Haussmann was in effect a regional chief executive officer. He was responsible for the city and for the surrounding districts of Saint-Denis and Sceaux, and he consequently supervised a huge staff that performed a wide variety of functions. It collected local taxes and customs duties, prepared budgets, and managed expenditures; it supervised railways and quarries, and maintained streets and highways; it operated public markets, parks, schools, hospitals, facilities for the elderly, the insane, and orphans; and it designed, planned, and managed the city's future.[11]

Haussmann was an experienced public administrator, and he understood that a great national capital was dependent on this vast bureaucracy to provide public services to a huge and growing commercial and industrial city. Part of his brilliance was to put his own stamp on the bureaucracy that ran Paris. He reorganized the Paris government into sixteen divisions plus forty-five bureaus to implement the work these administrative units managed.[12] So much needed to be done that without clear lines of authority there would have been no way to ensure efficient, cost-effective operations or accountability to the city's leadership. Equally important, he found exceptional people to run these offices, many of them professionals he had encountered during his years in the provinces. This was another aspect of Haussmann's brilliance—his swift recognition of talent, much of it underused. Among the most important members of his team were Eugène Deschamps, Eugène Belgrand, Jean-Charles-Adolphe Alphand, horticulturalist Jean-Pierre Barrilet-Deschamps, and the architects Victor Baltard, Jacques-Ignace Hittorff, and Gabriel Davioud.

Eugène Deschamps (1812–1880) was an architect and survey engineer who became key to the planning of the city's streets, sidewalks, and blocks of new buildings. Haussmann himself later said that "Deschamps was the Plan of Paris."[13] When he first encountered Deschamps, the latter was an obscure bureaucrat with the title of survey registrar. This young architect worked with five surveyors in a lackluster agency that proposed public works projects to representatives of the Ministry of Public Works and the Ministry of the Interior.[14] Haussmann recognized a dysfunctional agency when he saw one, and he also recognized Deschamps's talent. First he brought the agency into shape by doubling its size and dividing it into two departments (one for erecting public buildings and the other for surveying and creating public thoroughfares). Then he put Deschamps at the head of the new agency, in charge of surveying, designing, and laying out public roads.[15]

The surveying of Paris was no small task. At that time there was no reliable complete plan of the city. There were only partial surveys, which had been made as needed for widening a thoroughfare or for building one from scratch. Street alignments, too, were determined on an ad hoc basis. Haussmann asked Deschamps to prepare a triangulation survey of the city and to create a comprehensive map of Paris, including gradient alignments, legal lot lines, and accurate dimensions. Haussmann ordered publication of two versions of the map, one in the original 5-by-8-foot size, and one for public consumption at half that scale. [16]

Important as were Deschamps' technical skills and fastidious work, his discretion and integrity were even more vital. He was

A contemporary cartoon caricaturing surveying methods for the area around the zoo.

the repository of much confidential financial information, and, based on his work, decisions were made about payments of large amounts of money. He was responsible for the rights-of-way the government decided on, and he provided the information necessary for legislative approvals and judicial reviews. Payments were made for the negotiated purchase of property and for condemnation awards. Tenant indemnification payments from the resale of surplus property and expenditures for demolition and road construction were based on his work. Indiscretion could result in large-scale land speculation and fraud, but Haussmann had chosen his team well, and Deschamps was clean as a whistle. He retired with a meager pension, which Haussmann managed to improve, and he died a poor but honorable man.[17]

Haussmann first met the engineer Eugène Belgrand (1810–1878) in 1850, when he was still prefect of Yonne. Haussmann was impressed by a fountain Belgrand had designed, and he engaged him in a conversation about the geology and hydrology of the Pyrénées that convinced him this was an engineer of extraordinary talent. Thereafter he helped advance Belgrand's career. When he became prefect of the Seine, Haussmann brought Belgrand to work on his first memorandum on the Paris water system. In 1855, when Haussmann persuaded the Municipal Council to separate the water and sewer department from the agency in charge of public roads, he appointed Belgrand director of water and sewers for Paris.[18] Belgrand planned, designed, and managed construction of the water and sewer systems for which Haussmann was responsible.

The third and perhaps most important member of Haussmann's team was Jean-Charles-Adolphe Alphand (1817–1891), an engineer and landscape architect whose official title was chief engineer in the Services des Promenades et Plantations. Relative to the work of the other people on Haussmann's team, Alphand's probably did the most to alter the quality of life of the Parisians and visitors. Haussmann had worked with Alphand in Bordeaux and brought him to Paris to supervise the transformation of

Avenue Foch, Paris (2006).

the Bois de Boulogne from a royal forest pre-serve into a verdant and popular public park. He later put him in charge of designing and building the city's other parks, installing what we think of as distinctive Parisian street fur-niture, and planting the trees that everywhere soften the vistas of the city.

Haussmann sometimes had serious disagree-ments with his architects, but he knew how to bring out their best possible work. At the start of his prefecture, for example, Jacques Ignace Hittorf (1792–1867) showed him a plan for a 40-meter-wide, treeless Avenue Foch. Hauss-mann exclaimed, "The Emperor does not want that. . . . Triple it: 120 meters—add to your plan two [flanking] lawns . . . of 32 meters . . . which will allow me to plant groups of trees."[19]

He took a similar but more circuitous approach with the architect Victor Baltard

(1805–1874) for the creation of the city's public market (Les Halles). Construction of the first of eight market buildings had begun two years before Haussmann became prefect. It was halted the month he took office, however, because Napoléon III was dissatisfied with the masonry structure designed by Baltard, who happened to be a schoolmate of Haussmann. Baltard's plan called for heavy masonry; it was not the simple, functional pavilion the emperor had expected. Napoléon III ordered Haussmann to obtain a design of "iron, iron, nothing but iron."[20]

A number of architects were therefore invited to submit designs. Meanwhile, Haussmann had Baltard redesign the market with a broad traffic artery bisecting the site. This would carry the heavy traffic going to and from Châtelet and the bridge across the Seine. After Baltard had rede-signed the pavilions three times, Haussmann was finally satisfied. He presented the submissions of all the architects to Napoléon III, saving Baltard for last. When the emperor saw Baltard's revised plan, he exclaimed: "That's it! That's absolutely it."[21]

Haussmann possessed a combination of administrative brilliance, the ability to spot talent, and an uncanny understanding of what Napoléon III wanted. The rebuilding of Paris required more than the emperor's enthusiasm, however; it required understanding and cooperation from all the major players, in and out of government. This was particularly true of the new district that was to be created around the Central Market.

Haussmann wanted to be sure that everyone could see and understand the project's impact. He therefore requested a scale model of the entire neighborhood: the metal pavilions, the surrounding streets, sidewalks, carts moving produce, and pedestrians. Only when most of the relevant officials had approved what he had in mind did the prefect disclose that the plan was by the original architect, who had been dismissed.[22]

The model of Les Halles reveals an impor-

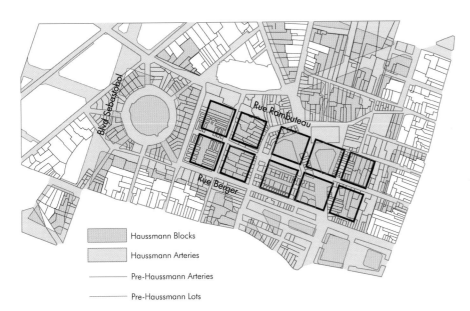

Les Halles, Paris (1800s). Creation of the city's central market required tearing out all the buildings on the site and its surroundings and piercing through major arteries that allowed huge quantities of produce to be shipped in and out.

Les Halles, Paris (1950s). Aerial view after completion.

Les Halles, Paris (1853).

tant aspect of Haussmann's method. He did not build isolated public works. Rather, he thought of them as part of a public realm framework for the continuing redevelopment of the entire city, and he was fortunate that his conception was shared by the minister of the interior, the Duc de Persigny. This conception of the public realm became the framework around which everything would grow—and it gave Haussmann leverage in capturing and guiding private investment. Part of the genius of the mid-nineteenth-century planning for Paris is that Paris and the public realm were conceived to be inseparable.

INFRASTRUCTURE FOR A MODERN ECONOMY

The public realm includes a great deal more than the scene admired by a tourist walking down the Boulevard Saint-Germain. It includes, as well, things that we do not see, but that make possible the growth of the city. Paris doubled in population between 1848 and 1870, in part due to the annexation of the faubourgs, but certainly made possible by the creation of a network of grand boulevards, like the Boulevard Saint-Germain.

When Haussmann's team set out to rebuild Paris with an eye to making it economically competitive, the city lacked two essential services: a reliable supply of clean water and an

effective system of waste removal. Its water came from many sources, but they were not easily accessible, and they were not related to each other. People got their drinking water from private water carriers, from 1,779 public street fountains, 113 commercial fountains, and 69 wells, from pumps located along the Seine, and from the Canal de l'Ourcq. Before Haussmann most people did not get their water from pipes or from delivery services. Private piping systems supplied a mere 7,771 registered customers, 160 of which were government entities and 223 of which were hospitals. Only one house in five was connected to water pipes, usually through a tap in the yard. Indoor plumbing was rare; a few houses had it, but pressure was so low that water rarely rose above the first or second floor.[23]

Haussmann's effort to provide Paris with a dependable supply of clean water faced opposition from the start. The emperor had no particular interest in creating a water distribution system. Moreover, critics on the Municipal Council argued that it was much easier and cheaper to pump water from the Seine and Ourcq rivers or to draw it from artesian wells than to build the expensive system of aqueducts, siphons, reservoirs, and pipes that Haussmann felt was necessary. Wells could never supply a city of 2 million. Some proponents of pumping river water admitted that it was contaminated, but they advocated filtration, which they claimed was cheaper than building Haussmann's proposed system. Other critics insisted that spring water caused tooth decay, stomach cancer, goiters, and other ills.[24] In addition, there was opposition from property owners who objected to condemnation or who claimed that the condemnation awards would be too low.

When Haussmann came to office, there were different proposals under consideration for providing the city with water. The one Napoléon III wanted him to submit for approval to the Municipal Council would have favored a well-connected private company. Haussmann argued him out of it, pointing out that "granting a direct concession to a single private enterprise, without an open bidding process would cause serious problems . . . [particularly because] this would seem to favor an entity proposed by the Emperor."[25]

With the help of Belgrand, Haussmann issued the first of four memoranda to the Municipal Council advocating his water supply proposals in 1854; he submitted the last in 1865, when his recommended approach was finally accepted.[26] A drought that year had brought the level of the Seine below the intake pumps, forced reduced use of water from the Ourcq, and resulted in new outbreaks of cholera. The drought and its effects accelerated the approval of his program.

The system Belgrand and Haussmann cre-ated provided 64 million gallons of fresh water per day, primarily from the Dhuis River valley, east of Paris, and from the Vanne River, southeast of the city.[27] Those two systems required construction of vast complexes of aqueducts, siphons, tunnels, bridges, and reservoirs. When the water arrived in Paris, it was distributed though a system of conduits five times the length of the system that existed in 1848. It was piped to virtually every building in Paris; because it had a natural pressure that forced water to a level of 230 to 260 feet above sea level, water could rise to the top floor of the six- and seven-story buildings that were being built throughout the city.[28] Nevertheless, the system only brought water to a building; it did not distribute the water inside buildings. Even after the new system was in place, half of the city's houses still lacked running water, and of those that had it, many did not have plumbing above the ground floor.[29]

Just as it needed a dependable water supply and distribution network, Paris needed a sewer system. There were sewers under only 82 miles of the city's 250 miles of streets when Haussmann took office. Most properties had masonry ditches or "less satisfactory" receptacles for sewage. Each night, carts picked up their contents and delivered the waste and refuse to La Villette, in the northeast of the city. There it was dumped into canal boats or delivered to pumps, both of which carried the sewage six miles farther to a disposal plant. The waste

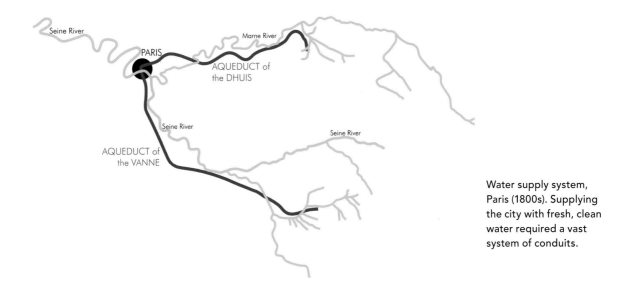

Water supply system, Paris (1800s). Supplying the city with fresh, clean water required a vast system of conduits.

Sewer system, Paris (1800s). Trunk sewer lines provided by Haussmann's team were able to connect with local sewers to service virtually every street in the city.

that was not collected ran down the streets in ditches and open gutters to the nearest sewer, if there was one. From streets or sewers the evil-smelling mass of household and business waste and human excreta flowed into the Seine. When the rainfall was particularly heavy, the overflow spilled into cellars, yards, and even into occupied sections of buildings.[30]

When Haussmann left office, virtually every street in the old city had underground drains, leading to 310.7 miles (500 km) of storm sewers.[31] The new sewer system discharged waste water into the Seine downstream from Paris, and river pollution was therefore no longer a problem within the city. The problem was solved, however, by shifting the pollution to communities below the capital.

PUBLIC THOROUGHFARES

Creating a system of streets and sidewalks for Paris was perhaps an even more awesome task than creating water and sewer systems, and the politics of the process was far more difficult. Piercing through a built-up city like Paris required purchasing properties with existing buildings and, if a negotiated sale was not possible, acquiring them by expropriation. Any property acquisition had to comply with legislation enacted in 1810, 1833, 1841, and 1852 that

required approval by the appropriate arrondissement mayor and national ministries, the Court of Cassation, the National Audit Office, as well as the Council of State and the Paris Municipal Council.[32]

According to laws approved by Napoléon I, the state could only expropriate property needed for a right-of-way if it provided fair compensation. Any challenge was subject to judicial review. Laws enacted by King Louis-Philippe required a public finding that the property was necessary to promote circulation (widening a street or correcting its alignment) or for construction of public buildings, military facilities, canals, or railroads. More important, it required legislative approval of the taking. Leftover property was a problem, because it might be awkward or impossible to build on the land that remained. Napoléon III dealt with this problem by issuing a decree in 1852 that broadened legal takings to include leftover and adjacent property needed for the healthy redevelopment of the surrounding district. It also formalized the process for approval and review.[33]

It is hard to overemphasize the difficulties involved in obtaining the necessary approvals, securing financing, gaining possession of property, forcing residents and businesses to leave their locations, and demolishing structures to create handsome, well-paved thoroughfares.

Haussmann's legendary persistence helped him to overcome those difficulties and to create a coordinated system of thoroughfares tying together all of Paris.

Haussmann's approach to the reconstruction of the university district on the Left Bank is an example of his ability to improve circulation throughout the city. Napoléon III had initiated the program of piercing major arteries through Paris before Haussmann became prefect of the Seine. One of the first new streets had been the Rue des Écoles, which would

Demolition for the Avenue de l'Opéra, Paris (1877).

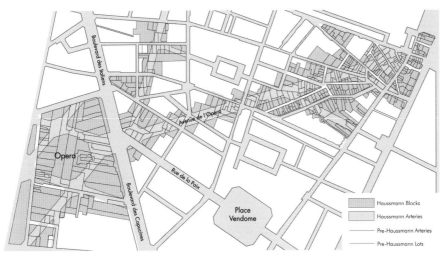

Avenue de l'Opéra, Paris (1800s). The reconstruction of the district around the Opéra and the avenues leading there required condemnation of hundreds of properties.

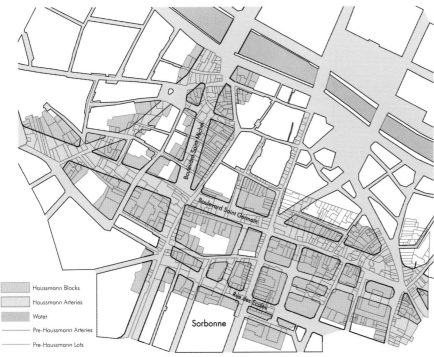

Redevelopment of the Left Bank, Paris (1800s). Haussmann was determined to connect the university district with major arteries crossing the city and, thus, with every section of Paris.

become one of the main streets of the university district.[34]

Haussmann, however, was intent on tying the Left Bank to the rest of Paris and transforming it from a district of insular institutions into a well-functioning part of the national economy. He believed the 72-foot (22-m) width of the Rue des Écoles, which Napoléon III thought essential to his redevelopment program, was inadequate for the intense traffic that had to traverse the district. Furthermore, the street did not lead to major destinations outside the district. Haussmann proposed making the 98-foot-wide (30-m) Boulevard Saint-Germain the area's primary artery. This would integrate the Latin Quarter with the arterial system in other sections of the city. Haussmann persevered until he convinced the emperor to give up the idea of making the Rue des Écoles the primary artery on the Left Bank.

Thus, the Boulevard Saint-Germain became one link in a loop encircling the center of Paris, beginning at the Place de la Bastille on the Right Bank, continuing along the new Boulevard Henri IV, crossing the Île Saint-Louis and the Pont de Sully, passing through the Left Bank to the Pont and Place de la Concorde on the Right Bank again, around the Grand Boulevards and back to the Place de la Bastille. Further, in order to connect the university district with neighborhoods to the south, Haussmann pierced the medieval fabric of the Left Bank with another regional artery, the Boulevard Saint-Michel. This north-south boulevard was an extension of the Boulevard de Sébastopol, which provided access north, through the Right Bank, to the northern gates of the city.

This combination of arteries shattered the insularity of the university district and made it an integral part of the administrative center of Paris. The arterial system also attracted support from constituencies interested in improving the movement of goods, providing access to and from the outskirts of the city, and reducing traffic congestion throughout Paris. Bringing these other players into the game was critical to implementing Haussmann's agenda.

There is a common misconception that the thoroughfares created during the Second Empire were based on a printed plan; they were based on careful planning, rather than a document. Indeed, Napoléon III had drawn a map of some of the arteries that were eventually created. He shared the map with Haussmann when he appointed him prefect of the Seine. It was not entirely original, for it included streets that had been proposed by others.[35] That map became the starting point for a much more ambitious network of tree-lined boulevards connecting railroad stations, bridges, city gates, parks, and other major destinations.

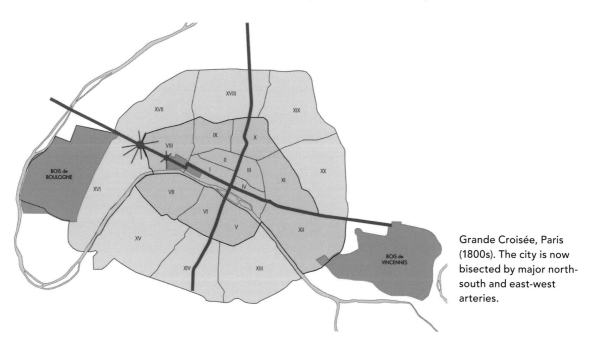

Grande Croisée, Paris (1800s). The city is now bisected by major north-south and east-west arteries.

Boulevard Saint Germain, Paris (2007). An inner loop of arteries connected the center of the city with the Grande Croisée.

Many commentators believe that the wide, straight streets that Napoléon III and Haussmann cut through old Paris had a military rationale. They point out that "between 1827 and 1851, the streets and alleys of Paris had seen barricades thrown up on nine separate occasions" and argue that "wide unbroken lines of streets were the best means of controlling incipient riots."[36] Presumably, the army using cannons and rifles could mow down demonstrators. This rationale was certainly accepted by political leaders of the day. But it was only one among many reasons for what happened.

Road construction programs have often been advocated for military reasons. The American interstate highway system, for example, was authorized in 1956 and funded by the National Interstate and Defense Highways Act, which was also approved for nonmilitary reasons. In the case of Paris, the anti-insurrection argument seems weak, because it is not clear why these same streets could not be used by demonstrators to shoot back at the soldiers. The army had heavy artillery and, thus, an advantage. In the heat of battle, however, the demonstrators could and did liberate cannons and use them.

In his comprehensive atlas of Haussmann's Paris, Pierre Pinon provides five reasons for creating these broad avenues: (1) to traverse the city from north to south and east to west; (2) to connect major destinations, such as railroad stations, bridges, and important intersections; (3) to bypass central Paris; (4) to create monumental axes to major buildings, such as the Arc de Triomphe or the Opéra; and (5) to open up the eight arrondissements annexed in 1860 to real estate development.[37] Other reasons include: extending existing arteries, widening heavily used streets, improving circulation within a neighborhood, and connecting to highways leading in and out of the city.

Many of the new avenues were part of the redevelopment of entire districts. Whether one believes that redevelopment of any particular section of Paris was intended to displace the poor or disperse potential insurrectionists; to create functioning districts for food distribution, government administration, retail shopping, or middle-class residence; or to establish

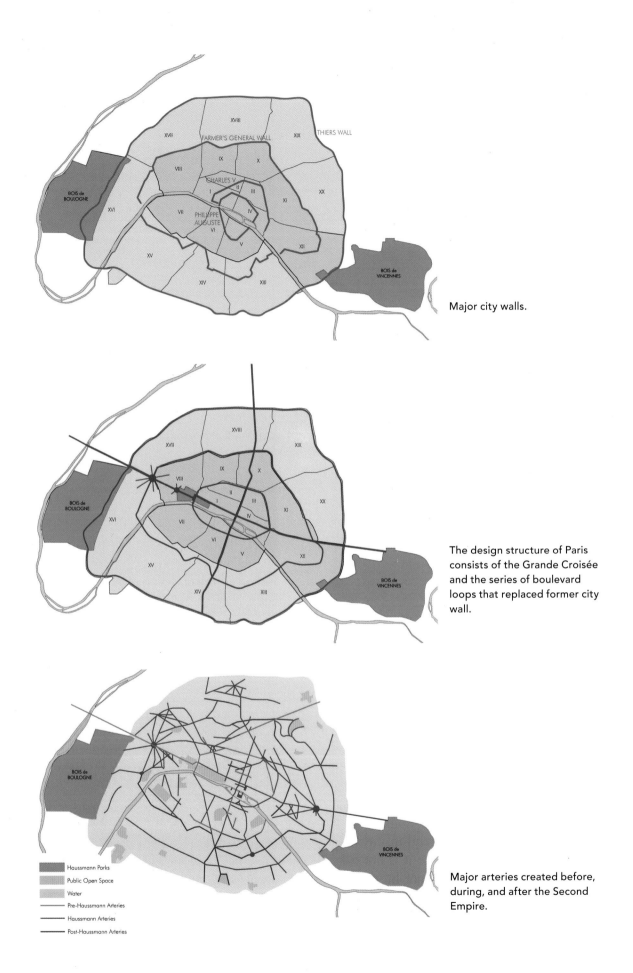

Major city walls.

The design structure of Paris consists of the Grande Croisée and the series of boulevard loops that replaced former city wall.

Haussmann Parks
Public Open Space
Water
Pre-Haussmann Arteries
Haussmann Arteries
Post-Haussmann Arteries

Major arteries created before, during, and after the Second Empire.

environments supportive of major institutions like the Opéra, the Louvre, Notre-Dame, and the Sorbonne, depends on one's point of view. There is some truth to all the explanations. The important thing is to understand that Haussmann's rationale for creating streets went far beyond the movement of vehicular traffic or any other single purpose. His reasons were as varied as the ultimate uses and users of avenues and boulevards throughout Paris.

One explanation for the boulevards that is often ignored is the creation of a design structure to provide residents and visitors alike with a method of orientation. There had been plenty of unrealized proposals for new streets.[38] One in particular had substantial support: the "Grande Croisée" (Great Crossing), a prominent east-west thoroughfare passing through Paris, crossed by a similar north-south artery. It had been evolving since 1616 when Marie de Médicis extended a path that would become the Champs Élysées from the Tuileries Gardens into the open fields to the west. It was transformed by landscape architect André Le Nôtre into a tree-lined approach to the Tuileries in 1667, and extended in 1724 by Louis XV past what is now the Place Charles de Gaulle (aka l'Étoile).[39] Napoléon I continued its trajectory, now in an eastward direction, when he authorized the creation of what is now the first part of the Rue de Rivoli in 1801.[40] It would be nearly completed by Haussmann, who also created the north-south thoroughfare along what is now the Boulevard de Sébastopol, passing across the Île de la Cité and continuing southward along the Boulevard Saint-Michel.

The rest of the design structure is provided by three circumferential boulevards, all created by tearing down city walls. The first loop was created on the site of walls that had been built in the fourteenth century, extended in the seventeenth century, and then torn down by Louis XIV in 1670 to create the Grands Boulevards. These included the Boulevard des Capucines, the Boulevard des Italiens, and the other boulevards extending eastward to the Place de la Bastille. Haussmann's contribution to the first ring was to add to it the Boulevard Saint-Germain on the Left Bank. Haussmann created the second ring by tearing down the Farmers General Wall (begun in 1785 by Louis XVI) to create the "outer" boulevards (including the Boulevards Montparnasse and Raspail on the Left Bank and the Boulevards des Courcelles and de Clichy on the Right Bank). The last ring is the "Périphérique" highway, completed in 1973 over the remains of the Thiers Wall, which was built in the 1840s and demolished between 1919 and 1929.

THE DESIGN OF THE PUBLIC REALM

Most people experience Paris's public realm without being aware of the Grande Croisée or the three encircling thoroughfares. During much of the nineteenth and twentieth centuries they were far more aware of Alphand's distinctive street furniture, most of which has been replaced by contemporary fixtures. Only the advertising columns remain from the nineteenth century. The public realm of contemporary Paris is built around characteristic building heights and styles, cafés, tree-lined avenues,

Street trees, benches, and advertising columns provide Paris with its distinctive appearance.

Boulevard de Sébastopol (2007). The public realm that dominates Paris is created by traffic arteries flanked by wide sidewalks, lined with retail stores in buildings whose heights are related to the width of the street.

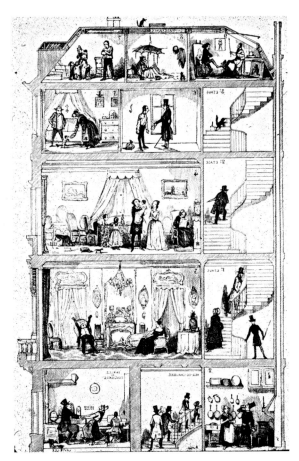

A contemporary cartoon caricaturing the life of the concierge on the ground floor, the upper classes on the next floor, and increasingly lower-class residences leading to the garrets at the top.

parks, and squares. Thus, the public realm is largely the product of the land uses and activities carried on in the surrounding buildings.

In the mid nineteenth century, Paris had height and setback requirements dating back a hundred years and more. They were conceived for a city with narrow streets, and once Haussmann and his team began to pierce wide avenues through the city, they needed new regulations. In 1859, Paris adopted a comprehensive building code that allowed building cornice heights to vary, depending on the width of the street. Cornice heights could now rise as high as 65 feet (20 m) on streets more than 65 feet in width.[41] Rooflines set back from that point at a 45-degree angle.

The new building height was suitable for a world without elevators; people were not willing to carry furniture or groceries much higher. Furthermore, the city was about to install a new water supply system, in which natural water pressure would reach about six stories above the sidewalk. This figure defined a natural limit for building heights, assuming that people would not want to pay to pump water higher than six stories. The ratio of street wall to street width also assured plenty of light and air at the pedestrian level. Building regulations

Boulevard Beaumarchais, Paris (2010). Boulevards in Paris are used for much more than just moving motor vehicles.

were altered somewhat in 1884, 1893, and 1902, but the basic principles held sway until 1967, by which time the building profile for Paris had been established and historic-preservation laws were in place.[42]

The vistas that one sees from street level are as important as the street walls to the unity, variety, and visual excitement of Paris. There are arteries, like the Rue de Rennes or the Boulevard de Sébastopol, that provide direct axes to visible destinations, such as railroad stations, but they are comparatively rare. In most cases topography, acquisition problems, political opposition, or some building that had to be retained kept Haussmann's team from creating the uniform façades and endlessly straight arteries that were fashionable at the École des Beaux-Arts. Those unexpected shifts in right-of-way have saved Paris from becoming a city of perfect axial vistas framed by endlessly repetitive façades, and they have assured Parisians a public realm full of serendipitous delights just around the next bend or behind some monument.

While Haussmann was prefect, the government created 90 miles of new streets between 65 and 100 feet (19 and 30 m) in width, and 700 miles (1,127 km) of broad, paved sidewalks, which provided plenty of room for the cafés that opened throughout the city.[43] As was the case with the boulevards, there had been cafés before Haussmann. The first one opened on the Left Bank in 1689, and by 1848 there were popular cafés along the fashionable

Grands Boulevards on the Right Bank.[44] Once the new boulevards spread through the city's twenty arrondissements, cafés opened everywhere. They promoted a particularly Parisian pastime: lingering over a glass of wine, a *café-filtre*, or a beer while visiting with a friend, or just watching the world go by. Without Haussmann, there would have been many fewer cafés in Paris and, of course, without the boulevards and cafés, Oscar Hammerstein could never have described Paris at the start of World War II as a place where you could hear "the laughter of her heart in every street café. . . ." [45]

GREENING THE CITY

Before 1850 the only open spaces that the people of Paris could use for recreation were some of the château gardens opened to the public during the Revolution (e.g., Luxembourg and Tuileries), adjuncts to public buildings (e.g., the esplanades attached to the Invalides and the École Militaire), and cemeteries. There were no public parks established and designed specifically for public recreation before the Second Empire.

In 1852, Napoléon III donated the Bois de Boulogne to the City of Paris. He wanted Haussmann to turn it into a public park that would rival the royal parks of London. At the time, it was neglected woodland, intersected by a number of formal, diagonal roads. Alphand and Haussmann spent five years transforming it into a rec-

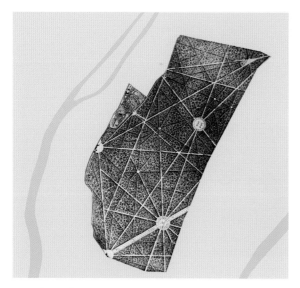

Bois de Boulogne, Paris (1700s).

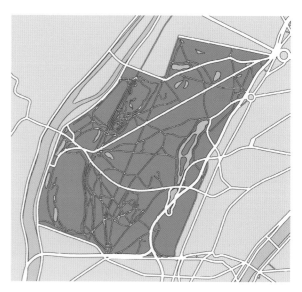

Bois de Boulogne, Paris (2000s).

reational destination for thousands of Parisians, eliminating all but a few of the diagonal roadways and replacing them with paved, curvilinear vehicular arteries and sidewalks. They regraded 438 acres (178 ha); installed water supply and drainage systems; planted more than 420,000 trees; excavated serpentine streams and lakes so they could be used for boating and skating; introduced smaller formal parks, like the Parc de Bagatelle with its spectacular rose garden; cre-

ated the Jardin d'Acclimatation (a combination zoo and amusement park); and built the Longchamps Racetrack.[46]

The gross project cost of what turned out to be a 2,090-acre (846 ha) park was 14.4 million francs, about two-thirds the cost of Haussmann's entire water system.[47] The net cost to the City of Paris, however, was far lower. Haussmann thought of parks, boulevards, and all of his public works as investments that would spur

Bois de Boulogne, Paris (2006). The lake in the Bois de Boulogne, like everything else in the park, was created to provide recreational opportunities for city residents.

Avenue Foch, Paris (2006).

Avenue Georges Mandel, Paris (2008). The wide, tree-lined avenues leading to the Bois de Boulogne became the city's most highly desirable residential districts.

real estate development. The surplus land was not needed because the Bois de Boulogne had gained value because of the transformation of the park. He sold this surplus land for 8.8 million francs to developers, who built tax-paying residential buildings. Another 2.1 million francs came from national appropriations for construction of the racetrack and from funds appropriated by imperial decrees. The cost to the city, therefore, was actually 3.5 million francs.[48]

Haussmann believed, correctly, that if the government invested intelligently in grand avenues leading to the new Bois de Boulogne, it could induce the wealthiest Parisians to move to the nearby Sixteenth Arrondissement. Accordingly, the city created the 460-foot-wide (140 m) Avenue Foch, with large park islands on either side of the roadway, leading from the Arc de Triomphe to the Bois. It also created the 110-foot-wide (40-m) tree-lined Avenues Georges Mandel and Henri Martin, leading from the Trocadéro to the Bois. These boulevards attracted many of the city's high-income residents to the western districts of the city, where they built fashionable mansions and apartment buildings.[49]

The Bois de Boulogne was balanced on the less affluent eastern side of Paris by the Bois de

Vincennes (2,458 acres [995 ha]). The Bois de Vincennes had also begun as a royal forest preserve and it, too, was donated by Napoléon III to the City of Paris. Haussmann's team transformed the preserve into a public park at a cost of 23.7 million francs, of which 12 million came from the sale of surplus property. At a net cost of 11.7 million francs, the residents of Paris paid three times the cost of the Bois de Boulogne to create the Bois de Vincennes.[50]

Haussmann conceived of these two regional facilities as part of a comprehensive park and boulevard system that would include three district parks: the Parc Monceau (20.3 acres [8.2 ha]), the Parc des Buttes-Chaumont (62 acres [25 ha]), and the Parc de Montsouris (37 acres [15 ha]); and twenty-four small neighborhood parks, inspired by London squares and in fact referred to as "squares."

The three district parks were conceived as part of the opening of whole new residential neighborhoods. The Parc Monceau, for exam-

Parc Monceau, Paris (before 1870). The territory around the park was purchased by developers who built apartment houses for the upper middle class.

Parc Monceau, Paris (2008) .

The red dots represent small parks (called squares) located throughout the city and designed for use by neighborhood residents and workers.

Square Laborde, Paris (2009). Although this neighborhood park is just under one acre in size, it is able to accommodate tots playing in a sandbox, seven-year-olds jumping rope, teenagers playing Ping-Pong, amorous young couples, students reading the newspaper, middle-aged businessmen discussing politics, and elderly singles sitting quietly in the shade.

ple, was just west of territory needed for the Boulevard Malesherbes and south of territory needed for the Avenue de Villiers.[51]

Haussmann sold some surplus land that he had bought for the park and nearby arteries to the Péreire brothers. The Péreires had been among the earliest businessmen involved in developing the railways. In 1852 they established the Société Générale du Crédit Mobilier and the Crédit Foncier de France, banks that invested in railroad, omnibus, gas, and real estate projects by tapping small as well as large investors. The brothers combined the surplus land they purchased from the city with other properties they owned, and they built the apartment buildings that would establish the area around the Parc Monceau as an upper-middle-class neighborhood. Much of the rest of the district was subdivided into streets by property owners who built apartment buildings themselves or sold their land to developers who did.

It was created on property that had once been a garden on the estate of Philippe d'Orléans.[52] Expropriated in the revolution of 1789, it was returned to the family by Louis-Philippe, the son of Philippe d'Orléans and the king of France from 1830 to 1848. The land reverted to the government, by agreement, in 1852. Haussmann purchased the rest of the property owned by the heirs of the estate in 1860, for 9.4 million francs. In the process he assembled a perfect site for the park, and he sold the land he did not use to the Péreire brothers for 8.1 million francs.[53] The public park that Alphand created remains one of the district's most popular recreational destinations. It includes broad meadows where children play while adults lie in the sun, shaded paths that are favored for strolling and jogging, and a variety of decorative attractions, some of which are relics of the eighteenth-century garden.

The squares, which range in size from .25 to

Boulevard Malesherbes, Paris (2006). Trees are as important to the character of the public realm as the stores that attract shoppers.

6.5 acres (0.1–2.6 ha), were also frequently the result of surplus property acquisition; Alphand transformed this surplus land into small parks. Each square has been modified over the years to meet the changing demands of the people who live, work, and shop in the surrounding neighborhood. The Square Laborde (1 acre [3,831 m2]), for example, was created out of land that was not needed for the creation of the Boulevard Malesherbes and the Place Saint-Augustin.

Alphand transformed the new avenues created by Deschamps and Haussmann into tree-lined boulevards where ordinary Parisians enjoyed a stroll, much as the fashionable upper classes enjoyed a promenade on the Grands Boulevards. By 1873 he had supervised the planting of 102,154 street trees and the installation of 8,428 benches.[54]

The trees, like the parks, performed an important function, perhaps less understood at the time but vital to sustaining a livable environment. They made the air fresher and cooler, especially on traffic-congested streets. Few people today think about the air quality in Paris. But in the nineteenth century Paris, in which the air was assaulted by "fetid odors that emerged from the middle of alleys, where muddy gutters served as sewers that periodically conveyed epidemic diseases,"[55] trees were essential to the creation of a livable city.

Although the first gaslights had been installed on the Champs-Élysées in 1828 and continued to be installed and maintained by the police department (outside Haussmann's jurisdiction), Paris was ill lighted and often dangerous in 1848. Eleven years later, in 1859, Napoléon III transferred responsibility for street lighting to Haussmann, who, together with Alphand, installed lampposts and luminaires that improved service. The additional 15,000 streetlights they introduced may be one reason Paris is often called the city of light.[56]

The importance of the benches cannot be underestimated in a city where whole families lived in a single room and toiled in overcrowded workshops that were broiling hot in the summer. Alphand also installed advertising columns, on which posters announce plays, art exhibitions, concerts, and all manner of coming events; kiosks, from which merchants sell newspapers and magazines; drinking fountains; litter bins; urinals; and small cafés in parks and squares. The advertising columns, based on a preexisting German design, have become emblematic of Paris and of France.

RECONSTRUCTING CENTRAL PARIS

Twenty-first-century city dwellers are accustomed to having schools, firehouses, and police stations in their neighborhoods. Paris in the

Third Arrondissement City Hall, Paris (2007). Community facilities were provided to every city neighborhood.

mid nineteenth century lacked these community facilities, and Haussmann was determined to provide them throughout the city. The needs of the original twelve arrondissements were different from the needs of the areas being developed in the annexed outer sections of the city, but they all needed schools, libraries, recreational facilities, government offices, and markets. Every facility had to be approved by the Paris Municipal Council and the relevant arrondissement council. While Haussmann treated council approval as a formality, he could not ignore its members. So it was difficult for

him to favor one member of the council over another. Nevertheless, rather than locating facilities on an equitable basis and distributing them evenly throughout the city, Haussmann tended to be opportunistic in selecting sites. He favored sites that were the most accessible, cost the least, and required the least disruption. Nevertheless, during his seventeen years in office his administration built, enlarged, or restored eleven local government centers (little city halls), erected small local markets throughout the city, opened seventy schools, five theaters, seventeen religious structures (including

Haussmann's fundamental reconstruction of central Paris connected the administrative, judicial, police, and university districts with the rest of the city.

two synagogues), and built nine scattered military barracks (which surely were intended to locate the military so it could provide protection against insurrection).[57] The government also built citywide facilities, including two hospitals and improvements to the Sorbonne, a livestock market at La Villette, and the 21-acre Central Market (Les Halles).

As important as it may have been to provide Paris with facilities similar to those being created at the same time in London and New York, Haussmann and his team went much further; they embarked on a program that completely rebuilt the city's historic core. If Paris was to become the capital of a modern industrial and commercial state, it needed a civil society with functioning national judicial, administrative, and university centers. Haussmann's conception went beyond simple area redevelopment. Haussmann thought of the reconstruction of the area around Châtelet and City Hall as part of a much more ambitious redevelopment, one that included virtually rebuilding the Île de la Cité and the section of Saint-Germain-des-Prés just across the Seine, as well as rebuilding the system of bridges that connected the Île de la Cité with the Right and Left banks. The purpose of all this rebuilding was to ensure that Paris could function as France's premier city.

Haussmann knew Saint-Germain-des-Prés well from his days as a student in the Latin Quarter. Consequently, he saw to it that the Boulevards Saint-Michel and Saint-Germain were streets wide enough to accommodate heavy vehicular traffic and also replaced or widened many of the Latin Quarter's narrow alleys, connecting the Latin Quarter with other parts of the city. The boulevards simplified circulation and the delivery of goods and services to the section of Paris occupied and used by university students. These wide arteries connected the district to the bridges across the Seine, to the major arteries being created on the Right Bank, to the administrative center of the city around Châtelet, and to the Central Market (Les Halles).

France, like England, the United States, and other major Western democracies, would

Model of Île de la Cité, Paris (pre–1850). The Second Empire tore out the densely packed slums that surrounded Notre-Dame Cathedral and created buildings to house the city's police department, the National Ministry of Justice, and a major hospital.

be increasingly dependent on the rule of law and on well-educated leaders in every field of endeavor. Haussmann therefore created spacious headquarters for the Ministry of Justice, the Commercial Court, and the police on the Île de la Cité.

Urban designers like to ascribe the current layout of the Île de la Cité to the desire for broad open public squares that would set off major public buildings, like Notre-Dame and the Palais de Justice. That surely was a consideration. As Haussmann explained, "one must have enough space around a monument to permit a visitor to grasp it in its entirety."[58] But Haussmann, like most Parisians, also wanted to eradicate what he called the "ignoble district" that dominated central Paris. When he began redevelopment of the historic core of Paris, it had become a notorious "refuge or meeting place for . . . criminals . . . rejects of the Parisian population . . . ex-convicts, swindlers, thieves, and murderers."[59] Haussmann and Napoléon III aimed to transform this slum into the political hub of "the world's leading city, a capital worthy of France."[60] At the same time, Haussmann believed that the lawyers, doctors,

Boulevard Saint-Michel, Paris (2010). Boulevards with cafés and stores animate the life of university students on the Left Bank.

public administrators, and business leaders who were so necessary to the transformation would not frequent the Île de la Cité until it was made safe and until it became easy to move around the area on foot.

The establishment and expansion of the administrative-legal-educational core of Paris would have occurred without Haussmann. It had begun before he became prefect of the Seine, it continued to be improved through the twentieth century, and it is still being enhanced. But without Haussmann, or somebody of his skill and temperament, the redevelopment of central Paris would have taken more time and been far less extensive. His great contribution was in understanding that rebuilding the city's historic core would be crucial to the future of the city, that it could not be accomplished all at once, and that it had to be linked together by a series of major thoroughfares. Those new thoroughfares not only connected major administrative, judicial, and educational districts of the city with the city's new produce market, railroad stations, and bridges; they led to the gates of the city and on to the rest of France.

PLAYING THE GAME

Design played an important role in transforming Paris into the city we know, but it was the way Haussmann played the planning game that got the job done. Haussmann was fortunate that he and Napoléon III shared a set of assump-

tions and were not pulling in different directions. The leaders of the Second Republic and the Second Empire believed that intelligently conceived public works were investments that would add value to surrounding property, trigger private real estate development, and generate more than enough additional tax revenue to pay for the public works. The government was able to sell bonds by dedicating this additional cash flow to payment of the debt service on the bonds it was selling.[61] This is similar to, but different from, what is commonly referred to today as *tax increment financing*, because tax revenues are not allocated exclusively to the district profiting from capital investment. In mid-nineteenth-century France, however, the idea of relating increases in property value to public investment, and the resulting increase in taxes to debt service payments on the bonds that paid for that investment was novel and, in the minds of many people, suspect.

The Second Empire financed three networks (*réseaux*) of street improvements by combining subsidies (approved by vote of the National Assembly and Senate) with bond issues (approved by vote of the Municipal Council). In each instance the Crédit Mobilier purchased a significant portion of the bond issue. The First Network was made up of arteries begun before 1858, some of which had been started before Haussmann came to office. It consisted of major parts of the Grande Croisée and other streets that received approval and

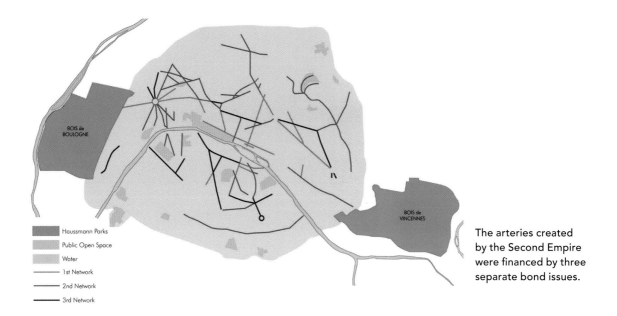

Haussmann Parks
Public Open Space
Water
1st Network
2nd Network
3rd Network

The arteries created
by the Second Empire
were financed by three
separate bond issues.

BOIS de
BOULOGNE

BOIS de
VINCENNES

appropriations at the national level (although not enough to cover the costs). The Second Network involved both national and city appropriations (though also not enough to cover the costs) for specific streets, which received legislative approval in 1858. The Third Network, which was entirely city-financed, was only approved when legislators came to believe that it was necessary to provide for the territory annexed to the city in 1860. Despite this explicit rationale, Haussmann used some of the money for streets in the original twelve arrondissements.[62]

Haussmann was unhappy spending time to obtain the approval of local and national legislators, many of whom he loathed as much as he loathed lobbying them. Like him, many of them wanted a cleaner, better Paris, but they also expected attention from the government and special treatment for their favorite projects. Haussmann felt he had better things to do and did not want to spend time courting legislators. Consequently, he employed three inventive ways to circumvent the legislative process: excess condemnation, turnkey financing, and floating short-term debt.

One way that Haussmann obtained funds without legislative authorization was to acquire more property than was absolutely necessary for a particular right-of-way, and then sell the surplus at a profit. The profit was essentially payment for the increment of value added by purchasing difficult-to-reach sites, often in poor, slum neighborhoods, and extending streets to them; it also derived from selling properties that public works had transformed into easily accessible development sites in attractive neighborhoods, now supplied with excellent water and sewer service.

A second device Haussmann used is what later came to be known in the United States as turnkey financing. In this case, rather than do its own contracting or pay for work as it is completed, a government will enter into a turnkey agreement that specifies the scope and character of the finished project and commits the government to pay for it upon the project's completion (when it receives the so-called keys to the property). This frees up cash for current spending and puts off expenditures (often for several years) until the project is complete. The contractor uses the signed agreement to obtain an interest-bearing loan that will supply money to pay all expenses until the government pays the contractor. This technique provides an incentive for the contractor to finish as quickly as possible (to reduce interest, insurance, and other payments prior to completion). It prevents the government from having to incur additional expenses to cover unforeseen costs or from having to take over a project if a contractor abandons it before it is completed. It also eliminates graft paid to government inspectors who certify progress payments for uncompleted or poorly done work. By the late 1850s, Haussmann was using this technique to contract for entire streets with builders who agreed to handle relocation, as well as the costs associated with demolition, construction, and resale of property outside approved rights-of-way.[63] Of course, Haussmann picked up additional opponents each time some contractor cut corners or engaged in questionable practices.

Haussmann's third device for protecting expenditures from prior legislative scrutiny came in the form of issuing short-term debt. Rather than pay contractors on completion of a street or other public work, he entered into an agreement to pay them in annual installments, sometimes over eight years.[64] The contractors, in turn, either borrowed the money to pay for the work, using the government's written agreement to pay in installments as collateral, or sold these agreements at a discount to some entity that then received city payments. Thus the contractor, not the government, borrowed the money, and therefore no legislative sanction for incurring debt was required.

Haussmann's clever financial operations, however, required breaking fundamental political rules of planning and led to his eventual demise. When Haussmann became prefect of the Seine he had the indispensable support of Napoléon III, Persigny, and the Bonapartist establishment. As time passed, that base of support grew to include the construction industry, property owners and bankers who had been enriched by his public works program, and the huge number of public employees whose incomes and working conditions were steadily improving as result of his policies. The importance of construction workers cannot be overestimated. People from all over France poured into Paris to find work. Napoléon III, Haussmann, and many others thought the best way to avoid demonstrations and insurrection was to provide them with work. Investment in the public realm accomplished that. There were 41,000 wage earners in the construction industry in 1848 (12 percent of the Paris workforce), and as a result of the government's program of public works, the number had grown to 71,000 (17 percent) by 1860.[65]

While Haussmann's political base had been growing, so had his opposition, whose numbers swelled year in and year out, as more and more people were displaced from their homes and businesses. The number is even larger if it includes as yet unemployed itinerant construction workers arriving from all over France, Parisians who could not afford to live in the new buildings, and thousands of residents who could afford lodging only in peripheral suburbs.

Haussmann's arrogant manner of dealing with public officials whom he considered incompetent, disloyal, or misguided caused him increasing difficulties as time passed, as did his desire for self-aggrandizement. In 1860 he persuaded Napoléon III to propose adding to his responsibilities those city functions that he did not yet supervise. But he overplayed his hand by demanding the title "Minister of Paris." The emperor, who was politically more adept than his prefect, asked for approval from the other ministers. They refused, and he complied with their wishes.[66] Five years later, when Napoléon III appointed a Municipal Council that included more of Haussmann's critics, the prefect opened himself (and the emperor) to major criticism by implementing a significant portion of his program without its express approval. He justified his actions by disdainfully informing the new council that their action was not always necessary because Paris was not "some ordinary community," but belonged "to the whole of France."[67]

As the number and value of public works expenditures outside the scrutiny of the National Assembly, the Senate, and Municipal Council increased, so did the opposition. Eventually, Haussmann incurred enough off-the-books financial commitments that it became impossible to keep them from being disclosed. His reputation was further damaged by Jules Ferry, a Republican deputy and an avowed enemy of the imperial government, when he published *The Fantastical Tales of Haussmann.*

The pun on E. T. A. Hoffmann's *Tales* ridiculed Haussmann's work.

Ferry was as incensed by Haussmann's underestimates of cost as by his failure to disclose the extent of his program. "What! So many millions in the hands of a single man! But two billion [francs], that is equal to the entire budget of France, and Mr. Prefect, over fifteen years you have spent not less than two billion."[68] Ferry went on to assert that the First Network of streets was supposed to cost 180 million francs but actually cost 410 million, and that the Third Network had been estimated at 350 million to be spent over ten years, when 634 million were spent between 1864 and 1868.

Ferry probably overestimated the cost overruns, unexpected construction problems, and government indebtedness. But his work did serious damage to Haussmann's reputation and triggered ongoing debate among legislators, as did gossip about his affair with a young dancer at the Opéra.[69] Ferry was right in attacking an absence of transparency that bordered on deception. But one has to question Ferry's objectivity when he also claimed that Haussmann's street network had "the unpleasing appearance of a Chinese puzzle," that the new buildings were an example of Haussmann's "bad taste," and that Haussmann had copied his program from proposals made by Voltaire in 1749 (before the invention

of the steam engine, industrialization, the existence of railroads, or the addition of twelve once-rural arrondissements to the city).[70]

The elections of 1869 increased the number of opponents of the Second Empire in the legislature. Napoléon III responded by giving the recently elected body a greater role in decision-making, and thus further weakened Haussmann's position. Some opponents gossiped about Haussmann and the dancer from the Opéra; others accused him of profiting from his government position. Once Haussmann left office, however, it turned out that he did not have a pension and had to support himself from his wife's dowry.[71]

With Haussmann support waning, the opposition demanded that Napoléon III jettison the prefect. Napoléon III appointed Émile Ollivier, leader of the opposition and a longtime enemy of Haussmann, to head the government, and the emperor dismissed his prefect on January 6, 1870. Nine days later a popular humor magazine featured a bitter cartoon on its cover, showing Haussmann with a pretty woman (ostensibly representing Paris), and the prefect exclaiming, "Is it possible, after I have loved you so, covered you with pearls and diamonds, and made you, so ugly before, the most beautiful woman in the world, that you should spurn me . . . You ingrate!"[72]

Avenue de l'Opéra (2010).

Boulevard des Italiens, Paris (late 1800s).

Boulevard des Italiens (2010). The public realm created for the nineteenth century was easily adapted to the activities of the twenty-first century.

SUSTAINING THE NEW PARIS

Sixty years after Haussmann left office, F. Scott Fitzgerald described an American directing his taxi to the Avenue de l'Opéra, to hear "the cab horns . . . [that] were the trumpets of the Second Empire," and watch clerks "closing the iron grill in front of Brentano's Book Store."[73] Nobody in the Second Empire could have foreseen motorized taxi service or an American bookstore on the Avenue de l'Opéra. Yet the city that Haussmann's team created easily accommodated both—and much else that appeared in the ensuing decades.

Surprisingly little has changed since Fitzgerald described the scene. Small children, teenagers, office workers, and the elderly still go to local parks, just as they continue to stroll and shop along tree-lined boulevards. Tourists and Parisians still sit at cafés on the city's broad avenues watching the world go by, attend performances at the Opéra, and stay in hotels in the sections of the city that Haussmann and his team rebuilt. Over nearly a century and a half, successive governments have accepted Haussmann's strategies and have continued to slice boulevards through congested districts, to extend the sewer and water systems, to create new parks, to redevelop obsolete sections of the city, and to create infrastructure to support new neighborhoods.

The Paris that Haussmann and his team created has been sustained and nurtured by succeeding generations. In many ways it is even more impressive today because it supports a very different population, whose economic life and activities were unimaginable in the 1860s. That era's array of public works could be expanded, extended, and adapted to the activities and desires of future generations at prices they could afford and were willing to pay. In words that will be eerily familiar to twenty-first-century environmentalists, their work met "the needs of the present without compromising the ability of future generations to meet their own needs."[74]

The new arteries are now used by motor vehicles and in many places have been retrofitted with special lanes for bicycles. Often they have been wide enough to accommodate the insertion of ramps leading to underground garages without interrupting the flow of traffic above.

The tree-lined avenues and boulevards have been popular with people of every social and economic class from the moment they were cre-

Avenue Georges V, Paris (2010). Nineteenth-century boulevards were large enough to accommodate late-twentieth-century underground garages.

ated. They have accommodated the changes in land use that accompanied a continually evolving economy. Even more impressive, the Paris created by the Second Empire proved capable of serving a much larger, much more decentralized twenty-first-century population and, still, all of France.

Nevertheless, the city is not exactly the same as it was in 1870, when the Second Empire ended. Subways, buses, trucks, and cars have replaced horses, carts, carriages, and horse-drawn omnibuses. Nor is Paris the same as it was in 1931 when F. Scott Fitzgerald described the Avenue de l'Opéra. Brentano's Book Store and the taxi horns are still there, but there are now high-rise buildings on the skyline, along with television antennas.

The Seine is no longer used for dumping raw sewage. Because of the higher embankments built by the Second Empire and later governments, flooding is no longer a problem. As a result, the river has become a major attraction for millions of tourists who enjoy trips on more than one hundred excursion boats that ply the river, something that nobody in Haussmann's day could have envisioned.[75] Since 2002, each summer the city has operated "Paris-Plages," a temporary beach created along the banks of the Seine, which by 2009 was attracting four million sunbathers annually.[76]

Few of the buildings that surrounded Notre-Dame in 1848 were still there at the beginning of the twenty-first century. Most of the Île de la Cité had been cleared for public squares, tree-lined boulevards, government buildings, and a hospital. The east-west axis of the Champs-Élysées has become part of a "Grande Croisée" extending from the high-rise office district at La Défense west of the city, for eight and one half miles to the Bois de Vincennes on the east. Its north-south arm begins in the north at two railroad stations (the Gare du Nord and the Gare de l'Est), continues along the Boulevard de Sébastopol, crosses the Seine, and goes down the Boulevard Saint-Michel into Montrouge, south of the city.

The most dramatic changes made to Paris by the Haussmann team were the transformation of a city of polluted air and water into one with a relatively healthy environment. They accomplished this by ripping out fetid slums (in the process causing considerable pain and economic distress to the relocatees) and replacing them with neighborhoods made up of five-to-seven-story apartment buildings along broad, tree-lined avenues; installing sewer and water distribution systems; and creating a remarkable network of public parks. When Haussmann left office, the city had one acre of parkland for every 390 inhabitants. The government has been adding parkland ever since. Paris may or may not be the greenest city in Europe, but it has more

Brentano's Book Store, Avenue de l'Opéra, Paris (2010).

Paris (2010).

trees (478,000) than any other capital on the continent.[77]

The capital investment strategy pursued by governments of Paris in the middle of the nineteenth century certainly set the city on the road to an increasingly sustainable environment. It also enhanced public health and the personal well-being of its citizens. But perhaps its most important role was in providing a public realm framework that attracted private investment and around which real estate development thrived. Cities and suburbs throughout the world have a great deal to learn from planners who, while creating thoroughfares that provided for the movement of goods and services needed by a modern industrial and commercial society, carefully adjusted their dimensions, layout, and accoutrements so that they served many other functions as well. Most important, their rejection of single-function planning and adoption of a public investment strategy that encouraged complementary real estate development provides a model that remains relevant for the twenty-first century.

Chicago (2008).

FIVE

THE PLANNING PROCESS THAT TRANSFORMED CHICAGO

Successful planning begins long before work on any specific plan starts, and continues long after that plan is published. There is no single correct method for the planning process. However, the process that resulted in the creation of the *Plan of Chicago* and the implementation of so many of its proposals contained all the elements of successful planning. They include: building a constituency for planning, creating an entity to do the planning, testing the validity of various government actions in order to establish the agenda set forth in the plan, creating an appealing and understandable image of the future, gaining public approval of the agenda, identifying the agencies that will implement the plan, obtaining the money needed to finance that agenda, and maintaining ongoing public support until that agenda has been implemented.

Every library is filled with documents presenting dreams of what might have been. Unlike most of them, the *Plan of Chicago* contained major proposals that were successfully implemented and that changed the face and character of the city. The success of the *Plan* resulted from a planning process that was classic in many respects but that was unique to its place and time in others. Growing out of the success of the World's Columbian Exposition of 1893, it took on a life of its own, and, therefore, the transformation of the city was in some respects quite different from the original plan.

In Chicago, as in most cities where planning has resulted in major change, the accompanying *planning process* was at least as important as the *Plan* itself. Together, the *Plan* and the process inspired remarkable public realm expenditures. During the ten years following publication of the *Plan*, its authors, the Chicago Plan Commission, its staff, and the proponents whom they inspired were able to convince voters to approve bonds in the sum of $61.5 million; legislators to approve $8.1 million in special assessments on properties affected by improvements to Michigan Avenue and Roosevelt Road; railway companies to spend $162.1 million, and the Forest Preserve to pay out $5.3 million to acquire and create parkland.[1]

Unlike Paris, Chicago had been built according to a rectilinear plan based on the Land Ordinance of 1785 and the Northwest Ordinance of 1787, which established a nationwide grid of one-mile squares.[2] From the time of Chicago's incorporation as a village in 1833, the extension of its rectilinear street grid proceeded bit by bit. It anticipated the real estate development that also

Downtown Chicago (2005) Like many American cities, the city's wide streets are placed at regular intervals and are oriented east, west, north, and south.

proceeded gradually outward from the Loop, in response to the demands of the city's growing population.

Improvements had been made to Chicago before the *Plan*. The city's water supply system had taken shape in the 1860s with the construction of a tunnel two miles into Lake Michigan that brought freshwater downtown, and a pumping station and tower that made possible its distribution through a system of underground pipes.[3] Between 1889 and 1900, the Metropolitan Sanitary District of Chicago invested in the 28-mile-long Sanitary and Ship Canal, which permitted the city to reverse the flow of the Chicago River and reduce the amount of raw sewage being dumped into Lake Michigan.[4] And in 1869, the state legislature took the first step in the creation of public parks when it established independent Lincoln, West, and South park commissions.

Among the players already in the planning game by the late nineteenth century were parks proponents, business organizations, civic and neighborhood groups, labor unions, designers, politicians, and quite a number of prominent individuals. Some, like Montgomery Ward, founder of one of the country's most successful mail-order retailing companies, spent years and substantial sums of money on successful litigation to keep Grant Park free of buildings so that it would be open to everybody.[5] Others, like Democratic Party leader Roger Sullivan, favored extension of utility networks as a way of skimming revenues from city franchise and construc-

tion contracts.[6] Landscape architect Jens Jensen, architect Dwight H. Perkins, and members of the Municipal Science Club (later renamed the Special Park Commission) sought to create a regional landscape preserve because they believed that naturally beautiful scenery should be maintained for its "own sake and scientific value, which, if ever lost, [could not] be restored for generations."[7] Players such as these had been active in Chicago and everywhere else in the second half of the nineteenth century.

In the 1890s a new set of players emerged who favored comprehensive planning. Until then Chicagoans had not seen any reason to do anything other than make separate, incremental public investments. A number of civic leaders, however, were inspired by the huge investment in public works made by the Second Empire in Paris. Investments in the public realm had transformed the French capital, improving conditions for the residents and for businesses in the city. More important, the Parisian planners provided a framework that shaped the city's future and allowed for activities that nobody at the time could have imagined. The example of Paris was one reason some people thought Chicago could do better. The other was the World's Columbian Exposition of 1893.

THE WORLD'S COLUMBIAN EXPOSITION OF 1893

It is possible to see the germ of comprehensive planning in Daniel Burnham's assertion that

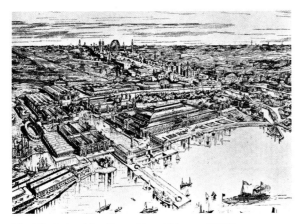

World's Columbian Exposition, Chicago (1893).

the Columbian Exposition "was the beginning, in our day and in this country, of the idea that the orderly arrangement of extensive public grounds and buildings [was] essential to material advancement."[8]

The impact of the Fair was enormous. It was a way to boost Chicago and to promote progress. All Chicago joined in the effort to make a visit to the Fair an unforgettable experience. The site selected had initially been acquired by the South Park Commission as parkland; when the event was over, the site of the Fair became Jackson Park.[9] Daniel Burnham, Frederick Law Olmsted, and some of the most famous architects of the day transformed 633 acres into an exhibition space with more than two hundred buildings. These contained exhibits prepared by nineteen national governments and thirty-eight states. The site included an artificial lagoon and a linear Midway lined with entertainment venues. The shores of the lagoon alone required "one hundred thousand small willows; seventy-five large railway platform carloads of collected herbaceous aquatic plants, taken from the wild; one hundred forty thousand other aquatic plants, largely native and Japanese irises, and two hundred and eighty-five thousand ferns and other perennial herbaceous plants."[10] As a whole, the Fair made what was described at the time as "a memorable impression of architectural harmony on a vast scale . . . [based on] the forums, basilicas, and baths of the Roman Empire, the villas and gardens of the princes of the Italian Renaissance, the royal courtyards of the palaces of France and Spain."[11]

The Fair received 27.5 million visits. The people who made those visits, including millions from other cities, saw a small, well-planned city unlike any other. Its fifty-seven miles of roads were lighted from the cornices of the buildings. Transit service was provided by an elevated, electric railroad that was powered, for the first time, by a third rail.[12] The Fair's significance was not in its lavish display, however, but in the belief it fostered in the efficacy of planning. People "from all parts of the nation came and saw and said: 'Why not these things in the building of our cities?'"[13]

Many visitors were dazzled by the magnificence of the Fair's architecture, and they conflated planning with the establishment of large formal gathering places enclosed by groups of civic buildings with a common cornice line, axial vistas, and an eclectic architecture: Roman in its civic presence, Renaissance in its surface decoration, and Baroque in its opulence. As a result, there are examples of this "City Beautiful" approach to urban design in civic centers throughout the nation.

Planning, as much as design, emerged as a star of the Fair. While visitors were dazzled by magnificent buildings, they were equally dazzled by a public realm lighted by 200,000 incandescent lamps; supplied by electricity, gas, and water from underground conduits; dotted with hundreds of fire hydrants and telegraphic alarm boxes; made accessible by an elevated electric railroad; and provided with coordinated police, fire, and hospital service. In fact, the Fair's impact on visitors from the rest of the country was magnified because, unlike Chicagoans, most Americans lived in communities with few paved streets and often without electricity or sewer service.

In Chicago the Fair resulted in "the emergence of a new type of civic pride."[14] A speaker at a dinner of major business leaders even announced that

Chicago stands without a parallel in the history of the world; second in population on this continent and soon to be first; fourth in population of the earth, and to be first within the lifetime of men here tonight; first in industrial activities and the financial and commercial center of an area larger, more productive and with greater potentialities of population than nations that loom big in the world's history.[15]

He was not alone. His fellow citizens expected the city to be home to "13,500,000 people in 1952."[16]

THE PLAYERS WHO TRANSFORMED CHICAGO

A year after the Fair closed, James W. Ellsworth, who had amassed a fortune administering mining, shipping, and banking companies, suggested to the architect Daniel Burnham that he make "a plan for a connection covering the eight miles of lakefront between Grant and Jackson Parks."[17] Two years later, when the plan had crystallized, Ellsworth invited George Pullman, Marshall Field, Philip Armour, and other prominent Chicago businessmen to a dinner, at which Burnham presented his proposals and ignited their enthusiasm for developing a park along Lake Michigan.[18] These powerful men all became supporters of creating a lakeshore park between the newly re-landscaped Jackson Park and Lake Park (now Grant Park) downtown. Over the next few years Burnham presented his ideas for improving the lakeshore and the park and street systems in formal papers at the Chicago Art Institute and the Chicago Literary Club, the Evanston Back Lot Club, the Commercial Club, and the Merchants Club.[19]

Business and civic leaders discussed the Fair and ideas for the future of Chicago in spontaneous conversations at informal gatherings and in the private clubs that had become centers of social power. At the turn of the twentieth century these clubs played a significant role in the lives of the upper middle class and of the business world in particular. Much of the business of Chicago was discussed there, particu-

larly at the staid and conservative Commercial Club and at the Merchants Club, which catered to younger, less established business and civic leaders. (It should be noted that the downtown clubs frequently restricted membership to men, and to white Protestant men in particular.)[20] Among the business and civic leaders who played particularly important roles in Chicago's planning process over the coming years were Daniel Burnham, Charles Dyer Norton, William A. Delano, Charles H. Wacker, and Walter D. Moody. Burnham provided the vision that animated their work, and he coordinated their efforts until his death in 1912.

Daniel Burnham was considered one of Chicago's major businessmen, and he found the private clubs to be an excellent source of clients. He was an obvious choice for membership in the Commercial Club, which he joined in 1901.[21] Burnham had had a long and highly successful career as an architect before turning planner. He and his business partner, John Wellborn Root, had designed nearly 150 buildings in Chicago, including the gate at the Union Stock Yards, the Monadnock Block, the Reliance Building, and the Rookery, as well as major buildings in Kansas City, Cleveland, Milwaukee, San Francisco, and elsewhere in the United Sates.[22] After Root died in 1891, Burnham renamed his business D. H. Burnham and in 1896 reorganized it as D. H. Burnham & Company. Practicing with various partners, he was involved in the design of several hundred more buildings, including the Marshall Field & Company Department Store in Chicago, the Flatiron Building in New York, Union Station in Washington D.C., the Ellicott Building in Buffalo, and Wanamaker's Department Store in Philadelphia.[23] Burnham was particularly admired by his fellow businessmen because, as chief of construction of the Chicago Fair, he had conceived and managed the administration of a huge development project.

By the turn of the twentieth century, D. H. Burnham & Company was the largest architecture firm in the United States and probably the world, with offices in Chicago, San Francisco, and New York.[24] The firm was also noteworthy in rejecting the artisan-artist approach common in American architectural practice. Burnham said that he wanted "to work up a big business, to handle big things, deal with big businessmen, and to build up a big organization." This required him to "delegate, delegate, delegate."[25] Louis Sullivan, one of Burnham's brilliant competitors, wrote that Burnham was the "the only architect in Chicago" who understood that corporate America tended "toward bigness, organization, delegation and intense commercialism" and "sensed the reciprocal workings of his own mind."[26] Perhaps that is why big business had an affinity for his firm's work and why the firm was so comfortable with corporate clients.

Burnham tried unsuccessfully to get the Commercial Club to produce a plan for the improvement of the city. When it became apparent that it was not going to proceed with his project, he accepted a commission from the Merchants Club. In 1907 the two clubs merged, expanding support for the project and providing the political depth that would be crucial to the *Plan*'s success.

Burnham was the obvious choice to coordinate preparation of the *Plan of Chicago*. His role as co-planner, co-designer, and chief of construction of the Chicago Fair was the formative experience that transformed him from a well-known architect into a prominent public figure and catapulted him into a career as a planner. In 1901–2, he had been involved in planning projects in Washington, D.C., along with architect Charles Follen McKim, sculptor Augustus Saint-Gaudens, landscape architect Frederick Law Olmsted, Jr., and editor Charles Moore. After Washington, Burnham prepared a plan for downtown Cleveland (1902–3) with architects Arnold Brunner and John M. Carrère; for San Francisco (1904–5); and for Manila and Baguio in the Philippines (1905).[27] Planning in San Francisco was cut short by the earthquake and fire, which destroyed all but a few copies of the city's plan before they could be distributed.

Thus, when Burnham took charge of planning for Chicago in 1906, very little had been built in any of the cities for which he had pre-

Chicago (1908). Daniel Burnham presenting images intended for the *Plan of Chicago* to committee members.

pared plans. His work was entirely on paper. Moreover, planning as a profession was in its infancy; Burnham and his colleagues in Chicago had to invent what they did as they did it. Burnham "surrounded himself not only with the best technical assistance obtainable in America, but he sought constantly the advice . . . [of] business men, among whom were the foremost captains of industry in Chicago."[28] Their task was to put the *Plan* together piece by piece, gathering ideas from a wide field of contributors, and to develop a comprehensive set of actions whose execution would be the responsibility of others. By then Burnham knew it would be his last and greatest work. His doctors had informed him that he was terminally ill with cancer.[29]

Burnham's work would be continued by extraordinarily able deputies, although two of them remained in Chicago only a short time. Charles Norton (1871–1923), who had made his career as an insurance executive, was the chairman of the Merchants Club Committee for the *Plan* and continued in that capacity after the club merged with the Commercial Club.[30] He thought of the *Plan* as "a business proposition" that should be developed under the direction and control of "business men," because "political administrations, whether city, county, or state, are subject to frequent changes of personnel and of policy."[31] Norton left Chicago in 1909 to work in Washington D.C. From there he moved to New York to become vice president of the First National City Bank of New York (now Citibank), where he led the effort to create the Regional Plan Association (RPA) and what became the 1929 *Regional Plan of New York and Its Environs* (see Chapter 6).[32]

Frederic Delano (1863–1953) was general manager and later president of the Wabash Railroad.[33] He was secretary of the General Committee, which oversaw the other committees working on the *Plan* and made final decisions. Like Norton, he moved to New York, where he participated in the creation of the RPA and succeeded Norton as its chairman. Delano continued to be a major figure in planning in Washington D.C., where he directed the National Capital Park and Planning Commission and chaired the National Resources Planning Board.[34]

Key members of the team remained in Chicago, however. Charles H. Wacker (1856–1929), a brewery executive, had been a director of the Chicago Fair and was active in civic affairs. He was the vice chairman of the General Committee from the beginning of the process until publication of the *Plan*. In 1909, Mayor Fred A. Busse appointed him chairman of the Chicago Plan Commission, believing, correctly, that he would promote and oversee implementation of the *Plan of Chicago*. It was in this position that Wacker, by then retired, exercised his greatest influence on planning in Chicago.

The Merchants Club Committee on the Plan of Chicago initially consisted of Burnham, Norton, Wacker, Delano, and three others, and when the two clubs merged, four more were added to the renamed General Committee. The wealth of highly placed input in the formulation of the *Plan* was extraordinary. When the General Committee met, a railroad president, ten of the world's greatest merchants, six bankers, an insurance official, six business owners, a real estate dealer, an iron manufacturer, newspaper publishers, two farm-implement manufacturers, a coal dealer, a bridge builder, a lumber dealer, a printer and publisher, a manufacturer of railroad supplies, and a ship chandler often sat in at the conference of the technical people.[35]

By 1909, the General Committee's final year of operation, there were six committees work-

Chicago (1908). Key members of the Commercial Club meeting to discuss *the Plan of Chicago* in Daniel Burnham's office.

ing on a plan for Chicago. Besides the General Committee, there were committees on Lake Parks; Streets and Boulevards; Railway Terminals; Interurban Railways; and Finance. Over a period of three years these committees met at least once a week, consulting regularly with the mayor, the governor, the Board of Commissioners of Cook County, members of the Board of Aldermen, the Drainage Board, the Board of Education, the South, West, and Lincoln park boards, representatives of all the city newspapers, and numerous architects, engineers, and other specialists.[36] Along the way, the club raised approximately $80,000, one-quarter donated by Burnham personally, from private sponsors to pay Edward Bennett (coauthor of the *Plan*), Charles Moore (the *Plan*'s editor), the draftsmen, Jules Guérin and Ferdinand Janin (the *Plan*'s illustrators), and for printing and other expenses. Burnham received no compensation for the hundreds of hours he devoted to the project.

PUTTING THE PLAN TOGETHER

Planning, as the hundreds of people who prepared the *Plan of Chicago* discovered, isn't easy. The men who put the plan together understood that in order to change the way Chicago made its public investments, they needed a vision of the future that would attract a constituency and inspire present and future generations of Chicagoans to implement its recommendations. Burnham worked with them to provide that vision, published in 1909 as the *Plan of Chicago*—America's first truly influential comprehensive plan (the nation's first comprehensive plan, *A City Plan for St. Louis*, was published in 1907).

There is a difference between planning isolated capital investments, however strategic they may be in triggering private real estate development, and genuine comprehensive planning. A truly comprehensive approach combines separate actions in a synergistic manner that transforms an entire neighborhood, city, suburb, or region into a coherent whole—one that is greater than the sum of its parts. It was comprehensive planning, the authors of the plan believed, that would make Chicago more competitive, keep its "people of means" at home, and that would act "as a magnet to draw those who seek to live amid pleasant surroundings."[37]

A particularly vivid example of this comprehensive approach was the transformation of Paris during the Second Empire. That was, however, accomplished without a printed master plan. While the people putting the Chicago plan together chose to emulate the Paris approach, they needed a document that would rally public support and guide the government agencies that would gradually rebuild Chicago. They chose to produce an explicit, printed blueprint for investments in the public realm.

In Burnham's view, a synergistic combination of public investments was not enough. He explained this best in what is the most famous epigram about city planning:

> Make no little plans; they have no magic to stir men's blood and will not be realized. Make big plans; aim high in hope and work, remembering that a noble, logical diagram once recorded will never die, but long after we are gone will be a living thing, asserting itself with ever growing insistency.[38]

The printed 164-page document that emerged consisted of eight chapters and an appendix on the "legal aspects of the plan." It begins with a particularly eloquent presentation of rationales for planning, presents a beautifully illustrated history of planning in ancient and modern times (including a tribute to Paris and a presentation of Burnham's prior city planning work), sets forth a carefully researched analysis of Chicago, and devotes individual chapters to the park system, transportation, streets, the heart of the city, and the plan itself. It recommended:

- transforming some suburban roads into major arteries encircling the city;
- establishing a quadrangle of major streets (Michigan Avenue, Roosevelt Road, Halstead Street, and Chicago Avenue) encircling the business district;
- piercing diagonal streets through the city;
- widening significant downtown streets;
- extending and widening Michigan Avenue north of the Chicago River;
- building a bridge across the river to connect north and south Michigan Avenue;
- establishing a grand civic center at the intersection of Congress Parkway and Halsted Street (now the site of a massive interstate highway interchange);
- consolidating railroad stations south of Roosevelt Road;
- moving freight yards from the center of the city and consolidating them into a central freight clearing yard;
- reorganizing commercial and industrial harbor facilities;
- straightening the Chicago River;
- creating a double-decker drive along the downtown riverbanks;
- creating a regional park system;
- reclaiming the lakeshore and transforming it into continuous parkland.

The watercolor illustrations by Jules Guérin in Burnham and Bennett's sumptuous document have never resembled Chicago. In part, this is because the illustrations were not intended to be specifically prescriptive; they were illustrations of the general character of future development.[39] In part, it is because the plan simplifies

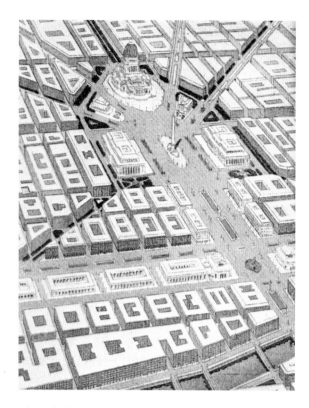

Plan of Chicago (1909). New diagonal boulevards were proposed to pierce through the city's existing rectilinear street system and provide access to a proposed new civic center.

the complexity of city development and the intricate interdependence of activities that had to be accommodated in widely different interior spaces in all sorts of buildings. In part, too, it reflects Burnham's philosophical insistence that planning always has to adjust to better information and changing conditions. But despite the repetitive character of the buildings, common building height, and abstract spaces illustrated in the images, the *Plan of Chicago* promoted ideas that led to important physical alterations, changed daily life in the city, and, like any successful planning venture, was one of the factors affecting the city's future.

PROMOTING THE PLAN

When the *Plan of Chicago* was released on July 4, 1909, it was hailed as "the most important civic event in the history of [the] city."[40] Four months later, at the request of the Commercial Club, Mayor Fred Busse appointed a 328-mem-

ber Plan Commission to direct the city's growth and to promote the plan; he named Charles Wacker chairman.[41] Wacker retained that post until 1926 and was an indefatigable proponent of the proposals until he died in 1929.

The proposals had immense governmental and business support. As Burnham and Bennett explain in the *Plan*, "[B]y invitation of the Club, the Governor of Illinois, the Mayor of Chicago, and many other public officials . . . visited the rooms where the work was in progress, and [became] familiar with the entire scheme as it was being worked out."[42] The interaction worked in both directions. Eight Commercial Club members were appointed by Mayor Busse to the Plan Commission. The interaction and the support these Chicago notables gave to the project were vital to gaining public approval for hundreds of millions of dollars in public spending.

The commission quickly began to promote the ideas in the plan and to draft implementing legislation. After Burnham's death in 1912, Walter D. Moody, the Commission's first managing director, was key to getting the recommendations accepted and implemented by the relevant public agencies. Moody (1856–1920) had previously been general manager of the Chicago Association of Commerce, and he used his extraordinary public relations skills in communicating the commission's recommendations to the public and bringing them to fruition.[43]

Moody conceived of his job as "scientific promotion."[44] Although many of the ideas in the *Plan of Chicago* were proposed before the Commercial Club took them up, most of them had been vetted by its committees, and all of them had been worked out, given shape, and publicized by Burnham and his colleagues.

Moody launched a public relations blitz that saturated Chicago with publicity favorable to the *Plan*. In 1911 the Plan Commission published *Chicago's Greatest Issue*, a 93-page condensation of the *Plan* which, Moody later wrote, "was distributed to 165,000 property owners and renters." The next year the commission provided articles that appeared in "575 magazines, periodicals, trade and club publica-

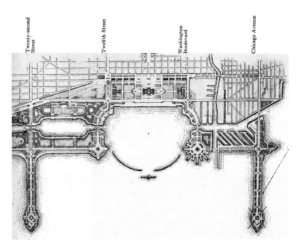

Plan of Chicago (1909). Burnham and Bennett's vision for the development of Grant Park.

Many Chicago streets were widened (violet) and some added (red) in response to the *Plan of Chicago*.

tions," including an article entitled *Fifty Million Dollars for Nothing* (which advocated using the city's waste material, which after all had to be dumped somewhere, to "obtain thirteen hundred acres of Lake Front parks, playgrounds, and watercourses").[45] The commission issued 70,000 copies of *Wacker's Manual of the Plan of Chicago*, which was actually adopted as a textbook by the city's Board of Education,[46] and in 1915 a movie version of the plan was screened in fifty theaters. By 1919, Wacker, Moody, and Taylor (then the commission's office manager) had delivered almost five hundred slide-illustrated lectures to about 100,000 Chicagoans.[47] It was a triumph of boosterism and advertising. As a result of the Plan Commission's promotional activities, public support was so strong that William Hale Thompson backed the Plan in his successful 1915 mayoral campaign. On

taking office he promptly began street-widening projects, notably of Michigan Avenue.[48]

Street widening was, in fact, one of the least noticed but most important of the *Plan*'s recommendations. Planners expected downtown congestion to become intolerable as the city grew, and consequently the *Plan* suggested widening a number of downtown streets. Approximately 120 miles of Chicago streets were widened, largely during the 1920s.[49] These street widenings were implemented because they were an easy way for the city's political leadership to demonstrate responsiveness while at the same time distributing profitable contracts to loyal supporters.

HOW THE PLAN CHANGED CHICAGO

The first two projects to be completed were 12th Street (now Roosevelt Road) and Municipal Pier No. 2 (now Navy Pier). The widening and elevating of 12th Street from Michigan Avenue to Ashland Avenue was largely completed by 1912. It eventually became a major artery going from Grant Park, Michigan Avenue, and the southern end of the business district to the western city limits. Municipal Pier No. 2 was one of two symmetrical piers flanking Grant Park illustrated in the Plan. Pier No. 1 became the site of Shedd Aquarium (1929) and the Adler Planetarium (1930). When Pier No. 2 opened in 1916, it was the largest in the world. It

Chicago River (1910). Actual conditions.

Chicago River (2008). The double-decker Wacker Drive envisioned in the *Plan of Chicago* was brought to fruition, although not precisely as illustrated in the *Plan*.

Plan of Chicago (1909). Burnham and Bennett's vision for the redevelopment of the Chicago River.

Chicago River (1918). The Chicago Plan Commission revised the original redevelopment scheme in light of better information and changing conditions.

was used by the U.S. Navy during World Wars I and II. After the First World War it was used for maritime cargo, but its use declined with the coming of the Depression and increased trucking. After a number of redevelopment schemes failed, it finally reemerged in 1995 as a major entertainment center.[50]

One of the most visible changes brought about by the plan was the straightening of the edges of a section of the Chicago River west of the Loop business district and the creation of the double-decker Wacker Drive along the Loop's northern edge. The first section of the Drive, which opened in 1926, resembles Guérin's watercolor illustrating the *Plan*.[51] It was extended in stages and was largely completed by 1958.[52]

There were three projects, however, that changed daily life for the citizens of Chicago in fundamental ways. Building a bridge across the Chicago River to connect Michigan Avenue and Pine Street (which became North Michigan Avenue) fostered expansion of the city's prime commercial and residential districts north of the Chicago River. Creating the Forest Preserve district provided residents with a unique regional resource for recreational use. But the plan's single most important achievement was promoting investment in 3,130 acres (1267 hectares) of lakefront parkland, which encouraged decades of real estate development along Lake Michigan.[53]

The idea of a major river crossing to connect Michigan Avenue in Chicago's downtown loop with a widened artery north of the Chicago River did not originate with the plan. For nearly two decades, Burnham had publicly promoted the idea of tying together the two sides of the river, and the inclusion of a Michigan Avenue Bridge in the 1909 *Plan of Chicago* provided crucial support for its construction.

Burnham's evolving proposals illustrate the complexity of the planning game. The proposal for a bridge over the Chicago River is a case in point. Chicagoans had been proposing similar projects since the early 1880s. At that time, a 36-foot-wide bridge with 7-foot-wide sidewalks connected Rush Street with the south bank of the Chicago River and handled about half of the city's north-south traffic.[54] Even then, without motor vehicles, the congestion was intolerable, and it was clear that additional crossings were necessary.

One early proposal, made in 1892, was for a tunnel under the Chicago River. Burnham incorporated the tunnel in presentations he made to the Commercial Club in 1896 and the Merchants Club in 1897. Two years later the idea was taken up by the chief clerk of the city's Board of Local Improvement, then by Mayor Carter Harrison, and in 1904 by the *Chicago Tribune*. A year later a committee of the city council voted to build a bridge over the river, connecting Michigan Avenue and Pine Street, but neither the tunnel nor the bridge materialized.[55] By 1906, Burnham had discarded the tunnel and was advocating first one and then another version of the bridge. Within a year he had the support of Mayor Busse and eventually of many (but not all) of the property and business owners of the district north of the Chicago River. His argument, made in the *Plan of Chicago*, was that extending Michigan Avenue north of the river "would enhance the value of the abutting real estate, because of the increased opportunities for . . . building structures of the highest class."[56]

By the time Burnham died, the proposal was facing opposition from building owners along Pine Street who didn't believe the condemnation awards for their properties would be adequate. Nonetheless, in 1913 the City Council passed an ordinance authorizing condemnation of private property along Pine Street, as well as a bond issue to pay for property acqui-

Michigan Avenue, Chicago (1918). Serious downtown traffic congestion was caused by the narrowing of Michigan Avenue at Randolph Street.

Plan of Chicago (1909). Burnham and Bennett's vision for a widened Michigan Avenue crossing the Chicago River.

sition and construction of the new bridge and boulevard.

The city began condemnation in 1916 and spent the next two years fighting off a series of lawsuits by outraged property owners, most of whom wanted more money for their property. Finally, in 1918 the city finished acquiring the necessary property along Pine Street and began demolition. By 1920 the bridge and the new Michigan Avenue were complete.[57]

Pine Street, Chicago (1918). The extension of Michigan Avenue north of the Chicago River by widening the existing Pine Street required substantial relocation and building demolition.

Lake Shore Drive, Chicago (1915). Some luxury residences were built in anticipation of the bridge connecting Michigan Avenue on both sides of the Chicago River.

Lake Shore Drive, Chicago (2010). By the twenty-first century the lakeshore had become the location of choice for the city's wealthier residents.

Building construction along the new avenue began even before the bridge was finished. When completed, the new buildings looked nothing like the illustrations in the *Plan*. They were shaped in large part by the zoning regulations passed in 1923, which allowed buildings along the avenue to rise to 264 feet along the street wall, and higher still in the form of smaller towers set back from the street.

The growth of automobile travel made the new avenue a critical traffic artery. In 1911 fewer than 10,000 vehicles per day crossed the Chicago River on the old Rush Avenue Bridge. In 1927, seven years after the Michigan Avenue Bridge had opened and Pine Street had been widened and renamed, 73,000 vehicles per day used the new bridge.[58] It opened the floodgates to development and expansion of the city north of the river.

In the 1920s, pent-up demand for office space created an enormous building boom. North Michigan Avenue was transformed from a narrow thoroughfare of warehouses and small shops into a "Magnificent Mile" of skyscrapers, department stores, elegant hotels, and high-end shops. That building boom, interrupted by economic downturns, has continued for decades. Today the district that grew up around North Michigan Avenue has become Chicago's premiere shopping, living, and business district.

At the time the *Plan of Chicago* was published, the area north of the Chicago River, espe-

cially near Lake Michigan, had become a popular location for wealthy Chicagoans to build single-family residences. The Michigan Avenue Bridge and the lakeshore improvements that were an outgrowth of the *Plan* accelerated the transformation of the so-called Gold Coast from a neighborhood of luxury mansions into a neighborhood of luxury apartment buildings with spectacular lake views.

The Michigan Avenue Bridge also altered patterns of business and tourism, as the city's prime offices and hotels gradually relocated from Michigan Avenue, opposite Grant Park,

North Michigan Avenue (1920s).

North Michigan Avenue (2010). During the second half of the twentieth century, North Michigan Avenue came to be considered the region's premier shopping district.

to North Michigan Avenue. Significant as that change was, it paled in comparison to the impact on retail shopping. At the beginning of the twentieth century, State Street had been the destination of choice for shoppers from all parts of the Midwest. By the third quarter of the twentieth century, most major retailers were leaving State Street and opening stores along North Michigan Avenue. It wasn't until the first decade of the twenty-first century, after several failed initiatives, that State Street finally emerged from its decline as a retail destination.[59]

The idea of creating a regional park system surrounding the city of Chicago had been around for some time when the *Plan of Chicago* was published. Six years earlier the Board of Commissioners of Cook County established an Outer Belt Park Commission to create a "line of parks and boulevards, encircling the city of Chicago and embracing the Calumet and Des Plaines Rivers and the Skokie Marsh."[60] Two years after that, the Illinois state legislature passed the Forest Preserve Act of 1905.[61] Its purpose was as much to create scenic highways through rural countryside as it was to preserve some of the natural landscape from development. Thus, when the *Plan of Chicago* recommended creating an "outer belt of parks and forest preserves" and "boulevards and highways connecting country towns with each other and with the city . . . [and] the Shore of Lake Michigan," the necessary legal and administrative mechanisms were already in place.[62]

Since 1913 the Forest Preserve District has been legally responsible for preserving undeveloped land in the surrounding Cook County suburbs. At the end of its first decade the Board of Commissioners of the Forest Preserve had spent $5.3 million on what had already become a 14,254-acre Forest Preserve District.[63] By 2007 the District owned approximately 11 percent of Cook County, or 67,800 acres (27,438 ha).[64] The pattern of ownership encompasses the main areas of scenic interest depicted on the map Burnham prepared for the *Plan of Chicago*, but the actual boundaries reflect the realities of acquisition. The Forest Preserve District was constrained by what property owners were

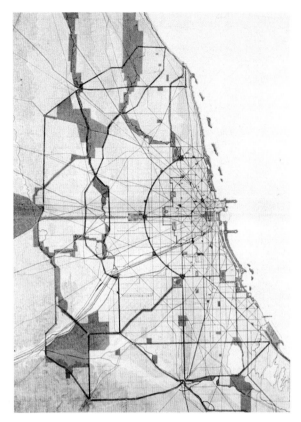

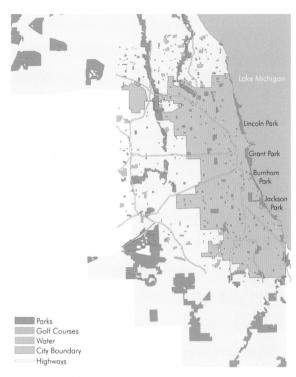

Parks
Golf Courses
Water
City Boundary
Highways

Chicago (2011). More than a century after the *Plan of Chicago* was published, the Forest Preserve and city park system together include more than 74,000 acres (29,947 ha) of parkland.

Plan of Chicago (1909). The authors of the *Plan* envisioned creating a 50,000-acre (20,234-ha) regional park system.

Forest Preserve, Glencoe (2010). Acquisition of tens of thousands of acres outside Chicago has provided residents with extraordinary recreational opportunities.

Chicago (2008). The parkland along Lake Michigan has provided a public realm framework of the city's development.

willing to give up, by asking prices and condemnation awards, available financing, and political pressures both for and against acquisition.

Much of the property has been left in its natural state, except for shelters and camping sites. Some cleared areas that were once farmland have been reforested. The rest has been set aside for golf courses, baseball diamonds, tennis courts, athletic fields, picnic grounds, swimming pools, and a wide variety of other facilities developed, operated, and maintained by the District. The extent of the District's acquisitions created a wealth of opportunities for active and passive recreation for residents of the city and county.

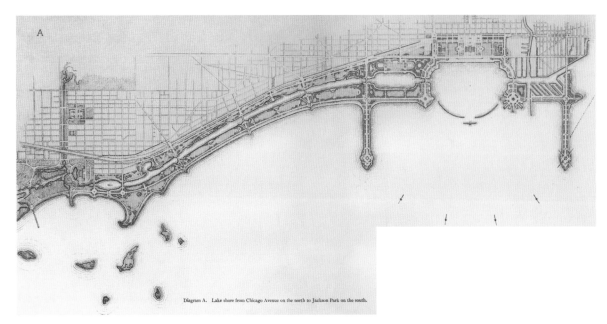

A

Diagram A. Lake shore from Chicago Avenue on the north to Jackson Park on the south.

ABOVE AND OPPOSITE: *Plan of Chicago* (1909). Burnham and Bennett envisioned a continuous park along the shore of Lake Michigan.

Link Bridge, Chicago (2010). The Outer Drive and Link Bridge, presented in a book prepared in 1929 by the Chicago Plan Commission, was eventually built and is now actively used by regional traffic.

Lake Shore Drive, Chicago (2010).

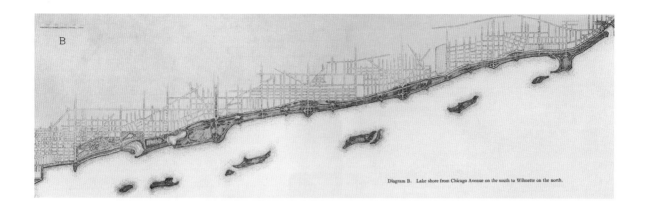

Diagram B. Lake shore from Chicago Avenue on the south to Wilmette on the north.

The single greatest transformative project in Chicago was the conversion of the shore of Lake Michigan into a nearly continuous twenty-four-mile strip of parkland. That work was started in 1869, when the state legislature authorized the creation of Chicago's South, West, and Lincoln park commissions. (These were consolidated with the city's various other park districts into a single Chicago Park District in 1934.) The South Park Commission turned the site of the Chicago Fair into Jackson Park in 1894–95, at which time sections of Lincoln Park formed the only other developed parkland along the lakeshore. The designation of the downtown shoreline as "Public Ground—Common to Remain Forever Open, Clear and Free of Any Buildings, or Other Obstruction Whatever"[65] was an example that was not followed elsewhere in the city. By the end of the nineteenth century much of the shore was given over to use by the railroads, and the rest was used as a dump.

Once developed into public parkland, the lakefront became the public realm framework around which Chicago would grow and develop. As a result of the efforts of Daniel Burnham, the Chicago Plan Commission, and others who came after them, most of the city's shoreline had been transformed by the second decade of the twenty-first century into thousands of acres of parkland, many public beaches, and countless other recreational facilities. The lakeshore had become "a great magnet . . . drawing people to it from all parts of the city and from great distances."[66]

The *Plan of Chicago* proposed taking a series of stand-alone parks and making them part of a continuous twenty-four-mile-long park

and parkway. With the plan as inspiration and the Plan Commission to promote it, this linear park came together in stages. The first part, named for Daniel Burnham in 1927, is a splendid complex of parks, beaches, boat harbors, and drives along the six miles from Jackson Park to Grant Park. It was created by the South Park Commission, based on negotiated agreements with the Illinois Central Railroad that resulted in the Lakefront Ordinance of 1920.[67] This work was partially financed with $20 mil-

Chicago (2011). More than 2,000 acres of lakeshore parks were created by landfill.

lion approved by Chicagoans in a 1920 referendum, and it was largely completed in time for the opening of the Century of Progress Exposition of 1933, which, like its 1893 predecessor, was completely relandscaped after the Fair.[68]

The critical piece of the park and parkway, planned to cover nearly the entire lakefront, was the link between Grant and Lincoln Parks. The Outer Drive and Link Bridge across the mouth of the Chicago River, first proposed in the *Plan*, were detailed in an elaborate book prepared in 1929 by the Chicago Plan Commission.[69] Later that year, just as construction was to begin on this eight-lane, double-decker bridge, the project was held up, but not stopped, by the Great Depression. It became the first Works Progress Administration (WPA) project in Chicago and was finally completed between Randolph and Ohio Streets in 1937.[70] During the early 1980s the southern approach to the Link Bridge was reshaped into an S-curve that greatly improved traffic flow.

Eventually, Lake Shore Drive was extended all the way north to the end of Lincoln Park. The real estate industry responded by constructing many buildings within view of the lakeshore. Most people want to live, work, do business, shop, or play as near as possible to this lakefront parkland. It has become the artery of choice for Chicagoans and visitors traveling north and south through the city and to destinations in town and along the shore. Traveling along any section of Lake Shore Drive is a unique delight for those coming and going to their jobs, shopping, visiting one of the city's cultural attractions, or just meeting with a friend in another part of town.

The lakeshore is really many destinations. It contains approximately 40 percent of the city's parkland, twenty-five public beaches, a dozen museums, three theaters, four band shells, a zoo, a planetarium, two water-treatment plants, the nation's largest convention center (2.67 million square feet or 248,000 m²), a 61,500-seat stadium, an amusement park, countless ball fields and playgrounds, and, since the start of the twenty-first century, all the attractions in Millennium Park. If Burnham could see what his vision triggered more than a century ago, he would surely be both amazed and delighted.

WHAT DIDN'T CHANGE

None of the images in the *Plan of Chicago* were intended to be implemented as depicted in the illustrations, as Burnham explained:

> Such radical changes . . . cannot possibly be realized immediately. Indeed, the aim has been to anticipate the needs of the future as well as to provide for the necessities of the present. . . Therefore it is quite possible that when particular portions of the plan shall be taken up for execution, wider knowledge, longer experience, or a change in local conditions may suggest a better solution.[71]

That open, flexible approach to implementing the *Plan's* proposals made it easier to adapt

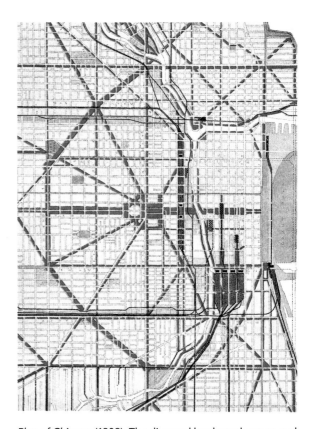

Plan of Chicago (1909). The diagonal boulevards proposed in the plan required too much property acquisition, relocation, and demolition to be financially or politically feasible.

Place de l'Opéra, Paris (2006). The inspiration for the grand civic square proposed in the *Plan of Chicago*.

Plan of Chicago (1909). The proposed Civic Center, centered on an 800-foot-high City Hall, seemed an extravagance even to Chicago's ambitious leaders.

them to economic and political realities. As a result, a remarkable number of the proposals became realities, even though they do not exactly resemble their illustrations in the plan.

Because the *Plan of Chicago* was responsible for so many of the changes, it is easy to overlook the proposals that failed. The rejected proposals are as important, in their way, as the plan's achievements, because they illustrate where the city's planning process failed. They include the pervasive City Beautiful aesthetic, the proposed street system, the civic center, and the reuse of railroad property.

The City Beautiful Movement, which had been promoted by the Chicago Fair, reflected the influence of Paris and its École des Beaux-Arts, where many of its architects had been educated. Burnham had been so deeply impressed by Haussmann's transformation of Paris that his earlier plan for San Francisco is sometimes described as Paris with hills. He probably understood better than anybody else that the physical character of Chicago was nothing like the Paris that Haussmann confronted in 1853. Nevertheless, the proposals in the plan failed to incorporate the difference between the two cities.

For example, the notion of diagonal boulevards in the *Plan of Chicago* went nowhere; most were not even proposed to the relevant public officials. Like the arterials that Haussmann pierced through Paris, these diagonals were intended to connect the city with the surrounding countryside and to make traveling easy between one neighborhood and another. But Chicago in 1900, unlike Paris in 1850, was not a cobweb of narrow, winding streets and densely built-up neighborhoods. It had broad, regularly spaced streets with compact blocks and large lots, accommodating modern office buildings, factories, and warehouses. Many of its residential neighborhoods were filled with handsome row houses with back yards. Thus, broad, diagonal boulevards piercing through a twisted maze of narrow streets made sense in Paris but was unsuited to the large-scale transport of goods and people required by a major metropolis, and so had far less appeal in early twentieth-century Chicago.

More important, expropriation of private property in America was then and is now more difficult than in France. At the beginning of Haussmann's work in Paris, excess condemnation had been an accepted government practice. In the United States, property not specifically needed for "public use" could not be condemned, because that would have violated the Fifth and Fourteenth amendments to the Constitution. Most important, piercing diagonal traffic arteries through built-up sections of the city would have caused dislocation and expense that were financially prohibitive, as well as politically explosive.

The civic center met defeat as well. Burnham thought the city needed a place that "would be what the Acropolis was to Athens, or the Forum to Rome . . . the very embodiment of civic life." He wanted it to play a role similar to the Opéra in Haussmann's Paris; all the city's main arteries would lead to it. The civic center would include office buildings for Cook County and for the United States government. There would be separate structures for the departments of police, public health, and public works, for the Hall of Records, and for the courts. At the center of it all illustrator Ferdinand Janin sketched an 800-foot-high domed City Hall, dominating the skyline. The federal, state, county, and city governments, however, were unlikely to coordinate their building programs in a manner that would make this massive civic center possible. But even if they had, the center depended on property condemnation for major diagonal boulevards, for which there was no support.

The *Plan of Chicago* emulated the Grande Croisée in Paris by proposing that two existing streets (north-south Michigan Avenue and east-west Congress Parkway) be made the primary

Plan of Chicago (1909). Construction of a system of regional roads had to wait for passage of the Interstate Highway Act of 1956.

axes of the city. This Grand Croisée was never created because Chicago's repetitive, orthogonal grid made a cross axis of this sort quite unnecessary.

Similarly, the suburban arterial ring roads in the *Plan* were intended to play a role in moving traffic, similar to the role of Paris's peripheral boulevards. But the regional circumferential roadways in the *Plan of Chicago* were like neither the Parisian Grands Boulevards nor the Périphérique. They looked good on the map, but they made sense only as abstract geometry.

Ten years after the plan appeared, there had been some progress in paving the circuit roads,[72] but after 1928 further advance would have required "the co-operation of certain authorities other than those of the city of Chicago."[73] That cooperation was not forthcoming, and it would be decades before the State of Illinois began to build toll highways and before the national government embarked on an interstate highway system to deal with regional traffic, which had changed drastically in the intervening years. The highways that finally emerged were neither in the same place nor intended to serve the same purposes as those illustrated in the *Plan of Chicago*.

Although Burnham had not been educated at the École des Beaux-Arts, he accepted most of its principles, including symmetry, axial vis-

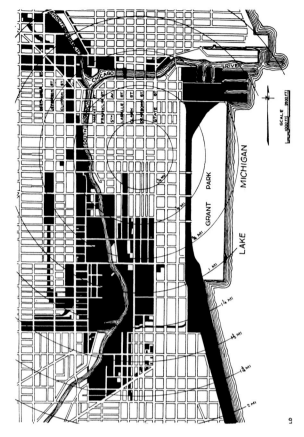

Chicago (1918). Property owned by various railroad companies.

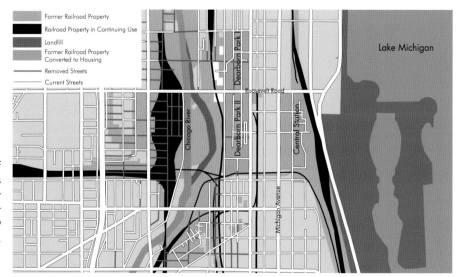

A great deal of railroad property was redeveloped after World War II in a manner unanticipated by the 1909 *Plan*.

tas, consistent building heights (except for major monuments), simple geometrical building forms and open space volumes, and Renaissance and Baroque architectural details. The placement of Piers No. 1 and No. 2, flanking the two ends of Grant Park, is a reflection of that commitment to symmetry. They do not look exactly as illustrated in the *Plan* because their design was modified to meet the functional, financial, and political realities of the day.

It was also because of commitment to City Beautiful design principles that the *Plan* depicts nearly all privately owned buildings occupying whole blocks or very large sections of them, all built to exactly the same height. This was totally impracticable, given the scattered, multiple ownership of the city's real estate; it would have been almost impossible to assemble such sites. Moreover, the city in which the skyscraper was invented would never be comfortable with simple height limits. In 1893, Chicago had adopted a 130-foot limit that was doubled in 1902 and then lowered to 200 feet in 1910. When Chicago finally adopted a comprehensive zoning ordinance in 1923, towers were permitted if they covered less than one-quarter of the site and contained less than one-sixth of the building's bulk.

Everyone who participated in the work of the Commercial and Merchants clubs thought they had presented effective prescriptions for improving freight and passenger rail service. But they underestimated the competition among the railroad companies with facilities in Chicago. Despite some improvements, the railroad recommendations were never implemented.

In other instances the proponents of the *Plan* compromised by modifying projects to meet the demands of their opponents. For example, when critics of the widening of 12th Street to create Roosevelt Road "did not want a street so wide that business would be lost," arguing that it should remain "a distinctive business artery," the planners reduced its width to 108 feet so it could accommodate retail customers, mass transit, and vehicular traffic.[74]

Unfortunately Burnham, Moody, and the other proponents of the *Plan* did not display the same combination of flexibility and persistence when faced with opposition to creating a consolidated railroad terminal for 12th Street, one and a half miles south of the Loop. They stood fast against all opposition. The idea was opposed by downtown merchants, who didn't want to lose their customers, and by the railroads, which did not want to incur the expense. Naturally, local politicians did not want to lose support from the railroads and the merchants. The planners' inflexibility doomed this part of the plan, as they were unable to put together the necessary coalition to win its approval.

HOW PLANNING BECAME ESSENTIAL TO CHICAGO

In 1927 the commission issued the *Chicago Plan Progress*, enumerating 110 projects with which it had been involved, from the aquarium to the zoo.[75] Some of these were not part of the 1909 *Plan*, though most of them were. By 1931 the commission had succeeded in obtaining voter approval of "eighty-six *Plan*-related bond issues covering 17 different projects with a combined cost of $234 million."[76] The equivalent of that sum in 2010 would be an amazing $3.4 billion.[77]

A number of factors contributed to the success of the planning process. The men who put together the plan produced recommendations that were practical, created a mechanism to build public support, and invested in a continuous lobbying effort in support of those recommendations. They ascertained its practicality by spending many, many hours checking their ideas against realities on the ground and with people who were knowledgeable about them—and changing their proposals to make them as feasible as possible.

The Commercial Club created a constituency for the *Plan* by consulting with many of the city's business, labor, and political leaders and involving as many other players as they could whose lives, work, and property would be directly affected by its proposals. Determined lobbying by the Chicago Plan Commission, its two chairmen (Charles Wacker and James Simpson), and its two executive directors (Walter Moody and Eugene Taylor) were critical to the success of the plan. Without their effort, the proponents would not have been able to overcome specific local opposition or to gain support from a city-wide majority. As Burnham explained:

It is "publicity," which, although unknown in older times, now exposes everything in the United States to open view. . . . [Thus] when the majority of the people of any town come to think that convenience and its consequent beauty are essential, they will have them, for a democracy has full power over men, land, and goods, and can always make its laws fit its purpose.[78]

Less discussed, but very important to the plan's success, is the fact that Chicago had public implementing entities that could execute public realm recommendations: its three park boards (established in 1869), the Forest Preserve District (established in 1907), and the Board of Local Improvements (established in 1897). For example, the *Plan* proposed two types of non-park projects: location-specific and city-wide. Local improvements, which primarily benefited the adjacent locality, were financed in whole or in part by a special assessment on the benefiting property owners. They were then implemented by the five-member Board of Local Improvements, appointed by the mayor and the City Council.[79]

There were, however, hindrances to implementation of the *Plan*, and especially to its financing. General improvements, which were of benefit to the entire city, were paid for by city budget expenditures or financed by issuing bonds and then implemented by the city's Commissioner of Public Works. These general improvements went through an elaborate process of public notice and hearings. Once the board voted for them, they had to have City Council and mayoral approval and were subject to all the vagaries of any political process involving large sums of money. Because these general improvements involved bond issues, they had to be approved by referendum. For the first decade and a half after publication of the *Plan*, bond issues that financed projects in the *Plan* were usually approved. The bond issue for widening 12th Street, for example, carried by a majority of 21,000 votes, despite opposition from ten aldermen. [80] However, implementation of the project, which had been proposed in 1909, was not speedy: the approval process took about a year, and construction, seven more.[81]

Furthermore, as time passed, it became evident that crooked politicians and businessmen were raking off money from the improvements. Condemnation awards, for example, required professional appraisals. Rather than pay the salaries of the appraisers or set a standard fee for each appraisal, the city administration paid 1 percent of the value of the reconstruction value of property on the streets affected. Over $2 million was paid for appraisals not "worth one-fortieth of the sum. One of the experts who made these appraisals received $577,000, another $460,000, another $544,000, averaging $1,900 per day for each expert."[82] The *Chicago Tribune* brought a lawsuit to recover the money. In 1928 the court held Mayor Thompson and his colleagues liable for $1.73 million.[83] That same year, when Thompson and the Plan Commission proposed thirty-one bond issues, all thirty-one were defeated by a two-to-one margin.[84]

Despite all the difficulties, it is amazing how much of the city's program of public improvements was enacted. By 1931, board projects to open and widen streets had required the acquisition of 939 properties. They cost a total of $54.4 million, of which $21.4 million was raised by special assessment of 188,200 affected properties; the other $33 million came from the proceeds of city-wide bond issues.[85] For the next decade, however, during the Depression, major public investments were based on the availability of federal subsidies from the PWA, CWA, and WPA, whose purposes were not necessarily consistent with those of the *Plan*.

Lakeshore Drive, Chicago (2005).

Gradually, the role of the commission itself changed. In 1939 the City Council replaced the informal 328-member City Plan Commission with a 26-member Plan Commission, twelve of whose members were agency and legislative leaders serving ex-officio, and gave the new commission a formal governmental role in planning public improvements, area redevelopment, and comprehensive planning. Although the council also established a 267-member Advisory Board to provide public input, the commission lost much of its independence and authority as a player in the planning game. The mayor and City Council were now firmly in control.[86]

Much had changed since the Commercial Club decided to produce the *Plan of Chicago*. Burnham had provided vision and coordinated a vast and complex array of information and ideas. A great many knowledgeable and strong personalities had been involved in developing the proposals that would forever change Chicago. Charles Wacker's and Walter Moody's political advocacy had resulted in the acceptance of an astonishing number of its proposals. The Commercial Club's greatest contribution, however, was not publication of a handsome document or even its powerful, practical ideas; it was in launching a planning process that reflected deep understanding of the political and economic rules operative in Chicago during the first quarter of the twentieth century.

New York metropolitan area (2007).

SIX

GROWING METROPOLITAN NEW YORK: IT WASN'T ALL MOSES

Paris and Chicago invested huge amounts of money over many decades, and they achieved remarkable results. Once their agendas were decided upon, however, the procedures they employed were the product of the particular political structure and economy of each of these cities. Paris was the national capital of a country with a centralized government, whose powers extended equally to the city and to surrounding communities. Most of the proposals in the *Plan of Chicago*, on the other hand, applied to the city itself, and for these it had a number of implementing vehicles already in place. Therefore, there was no need to devise new agencies to implement a regional agenda for Paris or Chicago. In the New York metropolitan area, on the other hand, an entirely new set of implementation vehicles had to be created to carry out its regional agenda.

The resources devoted to effecting change in the New York metropolitan area between 1920 and 1960 served two interdependent goals: to extend the region's public realm to accommodate its exploding population and vibrant economy, and to improve the quality of life for all its residents. Both were intended to strengthen the city's competitive position within an increasingly global economy.

To implement this agenda, the region invested in increasing the capacity and efficiency of its port facilities; improving access to and circulation within the region for trucks, buses, and automobiles; reclaiming and providing public access to the waterfront for recreational purposes; and adding to and improving the region's already significant inventory of parks and playgrounds. In some cases, such as creating a network of highways, bridges, and tunnels, the agenda achieved these goals simultaneously.

Unlike Chicago, New York's public investment agenda was not embodied in a comprehensive plan, carefully considered and cleverly marketed. Plans for New York published in 1914 and 1929 failed precisely because they were *not* a part of an effective marketing and implementation effort. Unlike the members of Chicago's Commercial Club, the authors of New York's planning documents were not plugged into the region's political system, nor were they the major figures in its business establishment. The New York metropolitan area had no official entity, like Chicago's Plan Commission, that was appointed by any of the region's political leaders to lobby for either plan's execution, nor was there a government agency, like Chicago's Board of Local Improvements, that had jurisdiction over all capital investments within the territory covered by those plans. What was unique to New York was neither the plans nor the larger agenda, which most people already accepted. The main story in New York was the pragmatic and incremental implementation of the agenda, as well the creation of governmental institutions specifically to be implementing vehicles.

THE PLANS THAT FAILED

Some thoughtful New Yorkers did try to emulate the *Plan of Chicago*. But there was no chance that they would produce a document that could determine the future of the sprawling, complex New York metropolitan region, managed as it was by hundreds of separate political jurisdictions and even more operating agencies.[1] Other New Yorkers thought that a regional government would have to be established before any plan could be formulated. This process seemed to have begun in 1898, when voters in Manhattan, Brooklyn, Queens, the Bronx, and Staten Island chose to consolidate into a single political entity, the "Greater City of New York." The consolidation of about forty separate local governments was the result of decades of effort to deal with transportation, utilities, shipping, finance, and administration on a regional basis.[2] Regional consolidation, however, never went beyond the five boroughs of New York City.

From the beginning, control of the government of the "Greater City" alternated between the Democratic Party machine and various coalitions of reformers. Power usually lay in the hands of the Board of Estimate and Apportionment (later the Board of Estimate), whose members and authority varied in accordance with the city charters of 1898, 1901, 1938, 1961, and 1975; the board was abolished entirely by the Charter of 1989, after the Supreme Court declared it an unconstitutional violation of one person/one vote.[3] Although the roles of its individual members changed with the charter then in effect, the board included the mayor, the comptroller, the president of the city council, the five borough presidents, and, in later years, the public advo-

cate. These officeholders were usually beholden to political machines, which controlled the nominating and electoral processes by which most public officials were chosen.

After 1898 the metropolitan area began to expand far beyond the political boundaries of the "Greater City." By 1919, New York City's population of 4.8 million surpassed London's 4.5 million, and the following year its metropolitan area, already estimated at 6.5 million in 1911, also overtook London's. New York became the world's largest urban agglomeration, surpassing London by 1920.[4]

Not surprisingly, many reformers believed the region's future success depended on taking steps to accommodate its exploding population and expanding economy. The broad regional government that they advocated through the twentieth century could not be created, however, given the region's chaotic political environment; community self-determination was ingrained in every aspect of daily life. This was perhaps to be expected in a population as large, as varied, and as contentious as the population of New York's metropolitan area.[5]

The region was dominated by political machines, particularly by Manhattan's Tammany Hall. With the exception of the mayoralties of John Purroy Mitchell (1914–17) and Fiorello LaGuardia (1934–45), Tammany controlled New York City's government until reformers began to reassert themselves late in the mayoralty of Robert F. Wagner, Jr. (1954–65). The machines' power was permanently reduced during and after John Lindsay's administration (1966–73), but through most of the twentieth century, virtually all decisions needed the approval of the relevant Democratic Party county leader, supported by his fellow leaders.

On Long Island the Nassau and Suffolk county Republican political organizations were even more powerful than the five borough machines. With occasional exceptions, they continued to control those counties into the twenty-first century, by which time both the political realities and the city itself had become quite different. New Jersey's counties and cities were similarly dominated by Republican or Democratic party organizations, depending on the locality and the era.

This pattern of regional politics was accompanied by pressure from reformers to eliminate what they perceived as widespread graft and corruption, to curtail the influence of political machines, to increase public participation in decision-making, and to establish government agencies that operated on merit. Sometimes reformers gained control of government and changed things, but neither the reformers nor their changes lasted very long. When the reformers left government, the same old practices returned with the players they had ousted.

During the time when a public investment agenda was beginning to take shape, two genuinely comprehensive plans were produced. The first plan, modest in comparison to Chicago's, was issued by the New York City government. The second was produced by an independent organization that had been established to advance the region's planning.

In 1914 the Committee on the City Plan of the New York City Board of Estimate and Apportionment produced a document titled *Development and Present Status of City Planning in New York*. This document had no impact whatsoever on what happened in New York,

Proposal for Brooklyn from *Development and Present Status of City Planning in New York* (1914).

but it included what is still a convincing rationale for planning:

> City planning does not mean the invention of new schemes of public expenditure. It means getting the most out of the expenditures that are bound to be made and saving of future expense in replanning and reconstruction. With or without a comprehensive city plan, the City will probably spend hundreds of millions of dollars on public improvements during the next thirty years. In addition, during this same period property owners will spend some billions of dollars in the improvement of their holdings.[6]

Its authors correctly believed that planning could accelerate or improve *what was likely to happen anyway* and that by making intelligent proposals, it could shape those inevitable actions. Instead, the 1914 plan emulated the unrealistic components of the *Plan of Chicago*, proposing diagonal boulevards, for example, that were as unlikely to appear in New York as in Chicago. The plan's scheme for consolidating waterborne shipping into a huge port occupying Jamaica Bay was as unrealistic as the consolidated rail-freight operations proposed in the *Plan of Chicago*.

Perhaps the document would have been more successful if it had lived up to its rhetoric or if its authors had concentrated on investments that, like the *Plan of Chicago*, reflected long planning and active constituencies. The 1914 plan did none of these things, and thus its supporters could not even propose creating an agency like the Chicago Plan Commission to lobby in its behalf.

Failure to understand what would be successful and what would not is particularly mystifying, since the chairman of the advisory commission for the 1914 City Plan was Charles Norton, who had been an active member of the Commercial Club when it produced the *Plan of Chicago*. A year after the 1914 plan was published, Norton began to advocate for a regional plan, including "the Atlantic Highlands and Princeton; the lovely Jersey hills back of Morristown and Tuxedo; the incomparable Hudson as far as Newburg; the Westchester lakes and ridges of Bridgeport and beyond, and all of Long Island."[7] That has been the unrealized dream of countless planners ever since.

Norton persuaded Frederic A. Delano to join him in advocating for a regional plan. Delano had been vice chairman of the committee that produced the Chicago plan and, like Norton, he had since moved to New York. Together, they convinced the Russell Sage Foundation in 1921 to eventually spend $1.2 million on the regional plan effort.[8] The following year Norton and Delano established the Regional Plan Committee (later the Regional Plan Association). The plan was largely the work of the staff, working under the leadership of Nelson Lewis, until he died in 1924, and then under Thomas Adams. Their product appeared as *The Graphic Regional Plan* and six other beautifully illustrated books, published between 1929 and 1931.

The *Regional Plan* proposed an orderly and rational scheme for growth. Its main proposal was a system of concentric highways, intersected by a regularly spaced grid of arteries running through the region, but for all the work that went into it, very little of the *Plan* was implemented. The exceptions were projects that had substantial support from the region's political leadership, were already underway, or had been previously approved. By 1929, when the first volumes were issued, the Port of New York Authority was already committed to building the Lincoln Tunnel; the New York City government was creating the West Side and East Side drives in Manhattan and had appropriated the first $5 million for the Triborough Bridge; and the Long Island State Park Commission was continuing to extend landscaped motorways toward state parks.

The *Regional Plan* answered the increasingly urgent demand for highways with a geometric diagram—an evenly spaced grid within a set of concentric roadways. The RPA claimed that this diagram had been modified to take account of topography, existing rights-of-way, and projects then under consideration or underway. Yet the 96 pages of maps printed in Volume I show a system that barely resembles either of the two accompanying diagrams. The maps showed designated new and existing express routes (like Manhattan's already approved West Side Highway), major regional routes (like Northern Boulevard in Queens), minor regional routes, important connections, parkways, and boulevards. This network seemed rational in the abstract, but it ignored the reality of the communities through which roadways would pass, and it failed to take into account the costs of property acquisition, the required displacement, and the scope of local opposition. The RPA plan greatly underestimated future population and economic growth. It proposed too few "express

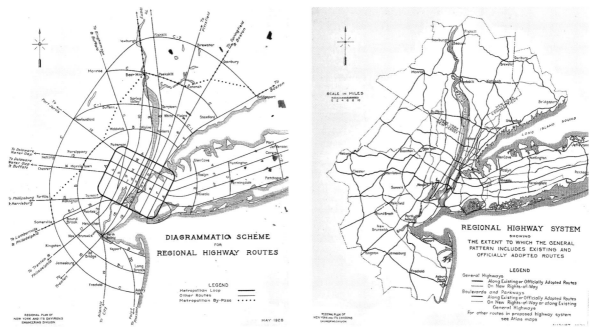

The Regional Plan of New York and Its Environs (1929) illustrated a highway network that would provide equitable service to everybody in the New York Metropolitan area.

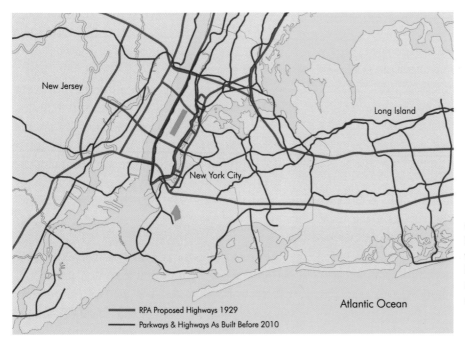

Comparison of actual highways as of 2010 with proposed highway locations from The Regional Plan of New York and Its Environs (1929).

routes" to accommodate the nation's largest and most productive metropolitan region, and it did not adequately accommodate interstate travel. Moreover, the other "major regional routes" could never have handled the additional traffic.

A second problem was that the central "express route" grid was based on a geometric diagram intended to indicate an even level of coverage. In Manhattan the routes along the East and Hudson rivers, which predated the 1929 plan, were implemented, but the rest of the diagram was profoundly unrealistic and was not. The RPA advocated four cross-Manhattan routes to link New Jersey with Long Island (as did the transportation establishment for the next four decades).

The southernmost proposed route would have connected the Holland Tunnel with the Manhattan Bridge by way of a Lower Manhattan Expressway. From its inception it was successfully opposed by community residents. The second route was similarly doomed; this one would have connected the future Lincoln Tunnel (opened in 1937) by way of a Mid-Manhattan Expressway to a proposed East River crossing. The East River crossing was built as the Queens Midtown Tunnel, which opened in 1940. There was even less chance of creating a third Hudson River crossing from New Jersey, to connect with the major regional artery designated by the RPA: a widened 125th Street leading to the Triborough Bridge. The only one of the four proposed routes that was actually built was the one connecting the future George Washington Bridge to the future New England Thruway, via the Cross Bronx Expressway. But this connector followed a different route from the one the RPA proposed.

The proposed extensions across Brooklyn, Queens, and Long Island would have caused such disruption that local officials did not seriously consider them. Like the 1914 Plan, the *Regional Plan* included projects that lived only in the realm of fantasy. These included erecting a terminal and office building more than 500 feet high, which would straddle the elevated subway that crossed the Sunnyside rail yards in Queens; creating "a new channel from the Passaic River east of Newark to the Hackensack River bend west of Secaucus Yards" in New Jersey; and lining the Brooklyn Heights waterfront with fifteen blocks of 30-story apartment buildings.[9]

The thoughtful, often brilliant intellectuals who put together the 1929 *Regional Plan* did not understand the rules of the planning game. Unlike Wacker, Moody, and the Chicago Plan Commission, they did not grasp Burnham's most important observation that proposals had to have a constituency and be actively promoted throughout the region, because once they went into execution, "wider knowledge, longer experience, or a change in local conditions may suggest a better solution."[10] Their proposals, unlike the projects presented in the *Plan of Chicago*, could not be adjusted to the realities of a later day. They were impractical from the start.

Moreover, the work of the RPA ignored the larger realities of its own day. The economy was entering the worst crisis of the twentieth century. Politically, potential players were focused on trying to keep the pluralist politics of the United States from following Germany and Russia into a totalitarian system. Given the gravity of the issues facing them, the region's voters and many of its leaders were not actively interested in the RPA's well-written, handsomely illustrated volumes.

Even had the Great Depression not begun just when the first volumes of the plan were released, there would have been no hope of obtaining the hundreds of billions of dollars that its 470 proposals required. The scale and the expense were simply too large. Furthermore, the plan covered 421 municipalities and 5,528 square miles, but there existed no entity with the requisite powers to act within all of their jurisdictions.[11]

IMPLEMENTATION

While most of the projects contained in the RPA plan were ignored, its intellectual framework had been generally accepted long before 1929. Publication of the plan helped to advance public acceptance of a regional agenda. Implementation, however, required the creation of new agencies, authorized to carry out different portions of the agenda (acquiring property by condemnation, issuing bonds, receiving federal funds, hiring expert consultants, entering into construction contracts, etc.). The most important common characteristics of these new agencies would be the ability to operate without specific approval from local or state governments and the political machines that ran them, reliance on revenue not appropriated annually from state and local governments, and dependence on personnel (leadership, staff, and consultants) who would be hired on merit.

There were precedents for broadly authorized regional agencies. Throughout the nineteenth century a number of states had established single-function implementing entities that operated on a regional basis. But the Chicago Sanitary District (1889), established to deal with storm water and sewage flowing into Lake Michigan, the Metropolitan Park Commission in Massachusetts (1892), established to create and operate a regional park system in the counties surrounding Boston, and other similar agencies had to obtain legislative sanction for their activities and sometimes approval by the voters as well. The Croton Aqueduct, which brought water to New York City, for example, was authorized by the New York State legislature in 1834 and approved in a referendum the following year. Even semi-independent entities, like Manhattan's Central Park Commission, established by the New York State legislature in 1857 as a way to prevent the Democratic machine from controlling the planning and development of Central Park, were unable to eliminate graft and corruption. Proponents of the post–World War I regional agenda were determined to prevent similar abuses. The most difficult problem, however, was the continuing demand for community control throughout the region's hundreds of independent political jurisdictions.

In an attempt to create agencies that could implement the reformers' agenda and override community control, the states of New York and New Jersey experimented with graft-ing semi-independent public agencies onto the region's existing political institutions. The most important of these were the Port of New York Authority, established in 1921 (renamed the Port Authority of New York and New Jersey in 1972), and the Triborough Bridge Authority (established in 1932 and later renamed the Triborough Bridge and Tunnel Authority). Unlike Chicago's Board of Public Improvements, these were not creatures of local political machines, and they were often independent of annual legislative appropriations or voter referenda. In some respects the new agencies were also free of legislative oversight and local government regulation.

In addition to the Port Authority of New York and New Jersey and the Triborough Bridge and Tunnel Authority (TBTA), the other primary vehicles that implemented the region's public investment strategy included the Long Island State Park Commission (1924), New York City's consolidated Parks Department (1934), the New York City Housing Authority (1934), and the New York City Committee on Slum Clearance (1948), all of which operated entirely within the structures and procedures of conventional government operations. Each of these new entities was subject to regulation by the federal government, which in many ways determined what they could do and often paid for what they accomplished.

These new agencies were successful when they followed the political and economic rules that govern planning; when they failed, it was usually because they ignored basic principles or failed to keep up with changes in the New York metropolitan area. For example, the Long Island State Park Commission (LISPC) successfully tapped the growing demand for recreational opportunities by collecting parkway tolls that paid for the creation and maintenance of its regional parks. The New York City Committee on Slum Clearance, on the other hand, was unable to gain approval for twenty-seven urban renewal projects because they were opposed by site residents, local communities, the county political machine, or some combination of the three.

The Port of New York
(2005).

THE PORT AUTHORITY OF NEW YORK AND NEW JERSEY

The first of these new agencies was the Port Authority of New York and New Jersey, whose purpose was to increase the capacity and efficiency of the region's port and transportation facilities. In 1917, in a preliminary bistate effort, the States of New York and New Jersey appropriated about half a million dollars to pay for engineering studies of harbor conditions.[12] The Authority's long-term agenda was to enable the Port of New York to compete advantageously with Baltimore, Philadelphia, and New Orleans. To this end, its planning efforts aimed to decrease congestion, improve efficiency, and reduce the cost of shipping from both sides of the Hudson.

Business interests and reformers who wanted "nonpartisan" administration of the port sought to reduce the power of parochial interests. It took two years to put together an agreement among 105 municipalities within the port district.[13] The deal seemed to be acceptable to both the Republican and Democratic parties, but it was in fact a shaky agreement, lacking support in New York City and in the mayor's office, in particular. Mayor John Hylan (1918–25) had defeated John Purroy Mitchell with slogans referring to reformers as misguided "efficiency experts." Not surprisingly, he opposed the creation of an agency that could operate within the city independent of local control. Worse yet, Hylan feared it would be run by "foreigners" from New Jersey.[14] This was a view shared by many New Yorkers at the time, and it would be echoed, in different words,

by many mayors over the next ninety years. It was for this reason that regional planning for the metropolitan area stopped at the Hudson River and that this chapter is largely devoted to New York City's five boroughs, plus Nassau and Suffolk counties, on Long Island.

Hylan's opposition was overcome by a fellow Democrat, Governor Alfred E. Smith (1919–20 and 1923–28). Nevertheless, the agreement had to be renegotiated and reworked, over and over again, with representatives of both states and both parties, until laws establishing the Port Authority passed both state legislatures in April 1921.

The Port of New York Authority was the first bistate agency in the country. It is governed by a twelve-member Board of Commissioners, half of whom are appointed by the governor of New York and half by the governor of New Jersey. To this day board members serve as public officials without pay for overlapping six-year terms. They appoint an executive director to carry out the agency's policies, to manage the day-to-day operations, and to administer the staff. There is a tacit understanding that the chairman of the board is appointed by the governor of New Jersey and the executive director by the governor of New York. In practice, decisions are largely the province of the Authority's skilled professional staff. In 2010 its staff numbered 7,000 people, its operating budget was $2.5 billion, and its capital budget was $3.1 billion.[15]

When the legislatures of New York and New Jersey voted in 1921 to create the Port Authority, they provided it with several unique powers. It is not subject to many of the laws of the municipalities in which it operates, and it does not need the formal approval of either state legislature for its operations. The Authority was given the right to charge fees for the use of its facilities and to issue bonds to pay for their development. It uses the revenue stream from the fees to cover the operating expenses of its many facilities and the debt service on its bonds.

Initially, the Authority's main objective was to increase the quantity, convenience, and efficiency of freight and passenger movement between New Jersey and New York. The staff of the agency in its early years, particularly Julius Henry Cohen, its counsel from 1921 to 1942, hoped to unify terminal operations with rail freight into a single system.[16] During the first few years, Port Authority engineers devised a number of rail freight routes involving bridges and tunnels; all of them were blocked by opposition from New York City and from the companies whose business they wanted to regulate. As in Chicago, the various railroad companies that serviced the region were never willing to coordinate operations with their competitors or to give up management of their business to technocrats.

Port facilities were the Authority's initial raison d'être, and subsequently its engineers devoted much time and money to studying rail service throughout its service area. Much of the Port Authority's impact, however, came from investment in bridges, tunnels, and airports. The first project to open was the Holland Tunnel in 1927. It was begun in 1920, before the establishment of the Port Authority, by two commissions created separately by the legislatures of New York and New Jersey. The tunnel was transferred to the Authority because reformers wanted an "impartial, objective, and efficient" nonprofit entity to coordinate all area transportation. Powerful New Yorkers refused to give the Authority control of anything that functioned entirely within the borders of either state. At the same time, Governors Al Smith of New York and George Silzer of New Jersey did not want a proliferation of bistate agencies, some of which they might not control.[17]

The success of the 2.6-mile Holland Tunnel catapulted the Port Authority into building additional connections between New York and New Jersey to improve motor vehicle movement and trade along the entire East Coast. The Holland Tunnel was followed by the Outerbridge Crossing (1928) the Goethals Bridge (1928), and the Bayonne Bridge (1931), which for decades, however, failed to attract enough traffic or tolls to justify the capital expenditure. The toll revenue that generated the necessary surpluses to pay Authority bonds came from the Holland Tunnel, the George Washington Bridge (1931), and the Lincoln Tunnel (1937).

The Port Authority became a model for the nonpartisan agencies that would be established to deal with regional issues, particularly when they involved more than one state. It was among the earliest government entities to pioneer the use of revenue bonds whose debt service was paid from fees and from tolls on the use of its facilities. Legislators in New York later copied major features of the Port Authority when they designed the Triborough Bridge and Tunnel Authority.

In 1947, despite opposition from prominent New Yorkers, Mayor William O'Dwyer transferred the operation of LaGuardia and Idlewild (now Kennedy) airports to the Authority. In addition to moving into airport administration, the Authority also opened major bus stations at the New York end of the Lincoln Tunnel (1950) and the George Washington Bridge (1963). Its most controversial New York State project, however, was the World Trade Center.

The Port Authority began to explore the idea of a World Trade Center in 1961, in response to pressure from downtown business interests, led by Chase Manhattan Bank's David Rockefeller and his brother, Governor Nelson Rockefeller, to revitalize Lower Manhattan by bringing international corporations to the city. At that time the Port Authority was not authorized to engage in redevelopment. Therefore in 1962, over the objections of Mayor Robert Wagner and a handful of public officials (who thought this was an unwarranted intrusion into city affairs), and from much of the real estate indus-

George Washington Bridge (2010).

try (which thought it was unfair competition for their customers), the state legislatures of New York and New Jersey passed enabling legislation authorizing the Port Authority to acquire 16 acres of Lower Manhattan for construction of the World Trade Center. What emerged in the mid-1970s was essentially a self-contained city with more than 14 million square feet of usable space, not just the two 110-story towers.

The difficulties that the Port Authority faced in doing anything in New York City came from the tensions inherent in any democracy between residents of individual communities, who desire and rely on self-determination, and people who advocate for what they perceive to be in the general interest of the region. From the very beginning, New Yorkers were suspicious of any agency that was not accountable to local legislative bodies or to voters. As mentioned above, this is one reason that most of the agenda for the New York metropolitan area originated and was implemented east of the Hudson River.

Most people could agree on the overall agenda, which was supplied by various reform groups. The implementation of that agenda, however, was dominated by new agencies created at the behest of and administered by Robert Moses.

ROBERT MOSES

Almost a century has passed since Robert Moses entered the planning game, and nearly half a century has passed since he held any significant office, yet he still dominates discussions of city planning in New York.[18] Any effort to examine the role he played is made more difficult by the fact that our understanding of him is encrusted with conceptions that persuasive interpreters have added over the years. Many of the things ascribed to Moses are in fact the work of others, while much of what he accomplished remains hidden from view. Furthermore, Moses, his supporters, and his critics have all exaggerated Moses's role.

No one in any city, anywhere, not even Haussmann, built more than Robert Moses. Within the seven counties of New York and Long Island, he administered the agencies responsible for building and maintaining at least 200 miles of landscaped parkways, six bridges spanning nearly 10 miles, and two tunnels extending nearly 2 miles. In addition, he was involved in some manner with about 160 miles of the seven counties' limited-access expressways, which were in fact built by entities he did not administer. As chairman of the Long Island State Park Commission from 1924 to 1963, Moses spearheaded the creation of fifteen major parks on Long Island, built 133 miles of parkways, and opened 24 miles of public beaches.[19] Between 1934 and 1960 he was also New York City parks commissioner, and under his administration the Parks Department acquired 20,200 acres of parkland in New York City, extended 133 miles of parkway, built 15 huge swimming pools, created 658 playgrounds, and added 17 miles of public beaches to the meager 1 mile the city owned when he came to office.[20] This inventory does not take account of his role as New York City's urban renewal czar, or the rest of his work in New York State and elsewhere, which includes building two bridges and a parkway near Niagara Falls, managing the New York State Power Authority, and consulting for Pittsburgh, Portland, New Orleans—and much else. Moses did not accomplish all this in a vacuum. He was pursuing an agreed-upon agenda that had received formal legislative sanction at the local, state, or federal level, and often all three.

Born in New Haven, Connecticut, in 1888, Robert Moses lived two blocks from the Yale University campus until he was nine years old, when his family moved to New York City. He graduated from Yale, then earned a masters degree in political science from Oxford and a Ph.D. from Columbia, in 1914. Many people think of Moses as a thoughtless but effective bulldozer. But he was well and broadly educated, as familiar with the writings of Pope and Shakespeare as he was with cost estimates for the latest playgrounds.

Moses began his career in government by enrolling in the Training School for Public Service of the Bureau of Municipal Research, one of the major organizations trying to reform New York City government. After John Purroy Mitchell was elected mayor in 1913, Moses

Fiorello LaGuardia and Robert Moses (to his right) at a ribbon cutting (1914).

joined the staff of the Mayor's Civil Service Commission, to which he brought a theoretical understanding of the British Civil Service, the subject of his doctoral dissertation. Mitchell lost his bid for reelection in 1917, however, and Moses was forced to leave the agency. In 1919 he became chief of staff to Governor Al Smith's Reconstruction Commission, and between Smith's terms, he was secretary of the New York State Association, another reform group.

With Smith back in office, Moses worked in Albany until the governor made him chairman of the Long Island State Park Commission and chairman of the State Council of Parks. During Smith's last two years in office Moses also performed the job of secretary of state. Throughout his career Moses held many jobs, often simultaneously. Among the most important of his posts were those of New York City parks commissioner (1934–60)—his only paying job during those twenty-six years; commissioner and chairman of the Triborough Bridge and Tunnel Authority (1934–68) in its various incarnations; chairman of the Mayor's Slum Clearance Committee (1948–60); and New York City coordinator of construction (1946–60).[21]

Because Moses was an effective public official, it is common, but mistaken, to think of him as a successful politician. He tried for elective office twice. In 1933 he thought he might get the Republican nomination for mayor, but he didn't stand a chance against Fiorello LaGuardia, who became the boss he admired almost as much as Al Smith. The following year, Moses won the Republican nomination for governor but lost the election.

Great politicians avoid making enemies, especially powerful enemies, and they always try to back winning candidates. Moses, on the contrary, did not suffer fools easily and was always eager to dazzle his audiences with a bon mot, often at the expense of somebody he considered a jackass. The press loved to print his colorful language, increasing the number of people who were aware that he thought them or their ideas foolish. His outspokenness contributed to a growing chorus of opponents. Moses's feud with Franklin Roosevelt is legendary.

The animosity originated in 1924–25, when Franklin Roosevelt was chairman of the Taconic State Park and Parkways Commission. It is unclear exactly why it began: whether because Moses channeled more money to the Long Island Park and Parkway Commission, of which he was the chairman, than to other commissions; or because at that time Moses was an idealistic political reformer offended by the idea of giving a "no-show" job to Louis Howe (Franklin Roosevelt's political mentor); because of some personal animosity; or simply because Moses was a Republican and Roosevelt a Democrat who went on to be governor and president.[22] When he became President, Roosevelt repeatedly tried to get Mayor La Guardia to dismiss Moses from the Triborough Bridge Authority and from other city jobs as well, but La Guardia never gave in to the President.[23]

In 1953, Moses failed to support Robert F. Wagner, Jr., in his successful campaign for mayor. Wagner, whose political guile usually triumphed, kept Moses on as parks commissioner but slowly began to chip away at his power. By 1956, opposition to what were considered Moses's urban renewal and highway projects had gained sufficient momentum for the mayor to begin plotting his downfall.[24] Eventually, in 1960, the mayor pressured him into resigning his city jobs, in order to "concentrate" on creating and operating the 1964 World's Fair.

Moses was seventy-seven years old when the Fair ended. He remained chairman of the Triborough Bridge and Tunnel Authority for another three years, until Governor Nelson Rockefeller chose not to reappoint him. Still, despite his age and his lack of an official role in the planning game, people continued to listen to what he had to say.

Moses himself created the legend that he was "the man who could get things done for New York."[25] The legend was credible because he usually implemented what he believed to be an agreed-upon agenda, adjusting it enough to minimize active opposition and making sure he had all the formal government approvals the projects required.

Perhaps the greatest of the misconceptions about Robert Moses is that he built highways. Moses administered the Long Island State Park Commission and the New York City Parks Department, the agencies that created and maintained parkways. He also administered the authorities that financed, built, and maintained bridges, tunnels, and the arteries leading to them. His authority over highways was indirect.

Under the New York City charters that were in effect until 1961, the five borough presidents and the Department of Public Works were responsible for building and managing public roads and highways. Routes required approval by the City Planning Commission, established by the Charter of 1938. While he was a member of the City Planning Commission, therefore, from 1942 to 1960, Moses voted on the mapping of highways. But highway routes then had to be approved by the commission and the Board of Estimate, which rarely overrode the president of the borough through which a given road passed. The Franklin Delano Roosevelt (FDR) or East Side Drive, for example, was created by staff under the supervision of borough presidents of Manhattan. Moses's involvement was the creation of the East River Park on landfill, along the edge of the drive, the extension and redesign of Carl Schurz Park, built on a platform over it, and the artery connecting it with the Triborough Bridge.

Moses undoubtedly had influence with the people responsible for highways, thanks to his reputation and his relationships with

Grand Central Parkway, Queens (2005). The parkways Robert Moses created were not simple traffic arteries but were also intended to provide recreational resources.

public officials, as well as his membership on boards and committees dealing with transportation. His influence greatly increased in 1946, when Mayor William O'Dwyer appointed him city construction coordinator. In that capacity Moses eagerly took on a major role, advising the borough presidents and the administration on the city's highway program. He was already an enthusiastic advocate for the system that had been proposed by state and federal engineers and that became the basis for the National Interstate and Defense Highways Act of 1956 (Public Law 84-627). He promoted those highways in speeches and articles for the *New York Times* and other periodicals.[26] Between 1946 and 1960, as construction coordinator, Moses spearheaded the effort to obtain approval of a system that was particularly contentious because it required the dislocation of entire communities. Mayor Wagner reduced Moses's involvement in highway planning by giving him the nom-

inal role of coordinator of arterial projects for New York City (1960–66); this role was terminated when John Lindsay became mayor. Nevertheless, despite the facts that the borough presidents played a primary role, that New York State transportation officials were intimately involved in the highway program, and that federal financing could only be obtained by meeting national locational and engineering requirements, Moses became indelibly associated with the city's highway program through his enthusiastic advocacy.

Moses was responsible for executing much of the region's agenda of public investments in parks, playgrounds, parkways, bridges, tunnels, and community redevelopment. His impact is obvious to anybody who goes to an Atlantic Ocean beach, drives along the Grand Central Parkway, visits a neighborhood swimming pool, attends a performance at Lincoln Center, or crosses the Bronx-Whitestone Bridge. Given his awesome inventory of public works, one has to ask: what exactly did he do and how did he do it?

THE MOSES METHOD

It took decades. In the beginning he had one title, chairman of the Long Island State Park Commission, and virtually no power. Over the years he amassed more and more titles, and with them, power. Power did not come from the titles; it came from his skill in playing by the rules of the planning game. Moses succeeded when he: (1) pursued an agreed-upon agenda that had received formal legislative sanction at the local, state, and federal level, and often from all three; (2) hired what he believed were the ablest professionals (without reference to political support) to design his projects; (3) obtained legislation creating an agency that he staffed with loyal civil servants to whom he entrusted project management and who could hire a staff competent and trained to implement that agenda, had the ability to hire people with the skills it might need in the future, and could engage consultants and companies to provide services it was unable to deliver; (4) established sources of revenue that allowed him to proceed without further legislative approval; (5) maintained the support of the relevant mayors and governors who had appointed him; and (6) played by all the other economic and political rules that apply to the planning game. He never deviated from the second, third, and fourth of these principles. His failures occurred when there was no longer general agreement on the agenda, as happened with the federal urban renewal and highway programs; when he lost the support of the mayor or the governor; or when he ignored one or another of the rules of the game.

As Moses explained, "esprit de corps, more commonly known as teamwork, is the most important factor in leadership." It doesn't just happen, he continued, "It must be earned."[27] The Moses team was made up of the leadership of the agencies Moses administered and the people they hired. On the first page of his book *Working for the People*, Moses wrote that "democracy's problem number one" was to

find a way "to get the right people into public service and to keep them there."[28] Within the New York City Parks Department and the Triborough Bridge and Tunnel Authority, he put together a highly competent staff of dedicated associates, whom he could put in charge of whatever projects needed attention. He said, "the ideal thing, of course, is to have first-class men operating first-class machines, but first-class men can operate any machine and third-rate people can't make the best and most modern gadget work.[29]

Moses did everything possible to maximize the productivity of agency staff. When he became New York City parks commissioner, for example, he inherited 69,000 poorly supervised relief workers. Six thousand of these were assigned to garbage dumps, and another 20,000, although on the payroll, had untraceable assignments. Moses knew that these people were a remarkable asset. He demanded the right to hire at least 500 supervisors who had technical training in architecture, landscape architecture, and construction. When he was told to use some of the relief workers as supervisors, he refused.

Within a week marked by resignation threats, Moses obtained approval from the mayor, the Board of Estimate, and the state government for the money to hire his technical supervisors. They began at once, and within three years Moses's team had developed 265 playgrounds, 12 Olympic-size swimming pools, and 8 golf courses.[30]

First rate administrative personnel were central to everything Moses undertook. On becoming New York City commissioner of parks, for example, he persuaded Gilmore Clarke (1892–1982), to become director of the New York City Parks Department Design Group. Clarke had been a member of the first board of design of the Long Island State Park Commission and thus he influenced the design of the parkways Moses built on Long Island. Clarke quit his other jobs and remained at the Parks Department until he entered private practice as a landscape architect in 1935. He continued his relationship with Moses after he left government office, designing the Henry Hudson Parkway, the grounds of the 1939 World's Fair, the Orchard Beach Bathhouse and Promenade and many other projects. He was not the only outside consultant with whom Moses had a continuing relationship. Othmar Ammann, whom Moses commissioned to design the Triborough Bridge (1936), went on to design the Bronx-Whitestone (1939), Throggs Neck (1961) and Verrazano Narrows (1964) bridges .

Moses went to extraordinary lengths to hire and maintain good relations with honest and productive contractors and with loyal subordinates. At one point auditors in Albany cut off funds for Jones Beach State Park because of a technicality. Moses and his chief engineer, Sidney Shapiro, "had personally to buy food" to keep the engineering staff from starving.[31] In 1929, Moses even borrowed money from his mother "to pay busted contractors," so the beach could open as scheduled.[32]

Moses insistence on creating agencies insulated from interference from political machines was as important as having the right personnel. This component of the Moses method began in 1923 with the establishment of New York State Council of Parks and the Long Island State Parks Commission, was repeated for the consolidation of New York City's five borough parks departments into a new city-wide Parks Department, and was expanded upon with the Triborough Bridge and Tunnel Authority. But, when Moses persuaded Mayor O'Dwyer and the Board of Estimate to establish the Committee on Slum Clearance to implement the city's urban renewal program, he turned over implementation to private real estate developers, whom he did not control, rather than loyal civil

Red Hook Recreation Area, Brooklyn (2005). The swimming pool erected in the Red Hook Recreation Area was one of hundreds of facilities the Moses team created using federal funds and workers on relief.

Orchard Beach, Bronx (2000). One of many New York City public recreation facilities designed by Gilmore Clarke.

servants. That proved to be a fatal flaw, which lead to his eventual demise.

In 1923, New York State possessed a collection of scattered sites that had been acquired "through accident, private gifts, or temporary enthusiasm of local people . . . [and were] administered by dozens of boards, societies, and ex officio and other commissions."[33] This new institution would be the central agency responsible for all state-supported lands, parks, forest preserves, and places of historic, scenic, and scientific interest. In that capacity, the council made plans for their acquisition, construction, maintenance, and management, as well as for new state and county highways connecting them. The Council consolidated all the agencies and parks controlled by the state. Its initial members included the state conservation commissioner, the heads of six newly-created regional commissions plus the head of the American Scenic and Historic Preservation Society, and the director of the State Museum. At its first meeting in 1924, the council elected Moses (who had already been appointed chairman of the Long Island State Park Commission by Smith) as its first chairman, and it made the New York State Association's plan the basis of its parks agenda. Moses continued to hold both positions (neither of which were paying jobs) for the next thirty-nine years.[34]

Moses applied to New York City parks the same pragmatic, management oriented approach he had used on Long Island. The newly elected mayor, Fiorello LaGuardia, wanted him to take responsibility for the city's parks. Moses was hesitant, because park functions were within the purview of the city's five borough presidents. He agreed to take the job, but only if LaGuardia secured passage of legislation in Albany consolidating all functions related to parks into a single department administered by a single commissioner, and authorizing the commissioner to hold other unsalaried offices so that he could "coordinate city, state, and metropolitan parks, parkways, arterial systems, and related developments."[35] As was often the case when he demanded something, the legislation was approved.

In anticipation of federal urban renewal legislation, cosponsored by New York Senator Robert Wagner, Mayor O'Dwyer in 1948 created a Committee on Slum Clearance. Its role was to operate the new urban renewal program. The mayor appointed Robert Moses chairman. Moses's approach to the program marked a major departure from all the other agencies he managed. The core of his method had been implementation by trusted, skilled civil servants working within government agencies that were generally created at his behest to be implementing vehicles. He shaped, staffed, and controlled those agencies. In his urban renewal projects, however, Moses relinquished control to the private sector. Thus, there was little he could do when any of the projects were prey to delay, mismanagement, and dishonesty.

As important as first-rate people and independent agencies were to the Moses method, without dependable, long-term borrowing it would not have worked. At first Moses relied upon government bonds backed by the full faith and credit of the State of New York. The first bond issue, approved by the voters in 1924, raised $15 million to pay for parks throughout New York State. This allowed Moses to get started. There would be other bond issues, but Moses did not want to be dependent on annual appropriations approved by the governor or the legislature. So he persuaded the members of the commission to finance park operations by having park users "pay reasonable charges for services such as parking, cabins, bathhouse lockers, games and other like facilities."[36]

During the Depression, Moses used a different approach to financing restoration, improvement, and expansion of New York City's park system. He continued to obtain whatever money was available from the city's capital budget (financed with bonds backed by the full faith and credit of the city) to pay for acquisition and development, and whatever was available from the city expense budget to cover operating costs. But, Moses used even more money that was appropriated by Congress for various New Deal programs. During his first year as park commissioner he obtained and spent $90 million (the equivalent of almost $1.5 billion in 2010) from various federal relief programs and used that money to put 86,000 men to work on 1,800 projects.[37]

Moses understood that shovel-ready projects would be likely to receive federal money. For that reason, the engineers and designers whom Moses kept on staff or hired on a consultant basis prepared construction documents for projects well before the money to build them had been appropriated. During the high point of those three years, Moses explained, "the planning section reached 1,800 employees, including architects, engineers, and landscape architects, who, working in the field and the drafting rooms, constituted one of the largest forces of this kind ever assembled."[38] Thus, whenever money became available from a suitable federal program, he was ready to use it.

In the case of the Triborough Bridge, city, state, and federal agencies struck a deal to obtain the necessary funds. The federal Public Works Administration would provide a $35 million loan (to be repaid from revenue bonds secured by tolls) and a $9.2 million federal grant. The remaining $16.1 million consisted of the $5.4 million already spent by the city plus another $10.7 million to be used for land acquisition for bridge approaches. After 1956, Moses also used federal funds available through the federal Interstate Highway system.

In the case of the urban renewal program, Title I of the Housing Act of 1949 authorized the federal government to pay two-thirds of the net project cost (determined by deducting the resale proceeds of the site from the cost of acquisition, relocation, demolition, and site preparation). In New York the local share was split between the state and local governments and, for nonprofit cooperative and limited-profit development, was accompanied by a 25-year tax exemption on any increase in the real estate taxes paid prior to redevelopment. Construction was usually financed by financial institutions whose long-term mortgages were insured by the federal government under the FHA 220 program.

In any examination of the planning game

it is a mistake to deal exclusively with process and ignore substance. The Moses method was effective only insofar as it implemented the region's agreed-upon agenda. Moses did not invent the agenda. It had evolved over decades. He usually had a profound understanding of the origins and purposes of that agenda. He also had a multi-functional approach that recognized the advantages of accomplishing different elements of the agenda simultaneously, and (possibly because he administered the agencies responsible for stewardship of projects after completion) the importance of the excellence and durability of any initial design, whether it involved parks, parkways, and playgrounds; or highways, bridges, and tunnels; or housing. Thus it is important to focus on the substance of his work with parks, the regional arterial network, and slum clearance individually.

PARKS, PLAYGROUNDS, AND BEACHES

The environmental-recreational agenda Moses implemented had not changed since the establishment of Central Park in the 1850s; as always, it was to improve personal well-being and public health, incubate a civil society, sustain a healthy environment, and provide a framework for development.[39] Its advocates had successfully promoted everything from playgrounds to national parks—always with scattered local opposition from businesses, real estate developers, and property owners determined to protect their investments and their way of life. Moses adopted that agenda when, as secretary of the New York State Association in 1921, he coordinated meetings that resulted in the acceptance of recommendations for parks throughout the state. These were embodied in the plan he prepared in 1922.

As he later explained, "mass production of automobiles, shorter working hours, and an enormous increase in outdoor activities, sports, and recreation" required an expanded role for government.[40] The New York State Association's plan called for increasing park acreage, opening new playgrounds, and consolidating manage-

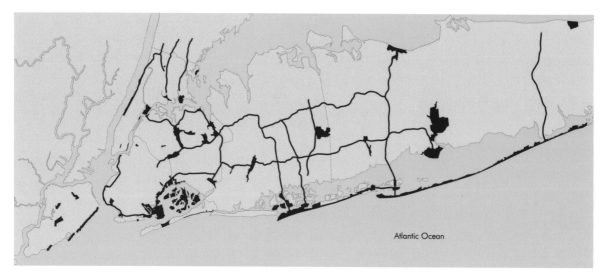

Atlantic Ocean

Sunken Meadow State Parkway, Long Island (2010). Long Island parkways were designed to provide a recreational drive to a state park.

Jones Beach (2010) provided the recreational facilities of a country club to people who could not afford the membership fee.

The designers of Jones Beach paid attention to the smallest details, even the garbage cans, which look like something from an ocean liner.

Moses added tens of thousands of acres of parkland, hundreds of playgrounds, 41 miles of public beach, and numerous parkways to serve more than 8 million people in New York City and nearly 3 million on Long Island.

ment within public agencies that were both honest and efficient.

Moses's objective was a park system for middle-class Long Islanders who could not afford membership in a country club, but who could afford to drive from their homes along landscaped, limited-access parkways to a state park. Both the parkways and the state parks were built and managed by the Long Island State Park Commission. People came in droves. During 1930, the first full year of Jones Beach's operation, for example, 950,000 cars took the new causeway to the beach; 1.4 million cars came the following year.[41] Most Long Islanders eagerly paid a few cents at the highway toll booth because they thought the visit to Jones Beach was a bargain.

His parks program was ahead of its time in its commitment to environmental sustainability. This is overlooked because it is inseparable from the other aspects of his multifunctional approach to public works. Moses explained, "I am a conservationist, but I object to lockup [sic] the wilderness against recreation."[42] Moses usually combined his environmental conservation agenda with other objectives. In 1925, for example, he entered into an arrangement with the New York City Department of Water Supply to add to the Long Island Park System more than 2,000 acres of streams, lakes, and parks that had been originally acquired for water supply purposes by the City of Brooklyn (prior to consolidation).[43] The deal permitted the property to be used for recreational purposes, in exchange for improving, maintaining, fencing, and properly policing the waterways.

Jones Beach State Park provides another early and striking demonstration of the characteristic Moses approach to public works. He thought about the present population that would use his facilities and about future generations as well. Eventually, Jones Beach became part of a 14.5-mile chain of state-operated public beaches. And in creating a park system on Long Island, Moses planned for a population far higher than the 235,000 people living there at the time.[44] In 2000 the population had grown to 2.75 million and Jones Beach was still successfully providing facilities for millions of visitors.[45]

The transformation of this spit of land— from a barren and almost unknown barrier island into a public park used by millions of people a year—required constructing access roads and bridges, raising the average island elevation from 2 feet to 14 feet above sea level by pumping 40 million cubic yards of sand from South Oyster Bay, planting hundreds of acres of beach grass to hold the sand in place, and building two huge bathhouses and countless other visitor facilities, all connected by a two-mile-long boardwalk.[46] The scale of the venture no longer seems out of proportion. But one

can only imagine the reaction in 1929 to a bathhouse containing 10,450 lockers.[47]

Acquisition of the land for Jones Beach proved to be difficult and contentious. The Long Island State Park Commission had the power to purchase any privately owned prop-

Hempstead Lake State Park, Long Island (2010).

Belmont Lake State Park, Long Island (2010). Environmental conservation of lakes and streams provided Moses with an opportunity to simultaneously create recreational facilities.

Jones Beach (2010). Millions of people flock to this public beach, which would otherwise be private property.

Heckscher State Park, Long Island (2010). There was opposition and litigation over the creation of most Long Island state parks.

erty it required for park purposes. If a property owner refused, the commission could obtain the land by exercising the right of eminent domain. Acquisition of property owned by a township, however, required a vote by its residents.

The rights to the sandbar and marshland that the commission wanted to transform into Jones Beach State Park belonged to the towns of Hempstead and Oyster Bay, in Nassau County, and Babylon, in Suffolk County.[48] In 1924, Robert Moses attempted to get the town board of Babylon to hold a referendum on the subject, but it refused. The Babylon state assemblyman conveyed the town's attitude: "We don't want people coming in and telling us where we shall have parks, when there is no public demand for them."[49]

The outcome was the same in the township of Oyster Bay. Resistance from the residents of the south shore of Long Island was similarly widespread. The governing boards of all the beachfront towns in Suffolk County refused to allow a vote. The problem was not simply opposition to outsiders; less interested parties also questioned the need for a park in so inaccessible a location. As Moses later pointed out, "the Regional Plan Association of New York bitterly opposed our program. . . . [It] advocated splitting up Jones Beach into minute subdivisions and selling them to cottagers."[50]

Moses thought he would have a better

chance of approval from the town of Hempstead, and in 1925 he convinced the Nassau County Republican leader to allow a referendum. It was roundly defeated, 12,106 to 4,200.[51] An editorial in the *New York Herald Tribune* declared that "the voters of the Town of Hempstead delivered a deserved rebuke" to what it described as the "blundering" Long Island State Park Commission.[52]

Moses would not give up. Instead, he took a more political route in preparation for another referendum in 1926. He worked out a deal, which remains secret to this day, with the Republican machine. This time the referendum passed, but the fight continued in court until the town of Babylon finally agreed to transfer its property to the commission. Only then could work on Jones Beach get started.

There were similar court battles over parks at Valley Stream, Hempstead Lake, Wildwood, Belmont, Sunken Meadow, and Orient Point. But Moses did not rely solely on persistence to get things done; he also knew when and how to compromise. He had always thought, for example, that Long Island's large estates and golf clubs could be transformed into excellent public parks. During the 1950s and 1960s, as he explained, time was "running steadily and inevitably in favor of profitable real estate subdivision," and public opinion was "a shifting matter, often dependent on misinformation about the loss of taxes."[53] Consequently, he made a series of deals, using a 1960 amendment to section 1-0713 of the State Conservation Law, which allowed park commissions that acquired large properties to permit estate owners and private clubs to remain in place for up to ten years after title was transferred. By this means, the Long Island State Park Commission was able to purchase the Daybreak (179 acres), Caumsett (1,750 acres), and Marshall Field (1,470 acres) estates and the Southside Sportsman's (3,400 acres) and Wyandanch (540 acres) clubs.

When he took over the New York City park system, Moses naturally rejected the automobile-oriented approach that was appropriate to Long Island. For one thing, the city had spent three-quarters of a century creating a complex and varied system of neighborhood parks and playgrounds. For another, when Moses became New York City parks commissioner, the country was in the midst of the Great Depression, and many people could not afford cars.

Given the scarcity of funds, Moses needed panoramic vision. He could not justify projects that had only a single purpose or would be used by a single group of people. So it was typical that he often embarked on one project and used it to implement other parts of his agenda.

The Shore Parkway in Bay Ridge, Brooklyn is a good example; in addition to providing a limited-access roadway, the project expanded neighborhood park acreage by extending bulkheads, filling in, and demolishing unnecessary buildings.[54] This created the opportunity to build ball fields, playgrounds, and a waterfront promenade with locations for amateur fishing.

Perhaps the most spectacular example of this multiple-project approach was the World's Fair of 1939. The fair was really an excuse to

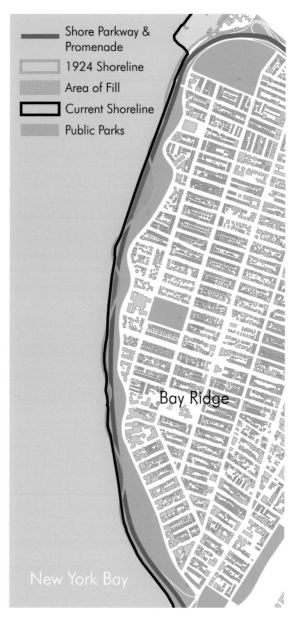

Shore Parkway, Brooklyn (2011). The requirement of smooth curves for driving allowed Moses to fill in sections of New York Harbor and add parkland to an existing facility.

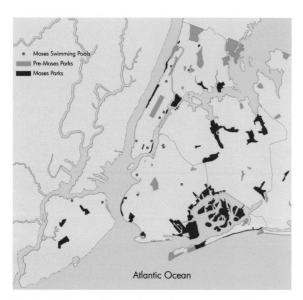

New York City public parks and swimming pools (1960). Moses doubled the size of the city's park system and built huge recreation centers with swimming pools in fifteen neighborhoods.

Flushing Meadows, Queens (1999). Transforming this former garbage dump into the World's Fairs of 1939 and 1964, providing convenient access by motor vehicle from the rest of the region, and operating facilities that would be used by hundreds of thousands of people required major public investments on-site and off-site. It also provided Moses with the opportunity to create a drainage system, a sewage-treatment plant, new roads, and the Bronx-Whitestone Bridge.

Highbridge Park and Swimming Pool, Manhattan (2005).

replace the giant garbage dump made famous by F. Scott Fitzgerald as the field of ashes in *The Great Gatsby* with the 1,255 acres of Flushing Meadows Corona Park. The other public works the fair accelerated included a drainage system for part of Queens; the Whitestone Bridge and Expressway, the Tallman Island sewage treatment plant, and the widening of Horace Harding Boulevard (now the Long Island Expressway).

When Robert Moses began his tenure as New York City's parks commissioner, the city had only a single mile of public beach. When he left office, there were eighteen miles of pub-lic beach, with bathhouses, boardwalks, swimming pools, tennis and shuffleboard courts, golf courses, playgrounds, and other facilities that had once been common only at private country clubs. Millions came to the city's new public beaches by bus or subway. Those who drove paid a parking fee. Entry, however, was free.

It fell to the Parks Department to manage and maintain the entire system. Moses consequently insisted on durable facilities throughout the park system that could service millions of people over many years. He spared no expense creating long-lasting facilities of this sort.

Shore Parkway and Jamaica Bay, Brooklyn (2004).

The Highbridge Recreation Center and Pool in Upper Manhattan is a good example of the sort of public facility he created. In his first year as commissioner Moses persuaded the Department of Water Supply, Gas, and Electricity to transfer to it the most spectacular 2.5 acres of what is now Highbridge Park. (Final assembly of the site continued in stages into the 1960s.[55]) Architect Aymar Embury II and landscape architect Gilmore Clarke restored the 1872 water tower that had been part of the aqueduct system supplying Manhattan. In addition to the pool and recreation center, the park included playgrounds, volleyball courts, handball courts, and sitting areas. Highbridge Pool was one of eleven grand public recreation centers combined with pools that the Parks Department opened in 1936 - all financed with funds from the federal Works Progress Administration (WPA).

Moses's insistence on environmental sustainability continued unabated. In 1938 the sanitation commissioner, having lost the use of the "Ash Heap" in Flushing Meadows, proposed creating an incinerator and garbage dump in Jamaica Bay. Moses was so adamant about preventing further environmental degradation that he had the Parks Department produce a booklet opposing "the blight of bad planning, polluted water, and garbage dumping" in Jamaica Bay, and he obtained legislation in Albany to insure this would not happen.[56] The region's

air, water, and wildlife have benefited greatly from the more than 2 million trees he was responsible for planting during his career, and from the 25,000 acres of shallow water, mudflats, marshes, and wetlands that are publicly owned and preserved in Jamaica Bay.[57]

Moses frequently used community complaints to help him fulfill parts of his agenda. In 1946, for example, residents living around Marine Park in Brooklyn complained about odors from garbage being dumped in the park. At first Moses suggested that the dump be moved out of the park. Then he convinced the Sanitation Department to cover the sludge with new sand instead, which would facilitate conversion of the sludge into topsoil. He argued successfully that making soil out of waste would save the city $7.5 million, which it would have had to spend on the purchase of

Playground, Pelham Bay Park, Bronx (1999).

topsoil.[58] Without the initial public complaints, the Sanitation Department probably would not have agreed to improve Marine Park. Because of Moses's efforts, it did more than the residents demanded; it also did what Robert Moses wanted it to do.

Insistence on multifunctional facilities, maximum use of federal funds, durable design, and environmental sustainability were all important factors in Moses's achievements as parks commissioner, but even more important was his stress on production. During his first year as commissioner, the Parks Department added 40 new playgrounds, with wading pools, comfort stations, swings, slides, and seesaws, to the 119 playgrounds then in existence.[59] When he left office, there were 777 playgrounds.[60] Such quantity was made possible by standardizing the design and by mass-producing the components. By the 1960s, everybody in New York could recognize the brick-and-slate-roofed comfort stations the Parks Department maintained in its playgrounds and parks.

THE REGIONAL ARTERIAL NETWORK

In the twentieth century the transportation agenda was developed in response to mass production of trucks and buses and to near-universal car ownership. Automobile registration in the United States rose from 78,000 cars in 1905 to 2.3 million in 1916.[61] Motor vehicles were becoming a major problem in the New York metropolitan area.

By 1921, of the 10 million motor vehicles in the United States, 582,000 cars, 140,000 trucks, and 32,000 buses were registered in New York State.[62] Passenger vehicles were crowding the narrow roads, making commercial deliveries difficult.

The solution seemed obvious: create an attractive alternative for private automobiles and free up space for commercial vehicles on public roads. The problem was finding a way to pay for them. Moses wanted sources of revenue that allowed him to proceed without legislative approval. So he copied the mechanism used by the Port Authority. The agencies he adminis-

tered had the ability to levy tolls on the motor vehicles who used their facilities. He used their toll revenues to cover the debt service on the bonds they issued to raise the money that paid for those very facilities. Moses began using this technique for Long Island State Park Commission projects and perfected the technique when he took over the Triborough Bridge and Tunnel Authority.

The ideas for most of Moses's endeavors had been discussed for years, even decades, before he came along. The idea of building a bridge to connect Manhattan, Queens, and the Bronx was no exception. A triborough bridge was first proposed in 1916 by the chief engineer of the New York City Department of Plant and Structures.[63] In 1929, when the city decided to build the Triborough Bridge (renamed in honor of Robert F. Kennedy in 2008), the project included sixteen lanes of vehicular traffic on two levels. It was to be entirely financed with city bonds and built by the Department of Plant and Structures. The 1929 design called for an ornamented, stone-clad structure with Gothic arches, similar to the nineteenth-and early-twentieth-century bridges that spanned the lower sections of the East River.[64]

Nothing happened for the next four years, except for the building of some unclad anchorages and a few piers. Given the decline in city tax revenue that accompanied the Great Depression, further investment in the bridge was at best problematic. Yet the need for an additional bridge across the East River was becoming urgent. In 1933, the four bridges linking Brooklyn and Queens with Manhattan carried 238,277 cars every day.[65]

Mayor John O'Brien (1933) persuaded Governor Lehman to approve state legislation establishing the Triborough Bridge Authority and appointed three Tammany loyalists to run the Authority. But when Republican Fiorello LaGuardia became mayor the next year, he announced, "We are going to build a bridge instead of patronage. We are going to pile up stone and steel instead of expenses. We are going to build a bridge of steel—and spell steel s-t-e-e-l instead of s-t-e-a-l."[66] He began by replacing two of the three members of the authority and making Robert Moses, whom he had just appointed commissioner of parks, its secretary and chief executive officer.[67]

Moses dismissed the old staff and hired Othmar Ammann, who had designed the George Washington Bridge, to replace the original designer. Although the Triborough Bridge was planned with the idea of adding a second level at a later date, Ammann eliminated the second level, removed the Gothic arches and stonework, and replaced them with the much less expensive, streamlined Art Deco detailing we see today.[68]

At first Moses wanted to move the Manhattan entrance that had been selected for the Triborough Bridge but then decided that it was not worth the fight. As he explained:

> Any child could see it belonged much further downtown at 103rd Street, in a direct line from Queens. This would have avoided disruption of the Randall's Island institutions. But the same forces, namely, the Hearst real estate interests, that had procured the 125th Street arm . . . would have stymied the entire project if we had insisted. We reluctantly accepted 125th Street, on the theory that a misplaced arm is better than no bridge at all."[69]

By avoiding this conflict, Moses, acting as parks commissioner, prevented opposition to his using money earmarked for land acquisition to create parks on Randall's Island and in Astoria, where the bridge descended into Queens.

Three years after Moses was entrusted with building the Triborough Bridge, it opened to the public. Eleven million vehicles crossed it during its first full year of service. By 2005 the number was nearly 63 million.[70] Tolls provided more than enough revenue to repay the bonds, to cover improvements and maintenance, to provide cash for other Authority projects, and eventually to subsidize New York City subways.

The bridge itself proved essential to the economic growth of the city, saving time and money for the businesses in Manhattan and the Bronx that used its trucking routes to supply customers on Long Island, and for businesses in Queens that had customers in Westchester and New England. The bridge also shortened the commute from Long Island to Manhattan. Since land was cheaper in Nassau County than in New York City, the Triborough Bridge opened the door to less expensive real estate development by making the commute more convenient.

Without Moses, the Triborough Bridge would have been built, but construction would have taken much longer. Moses knew when to jettison staff and designs, when to accept political reality rather than fight, and how to find colleagues who could make things happen. The major achievement of his work on the bridge, however, was institutionalizing the financial and administrative procedures that would be used later by the Triborough Bridge and Tunnel Authority to reshape the entire New York Metropolitan area. In 1940, the Triborough Bridge Authority merged with the authorities that operated the Henry Hudson Bridge and Parkway and the Marine Bridge and Parkway, all run by Moses. Moses also stepped in to complete the Queens-Midtown Tunnel when the New York City Tunnel Authority ran out of money.[71] The Tunnel Authority eventually merged with the other authorities to create the TBTA. It was the ability of this enormous new agency to issue and sell tax-exempt bonds backed by toll revenues that made Robert Moses a giant in the worlds of local politics and public finance.

The planning of the arterial system was as important as its financing. Government agencies had to select routes, establish design standards, acquire property, and build entire arterial networks that were separate from existing local thoroughfares. The form and character of these new roads, however, was in doubt. The typical road built by state highway departments and local agencies had been a relatively narrow concrete corridor with minimal shoulders. One alternative to this model was to build landscaped, limited-access arteries modeled on

Triborough Bridge (1999).

the Bronx River Parkway. The other alternative was to build limited-access arteries, designed for easy driving and maximum driver visibility at speeds of 65 miles per hour or more; these would consist of broad, continuous curves with small changes in grade.[72] New York, New Jersey, and Connecticut chose to invest in both.

The earliest parkways in America were designed by Frederick Law Olmsted and Calvert Vaux for Brooklyn, Buffalo, and Chicago.[73] They were intended to initiate the park experience as soon as people left their homes or places of work. People would travel along landscaped roadways that eventually led to public parks. The resulting public realm additionally provided a framework for private real estate development along the parkways. A parkway therefore had a double effect. It turned driving into a pleasurable recreational activity, while at the same time insulating nearby residents from the noise and pollution generated by commercial traffic.

It was the Bronx River Parkway (completed in 1923), however, not Olmsted's landscaped boulevards, that served as the model for the limited-access parkways built in Connecticut, New York, Maryland, Virginia, and North Carolina during the 1920s and 1930s. These achieved the same goals as Olmsted's parkways, but they were engineered for higher traffic speeds, they eliminated most grade crossings in favor of overpasses, they limited access to automobiles, and they provided broad scenic vistas wherever

possible. Gilmore Clarke, who played a major role in creating the Bronx River Parkway and who became one of Moses' most trusted colleagues, explained that its design was intended to preserve existing amenities, control floods, and eliminate "dumps, billboards, and other unsightly features."[74] That could just as easily describe Moses's parkways.

When Robert Moses took charge of the Long Island State Park Commission, he inherited a completely inadequate road network. (He faced similar situations when he took over the Triborough Bridge Authority and the city's Parks Department.) The Moses approach to the location and design of a network of roadways can be summarized with the same words he used in discussing parks. "Sensible, practical people know that [it] depends upon the actual problems of the city in question."[75] He rejected equitable distribution of highways based on mathematical calculation, as proposed by the Regional Plan Association. In fact, Moses detested the RPA. In a 1938 letter, which he wrote to the Bronx Chamber of Commerce and provided to the *New York Times*, he advised not to "waste time with the Regional Plan. Every so often these boys have to get out reports claiming credit for everything good that

Bronx River Parkway (2011).

Grand Central Parkway, Queens (2009). As parks commissioner, Moses was responsible for the creation of all New York City's parkways.

has been accomplished, criticizing plans of public officials which have not been carried out."[76]

One of Moses's objectives in everything he did was to maximize the constituency of each project. To this end he employed the strategy he had used with the parks. Whenever possible he combined a transportation project with other local objectives. He used the property acquired to build the approaches to the Triborough Bridge in Queens to create Astoria Park at

the same time. Similarly, while laying out the Cross Island Parkway, he created a landscaped waterfront promenade running along Little Neck Bay in Queens.

The legislation creating the consolidated New York City Parks Department also authorized the commissioner to create parkways. Moses accomplished this task by selecting largely unoccupied land along the shoreline of Manhattan, Brooklyn, and Queens or selecting routes along

East River Park, Manhattan (1999). While several successive borough presidents of Manhattan were building what is now the FDR Drive, Parks Commissioner Moses used the opportunity to fill in parts of the East River to create additional parkland.

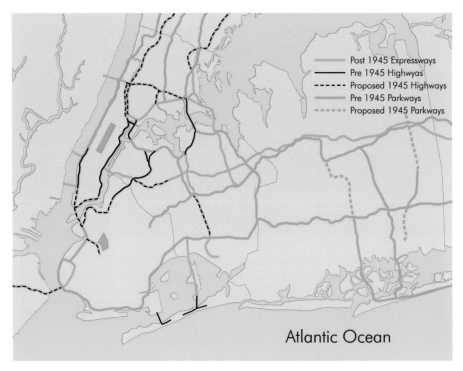

	Post 1945 Expressways
	Pre 1945 Highwyas
	Proposed 1945 Highways
	Pre 1945 Parkways
	Proposed 1945 Parkways

Atlantic Ocean

By 1945, engineers working for the city and state governments had devised a network of new highways that would provide the construction agenda for the next three decades.

the edges of parks that he was creating. These parkways were both roadways and broad, linear parks very much like the Bronx River Parkway. Because they ran along waterways, however, they could be acquired with minimal acquisition of private houses and businesses.

During the period in which New York, Connecticut, and other states were creating landscaped parkways, transportation engineers were conceiving of an entirely different form of artery: broad, limited-access highways that could be used by trucks, buses, and cars traveling considerable distances at high speeds. Because they passed through densely populated urban areas, major displacement was inevitable. New York City had begun to build them but lacked a generally accepted set of principles for their location, design, or dimensions. The one exception was minimizing the width of these highways, so as to minimize expensive property acquisition, relocation, and the inevitable community opposition that they generated. The West Side Highway (later known as the Miller Elevated Highway) and the East River Drive (later known as the FDR Drive) were the first of these.[77] Once a highway route was approved by the city's Board of Estimate, the appropriate

borough president became responsible for the highway's design and construction.

A new charter for New York City was approved by the voters in 1938. It set up a new agency, the City Planning Commission, which would vote whether to recommend proposed highway routes to the Board of Estimate. Thus, when Moses was appointed to the commission by Mayor LaGuardia in 1942, he gained a role that he had not previously possessed in influencing the routes of highways. Neither the mayor nor the borough presidents wanted the commission to carry much weight in these matters, and at first Moses had to be very careful about influencing highway location and design. Nothing prevented him, however, from pretending that his role was larger than it was, nor neighborhoods from believing that he was the chief player. The selection of the route for the Brooklyn-Queens Connecting Highway as it passed through Brooklyn Heights illustrates how Moses's skills made him an effective player in the planning game.

In 1931, three years before Moses entered city government, the borough presidents of Brooklyn and Queens had recommended approval of a $75 million highway scheme. It had no future, because it required too much dislocation and could not be financed.[78] Gradually, a more suitable project began to emerge, one that would connect the Belt Parkway (which Moses built in his capacity as parks commissioner) with the Southern State Parkway (which Moses built in his capacity as chairman of the Long Island State Park Commission). This highway provided a link between Long Island, in one direction, and the Triborough Bridge (which Moses built in his capacity as chairman of the TBTA), the Bronx, and the Westchester parkways in the other direction. Unlike the parkways, it was designed to handle trucks and buses in addition to private automobiles.

Construction began in 1938 on a section of the highway in Queens, and a year later construction began on another section connecting the Brooklyn Bridge with the Queens Midtown Tunnel (one year before it opened). It still had not been decided how to continue the highway from the Brooklyn Bridge to the Brooklyn Battery Tunnel, and thence to a Verrazano-Narrows crossing to Staten Island, where the Verrazano Bridge would be opened in 1964. Traffic coming from southern Brooklyn, and later from Staten Island, heading for the Brooklyn Bridge, the Queens-Midtown Tunnel, or the Triborough Bridge had to pass through Cobble Hill and Brooklyn Heights. Any route was bound to be expensive and contentious (see map above).

The most direct route would cross the Gowanus Canal. Then, after removing all the buildings on one side of Court Street, it would connect with Adams Street and would lead to the Brooklyn Bridge and the Brooklyn-Queens Connecting Highway. This route would have destroyed one of Brooklyn's shopping streets, cost a substantial amount of money to pay for condemnation, and would have called for unacceptable levels of relocation. Consequently, it made more sense for the highway to be continued along Hamilton Avenue and then to swing north, taking out, on its way, the west side of Hicks Street. This route separated a residential section from the rest of Cobble Hill, but planners pointed out that, in addition to sav-

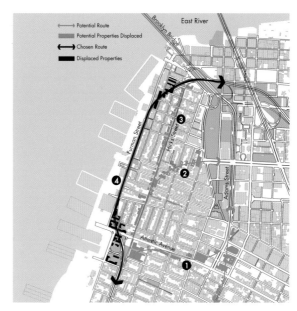

Brooklyn Heights (1943). Alternate routes for the Brooklyn-Queens Connecting Highway.

ing part of downtown Brooklyn, the highway would shield the bulk of the residential neighborhood from the noisy shipping, warehousing, and manufacturing along the waterfront. But the toughest decisions were still to come, and they involved routing the highway past Brooklyn Heights.

Once the Hicks Street leg had been selected, there were four possible routes (see map): (1) The new leg of the highway could follow an S-curve, swinging east onto Atlantic Avenue and then north on Adams Street, and continuing on to the Brooklyn Bridge, or on to the rest of the highway; (2) It could continue along Hicks Street, sweeping east to Tillary Street. From there it could turn left onto Adams Street and the Brooklyn Bridge, or it could continue straight and connect with the rest of the highway; (3) It could continue to the end of Hicks Street, from where it could either curve onto the bridge or continue east to connect with the rest of the highway;. (4) Finally, Furman Street provided three potential routes—one at grade, which would eliminate the marginal service road serving six busy piers (now Brooklyn Bridge Park), another above Furman Street on an elevated platform supported on columns, and the solution ultimately selected, a triple-decked cantilevered highway and park combination projected over Furman Street.

To meet the highway standards of the day, all four routes required broad curves, as well as complex shifts in elevation. The first route would have demolished all the buildings in its path until it reached Adams Street. The second and third routes would have required the acquisition and demolition of even more buildings. These routes were also very expensive, and they would have split Brooklyn Heights into two neighborhoods. Of the four, the Furman Street route clearly was the least disruptive.

There is a widely believed legend that Moses favored either the second or third alternative.[79] What really occurred is difficult to pin down. It is clear, however, that the Furman Street route involved less property acquisition, relocation, and demolition and was the least expensive alternative. It also aroused considerably less opposition from neighborhood residents. One has to wonder whether the other routes were ever seriously considered.

Creating an at-grade, six-lane highway with service roads on Furman Street would have required disrupting so much port activity that it was quickly rejected. The issue to be resolved, therefore, was whether to create an elevated highway or a cantilevered structure extending over Furman Street. In 1939 a member of the staff of the City Planning Department proposed a double-decker cantilever with three lanes of traffic in both directions.[80] By February 1943, the engineering firm of Farley & Andrews, which prepared construction documents for the project, was proposing a triple-decker version with a promenade on the top level.[81] The firm's senior partner, W. Earle Andrews, was close to Moses, having been chief engineer for the Parks Department before leaving to take on the same role for the 1939 World's Fair. So it is more than probable that Moses was aware of the triple-decker version before the city planning commission scheduled its public hearing on the highway in March 1943.

At the hearing, Roy Richardson, representing the Brooklyn Heights Association, argued

Brooklyn Heights (2005). During World War II no responsible public official would have countenanced building a highway that cut off access to busy East River piers.

that an elevated roadway would be detrimental to property owners and that "people walking along there... [had an] enjoyable view of the opposite side of the River."[82] Moses interjected, "You mean you can go to the street ends and look out from there; that is not a promenade." When the project was approved, Parks Commissioner Moses had the responsibility for creating the promenade.

Once again community residents thought they had won. In fact, they had made possible a result that Moses clearly preferred: the triple-decker design with a promenade (the design that Moses referred to at the public hearing). This provided what is now one of the city's most popular linear parks, with spectacular views of the lower Manhattan skyline. Although he had no official role in building the highway, Moses transformed it into much more than a single-purpose roadway. Borough President John Cashmore, who wanted to dampen opposition to the highway, persuaded the willing Parks Commissioner to build twenty-six playgrounds between Atlantic Avenue and the Brooklyn Navy Yard. Or was it Moses who used the highway as pretext for creating recreation facilities? Whatever happened, the borough president announced that there was no other "highway in the world with similar recreational facilities along its path."[83]

The Brooklyn-Queens Connecting Highway was, to some degree, the model for the Cross Bronx Expressway, the Major Deegan Expressway, the Van Wyck Expressway, and other limited-access highways built after World War II. By the time decisions for these arteries were made, Moses had become an indispensable member of the informal group of federal, state, and city officials whose consensus determined highway policy. Further, Mayor William O'Dwyer appointed him city construction coordinator in 1946, a post that gave him formal authority over all city construction. Yet, because of the financing and safety requirements of federal and state funding, Moses would never again be able to manipulate participants into approving the kind of complex park-and-highway combinations that he had formerly been

Brooklyn Heights (2010). The Promenade became a public park on the top tray of the triple-decker, cantilevered highway structure. People enjoy strolling through the park, which provides glorious views of the lower-Manhattan skyline. It also makes space for a children's playground.

able to create. Worse, he soon began to make mistakes in matters of judgment.

When the Cross Bronx Expressway went through its approval process in 1953, Moses was at the height of his power. As construction coordinator, he had far more power than he had had when he was dealing with the Brooklyn Heights Promenade. This time he played the planning game differently, but no less skillfully.

The Cross Bronx Expressway was built to provide a way for interstate travel to bypass New York City. The expressway began at the George Washington Bridge, cut through the Bronx, and connected with what was to become the New England Thruway. Its origins lay years earlier, when the Port Authority decided to build the George Washington Bridge. Once that decision was taken, a direct extension to New England became the logical next step.

Construction of a truly limited-access highway involved building a roadway over or under about one hundred streets. The transportation

Cross Bronx Expressway (1953). The route recommended by the RPA (lower red artery) was rejected by state and federal highway officials who succeeded in getting approval of a right-of-way for the Cross Bronx Expressway (upper red artery) that minimized acquisition, demolition, and relocation by taking property only on one side of 177th Street.

fraternity had to face two issues: the cost of the project, already estimated in 1949 at more than $50 million, and the enormous number of people and businesses that would have to be displaced.[84] Nothing of this scale had been attempted since Haussmann built boulevards through the neighborhoods of Paris.

The Regional Plan Association had proposed a bypass route in its 1929 plan, but transportation officials rejected it. It had looked good as a diagram, but it involved far too much property acquisition, it cut through the middle of too many blocks, and necessitated much too much relocation. The route the New York transportation fraternity ultimately selected was influenced by high speed limits and 12-foot lane widths. For the most part, their route followed an existing right-of-way: 177th Street. By condemning the 100-foot-deep lots on one side of the street, while leaving the other side untouched, relocation was reduced to a minimum.

State and federal officials may have thought the relocation load to be manageable, but Bronx residents were outraged. Thousands of households would be displaced. A group of residents convinced Bronx Borough President James Lyons to advocate altering the route. By supporting this group of constituents, Lyons found himself in a fight with Robert Moses in his role as city construction coordinator. Moses was in a

Cross Bronx Expressway (2005). The trucks, buses, and cars in the below-grade section of the expressway have little impact on daily life in the Bronx.

different position from the one he had occupied a decade earlier, when the city was selecting a route for the Brooklyn-Queens Connecting Highway.[85] Now Moses was responsible for getting highways built—and he was determined to have the route approved.

Redesign would have delayed the project, but a greater worry for Moses was that federal and state officials would not agree to changes because of the greater costs they would incur. The Cross Bronx Expressway was part of a much larger system linking together the different parts of the New York metropolitan region and connecting it with the rest of the nation. The state and federal governments had agreed to put up three-fourths of its $400 million cost—

a huge stimulus to the city's economy. Moses argued that if unacceptable designs or "unjustified" increases in costs forced the federal and state governments to withdraw from the highway program, the city would have to come up with the $300 million those governments had agreed to contribute, or else eliminate a large piece of the highway network, which was crucial to the region's future.[86]

Moses believed it was important to retain the route that state and federal officials had agreed upon, and he knew that he needed to create support for his position. To do this, he used one of he favorite ploys; he threatened to resign. As he explained, if "borough politics" interfered with carrying out his responsibilities as construction coordinator, he could not perform his duties.[87] Whether because of the risk of losing the federal and state money, the threatened resignation, two months of behind-closed-doors politicking, or some combination of the three, the Board of Estimate in May 1953 voted to approve the original route.[88]

Moses had had to fight hard for the Cross-Bronx Expressway, and outright defeats were to follow. His biggest highway defeat came after Mayor Wagner had forced him out of city government, when he no longer had any direct control over the location or design of highways. He was so towering a figure that the highway is often referred to as the Moses Lower Manhattan Expressway (Lomex). Moses certainly was its most vociferous proponent during the 1950s and 1960s. As with most of his projects, he was not the originator of the idea. This proposed highway was initially discussed during the 1920s by the Regional Plan Association, by the engineering staff of the Board of Estimate and Apportionment, and by Borough President Julius Miller. In fact, the idea of connecting the Holland Tunnel with the Williamsburg and Manhattan bridges was approved in 1941, before Moses had been appointed to the City Planning Commission.

During the 1950s, when he was chairman of the Triborough Bridge and Tunnel Authority, Moses commissioned models and drawings of what the Lower Manhattan Expressway might look like,[89] but the route was not approved until 1960. Opposition to Lomex was fierce, and it increased as time passed. During a stormy Board of Estimate hearing in 1962, forty-four speakers presented testimony. Opponents included the assemblymen and city council members representing the area; four congressmen, among them John Lindsay; and Jane Jacobs, acting as chair of the Stop the Lower Manhattan Expressway Committee. Most of the other speakers also opposed Lomex, pointing out that it would result in the relocation of 1,972 families and 804 businesses.[90] At the request of Mayor Wagner, the decision on Lomex was postponed.

The following year Moses, in his capacity as Mayor Wagner's representative on the planning of arterial highways, and working in concert with the Citizens Union and the Downtown Lower Manhattan Association, began a campaign to salvage Lomex. Proponents argued that because 90 percent of its cost was coming from the federal Interstate Highway Program it would provide a stimulus to the city's economy.[91] In 1964 the board approved the project.

But in 1968, when Moses was eighty years old, "his" Lower Manhattan Expressway was finally killed. By that time he had been out of city government for eight years and was no longer on the board of the Triborough Bridge and Tunnel Authority. Mayor John Lindsay and Governor Nelson Rockefeller agreed to give up Lomex in exchange for federal mapping of an interstate highway from the Brooklyn-Battery Tunnel to the Lincoln Tunnel (later known as Westway). Lomex was formally demapped in 1969.[92]

Most observers identify the region's arterial network with Robert Moses. He was certainly responsible for its bridges and tunnels and the access ramps leading to them, except those connecting with New Jersey. He was also responsible for all of the New York City and Long Island parkways. But his role in creating limited-access highways is far more difficult to pin down.

Two things are important to keep in mind: (1) most highway routes had been discussed for years by government engineers, and (2) the highways were not only part of the New York metropolitan transportation network; they were necessary links in a national system. Engineers who worked in the agencies that paid for the highways were devoted to the concepts of efficiency and economy in highway location and design. Thus, they insisted that federally assisted highways had to have standard lane widths of 12 feet and generous shoulders, rather than the narrower profiles that characterized early parkways. Slopes and curves had to conform to federal engineering standards that guaranteed safe driving at the higher speeds that had become common. The engineers believed that there was neither the need nor the money to acquire more land than was absolutely necessary to meet the minimum standards they required.[93] As Moses vividly explained, "The average engineer's idea of landscaping is something to make the angels weep."[94]

Since most of the highways went through densely built-up areas of the city, they inevitably generated disruption, dislocation, human hardship, and opposition—everything that Moses had done his best to avoid while creating the parkway network. As a young reformer, he had been an active participant in the civic organizations that fashioned the parkway agenda. The highway agenda with which he is most identified was devised by transportation engineers, federal officials, and business interests (particularly from the trucking industry) with little input from the communities that it would inevitably disrupt.

For two-thirds of a century, financing for a safe, convenient, high-speed arterial network had never been in doubt, whether the source was toll-based bonds or appropriations from local, state, and federal budgets. By the mid-1960s, however, community opposition had begun to stall highway construction in New York, as well as in Boston, Baltimore, Memphis, San Francisco, and other major American cities. If people had asked Moses during the last years of his life how to get an arterial network implemented, he might well have replied that it was no longer pos-sible because highway construction was no longer part of a generally agreed-upon agenda.

SLUM CLEARANCE

Improvement of New York City's housing had been part of the reform agenda since the middle of the nineteenth century.[95] During the LaGuardia administration, it took the form of clearing slums and building public housing for people of low income. The implementing agent was the New York City Housing Authority (NYCHA), established in 1934. As of 2010, the NYCHA owned and operated 178,000 apartments, occupied by more people than live in Boston or Seattle.[96]

Moses believed in that agenda. He wrote in 1968 that if its slum clearance program "had been adopted and implemented between 1934, the first LaGuardia year, and 1946, when he left office, we would now be rid of half at least of all the old rabbit warrens and rookeries and well on the way to demolition of the other half."[97] Nevertheless, LaGuardia and every mayor after him kept Moses from having any role in the construction or operation of public housing.

After World War II the regional agenda was altered to help cities create attractive residential opportunities that could compete with the suburbs. Many designers, public officials, and developers believed that a green setting for apartment buildings, with plenty of light and air, would be an attractive alternative to single-family houses in the suburbs. The image was based on Le Corbusier's "towers in the park" (see Chapter 2), and it was grafted onto the rest of the housing agenda.

In 1948, when Mayor William O'Dwyer appointed Moses chairman of the Committee on Slum Clearance, Moses thought he had an agreed-upon agenda for housing redevelopment. The financing was provided by a combination of local, state, and federal governments. Because the state legislature had passed the Redevelopment Companies Law of 1942–43, establishing a similar program but without federal subsidies, in anticipation of the Stuyvesant Town housing

Corlear's Hook Urban Renewal Project, Manhattan (2005). The first urban renewal projects executed by the Committee on Slum Clearance adopted the "towers in the park" objectives recommended by Le Corbusier.

and later projects, Moses believed he had the necessary legislative sanction. He thought project approval seemed certain because all the appropriate officials were members of the Committee: the chairman of the City Planning Commission, the commissioners of Real Estate and Buildings, the chief engineer of the Board of Estimate, and the Borough President responsible for the project's location. Besides, since every project required an affirmative vote of the City Planning Commission (of which Moses was a member) and the Board of Estimate (whose representatives would have already agreed to the project), he would be guaranteed all necessary approvals.

Instead, every time Moses announced a new project, he added to the growing and increasingly angry opposition from site tenants, their friends and relatives, neighborhood activists, and many of the public officials who represented them. Moses thought he was advocating just what good government advocates had spent years fighting for. The aggregate amount of

new housing (although not necessarily on each site) was to exceed what had been demolished, guaranteeing a net gain in available apartments. But he did not have the public with him.

The idea behind the program was that government would do the heavy lifting—acquiring property, investing in necessary site improvements, managing the site until all the approvals were in hand, forgoing taxes, and covering all costs until it was sold to private companies. The new owners would design, build, and manage the new construction.

The Moses method, however, differed from the approach taken in other cities, and here he made a major mistake. He believed that government agencies were less efficient, took more time, and spent more money than private developers. Consequently, he uncharacteristically reduced the role of government. Once the redevelopment plan had legislative approval, the sites were to be turned over for development to for-profit or not-for-profit companies.

APPROVED	DEFEATED
Corlear's Hook	South Village
Harlem (Lenox Terrace)	Williamsburg
North Harlem (Delano Village)	Delancey Street
West Park	Battery Park
Morningside	Gramercy Park
Columbus Circle	Riverside Amsterdam
Fort Greene	Division Street
Pratt Institute	Mid Harlem
NYU Bellevue (Kips Bay)	Mott Haven
Washington Square SE	South Brooklyn
Seward Park	Houston Street
Lincoln Square	Chelsea
Park Row	Jamaica
Seaside	Battery Park North
Hammels	Heyward Bedford
Penn Station South	Fulton Market
Cadman Plaza	Atlantic Avenue
Park Row Extension	Willowtown
Seward Park Extension	Battery Park North
Cooper Square (reconceived)	Flatbush Avenue
Bronx Park	Soundview
Lindsay Park	South Brooklyn
Brooklyn Bridge South	Cathedral Parkway
(reconceived)	Plymouth
Bellevue South (reconceived)	Central Park Northeast
Washington Street (reconceived)	York Avenue
Arverne (incomplete in 2010)	Northern Boulevard

Fewer than half of the 53 urban renewal projects proposed were able to proceed.

In order for his method to work, Moses had to prenegotiate the deal with an appropriate developer. The deal was then formalized in a detailed brochure with plans, financial calculations, and renderings, prepared by some of the city's premier architectural, engineering, and real estate firms. At that point it was presented to the City Planning Commission and the Board of Estimate for approval.

From that point on, the developers had to pay taxes, manage occupied property, arrange for relocation, pay for demolition, and cover all costs until construction began. Moses correctly believed that this provided a powerful incentive for them to move as quickly as possible, reducing carrying costs. Early sale had the added benefit of diverting political pressure from public agen-cies to property owners to take care of site tenants, prevent destruction of beloved buildings, and anything else that might slow things down and cost more money.

Moses anticipated opposition, but not its virulence. He did not expect to get city approval for only twenty-six of the fifty-three redevelopment projects he announced (one of which could not proceed for several decades because of community opposition).[98]

Only two of the first five projects he announced were executed: Corlears Hook and Harlem–Lenox Terrace. Despite support from nearby Columbia University, Union Theological Seminary, and the Juilliard School of Music, it took two years to overcome vocal opposition from a "committee to save our homes" and obtain approval for Morningside-Manhattanville, a 976-apartment nonprofit cooperative. The developers of NYU-Bellevue (Kips Bay Plaza) and Lincoln Towers were unable to fulfill their obligations and had to be replaced. Manhattantown (Park West Village) was the subject of a widely publicized investigation by a committee of the U.S. Senate headed by Estes Kefauver.[99] Moses replaced the developer, but some held him responsible for the developer's misdeeds. His reputation was tarnished by the affair.

Moses had one real success in urban renewal: Lincoln Center for the Performing Arts. Its success was the product of implementing an agenda of some of the nation's most important cultural institutions and depended on the strength of those institutions for its realization. Moses knew that the Metropolitan Opera occupied a much-beloved building but that it had hundreds of seats with obstructed views and inadequate means of egress in case of fire. The opera had tried and failed to relocate to Rockefeller Center, to West 57th Street, and to several other locations.[100] In 1953, Moses tried to convince both the opera and the future Guggenheim Museum to relocate to a Title I project that he was going to propose for Lincoln Square, a few blocks north.[101] This eventually became Lincoln Center, and the Metropolitan Opera has occupied prime space there since it opened. In addition, Moses secured the Ameri-

Proposed South Village Urban Renewal Project (1951). One of the twenty-seven urban renewal projects Moses announced that were never approved.

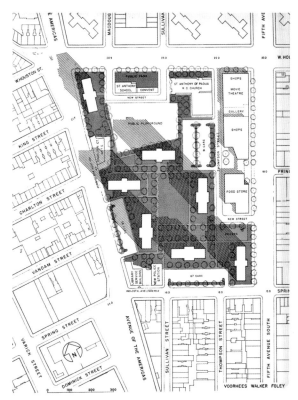

Site plan for the proposed South Village Urban Renewal Project (1951), never approved.

can Red Cross, the New York Philharmonic, the New York City Opera, the New York City Ballet, the Juilliard Music School, Fordham University Law School, a new repertory theater, the performing arts library, and two public high schools. With them came a coalition of powerful supporters, including not only the Rockefeller family, key charitable foundations, major financial institutions, media giants, "the liberal wings of the Democratic and Republic parties . . . [and] the classic WASP establishment, but Jewish and Catholic power centers as well."[102] Moses failed, however, to make a deal with the Guggenheim, nor did he realize his plans for a complex of five commercial theaters, a skyscraper hotel, and a shopping center.

In 1955, Moses publicly announced plans to clear eighteen blocks for the Lincoln Square Urban Renewal Project, just north of the Lincoln Center site. The more than 5,200 households (families and single individuals) who would be displaced were incensed, as were the seven hundred businesses.[103] They all demanded that clearance "be accompanied by the building of low-cost housing for the tenants" and "machinery to safeguard displaced residents against abuses of unfair relocation practices."[104] Their complaints were supported by city-wide tenant organizations, Spanish-American and African-American organizations, thousands of relocatees from other urban renewal projects (who were

VI COST ESTIMATES & FINANCIAL PLAN

SOUTH VILLAGE SITE

ESTIMATED COST OF PROPOSED REDEVELOPMENT

LAND:		
	Appraised Resale Value as if Cleared	$ 2,980,000
	Less: Demolition and Tenant Relocation	925,000
	Resale Value of Land in its Present Condition	$ 2,055,000
BUILDING:		
	Field Cost of Structures	$ 8,805,500
	Architects' Fee	300,500
	Total Structural Cost	$ 9,106,000
	Cost of Landscaping and Site Improvements	411,500
	Total Cost of Buildings and Site Improvements	$ 9,517,500
PROJECT:		
	Interest on Land during Construction	$ 178,800
	Interest on Building during Construction	285,525
	Total Interest on Working Capital	$ 464,325
	Real Estate Taxes on Land during Construction	166,470
	Finance, Legal & Organization Expense	190,350
	Total Interest, Taxes & Financing during Construction	$ 821,145
	Total Estimated Cost of Building	$10,338,645
TOTAL ESTIMATED COST OF PROJECT		$13,318,645

FINANCIAL PLAN FOR PRIVATE DEVELOPER

Cost of Land at Appraised Resale Value as if Cleared	$ 2,980,000
Estimated Cost of Buildings as of date of completion, including all fees, taxes and financing	10,338,645
Total Estimated Cost of Project	$13,318,645
Estimated Rental Value	
Apartments: 3275 rental rooms @ $33. per room per month or $396 per room per annum	$ 1,296,900
Stores: 55,000 sq. ft. basement @ 50c	27,500
55,000 sq. ft. grade fl. @ $3.50	192,500
Commercial Space: 20,000 sq. ft. basement @ 50c	10,000
20,000 sq. ft. grade fl. @ $3.50	70,000
Theatre: 900 seats @ $75 per annum net	67,500
Parking Space: 241 cars @ $120	28,920
Total Estimated Rental Value	$ 1,693,320
Less: Vacancy Reserve of 7%	118,532
Effective Rental Value	$ 1,574,788
Operating Expenses:	
Apartments: 3275 rental rooms @ $90	$ 294,750
Stores: 110,000 square feet @ 20c	22,000
Commercial Space: 40,000 sq. ft. @ 20c	8,000
Total Operating Expenses	$ 324,750
Real Estate Taxes:	330,000
Total Operating Expenses and Taxes	$ 654,750
Net Return on a Free and Clear Basis	$ 920,038
Percentage of Net Return on Investment	6.91%

Financial projections for the South Village Urban Renewal Project (1951).

Lincoln Square Urban Renewal Project and Columbus Avenue, Manhattan (1966). At first Lincoln Center had little impact on the surrounding neighborhood.

more than justified in protesting the damage that had been done to them and their communities), liberal reformers like Jane Jacobs, and politicians like council member and former Borough President Stanley Isaacs.[105]

By the time the 49.6-acre Lincoln Square was approved for federal funding in December of 1957, Moses had eliminated from the project the four blocks between 66th and 70th Streets, from Broadway to Columbus Avenue and had added 420 new apartments, increasing the number to be built from 3,840 to 4,260.[106]

In an attempt to weaken the opposition to urban renewal, Moses began to propose projects on predominantly vacant sites, many of them away from the center of the city. Mayor

Lincoln Square Urban Renewal Project and Columbus Avenue, Manhattan (2007). Half a century after completion of Lincoln Center, life on the Upper West Side had changed significantly.

Wagner, however, was unsatisfied, and he appointed J. Anthony Panuch, assisted by a professional staff, to assess the situation. Their first recommendation was to transfer responsibility for relocation from property owners to a newly established city Department of Relocation; their second was to replace the Committee on Slum Clearance with a city agency specifically charged with managing urban renewal.[107]

Moses had been considered the most effective redevelopment executive in the country, because while he was in charge of New York City's program, it accounted for 32 percent of all Title I urban renewal construction in the nation.[108] But New York City government officials had a different opinion, since they had to deal with intense public opposition that was stalling completion of the program.

In 1960, while Lincoln Center was under construction, Mayor Wagner pressured Moses to abandon slum clearance in order to create the 1964 World's Fair. In one sense Moses was an obvious choice, having transformed the "ash heap" for a similar event in 1939. But the reality was that Moses had been unable to complete urban renewal projects quickly enough to stay ahead of the debilitating opposition. The cumulative impact became too intense, especially when opposition to urban renewal combined with resistance to the federal highway program, which Moses eagerly (and less than truthfully) claimed to be his responsibility. Opposition was becoming so intense that the seventy-two-year-old began to lose his enthusiasm for the fray. At that time only three of his urban renewal projects had been completed; thirteen were still underway.[109] Eight of the other projects he announced would be approved after he was no longer in charge of the program.[110] Moses likely understood that he would be unable to complete his proposed redevelopment program or to continue the arterial highway program. So, under pressure, he resigned all his city positions to "concentrate" on retrofitting Flushing Meadows-Corona Park for the Fair.

It is difficult to separate Moses's downfall from the inherent problems of the urban renewal program he thought of as an agreed-upon part of the regional agenda. The urban renewal program,

Penn Station South Urban Renewal Project, Manhattan (2005). While displaced residents and businesses paid a heavy price for the creation of thousands of new apartments, the future economy and life of New York City were barely affected by the slum clearance program.

however, differed from Moses's other projects in two major respects. It was not accompanied by the creation of governmental agencies controlled by Moses. And, unlike parkways, bridges, and tunnels that Moses created, the urban renewal program was not meant to make business more efficient or New York more competitive. In fact, it had little impact on the economy or the quality of life in the New York metropolitan area. Of the 391,525 apartments that were completed while he was chairman of the Committee on Slum Clearance, only 8,946 (2 percent) had been completed in the federally assisted urban renewal projects that he initiated.[111] The private sector produced far more housing without assistance from urban renewal.

But it is also correct to say that more housing was produced more quickly in New York than in any other city receiving Title I assistance. The first ten housing redevelopment projects eventually yielded nearly 18,000 apartments, most of them built after Moses had left city government. Six of them included 7,244 nonprofit cooperative apartments among their 10,503 dwelling units. The other four contained an additional 7,440 rental apartments.[112]

The urban renewal projects caused hardship to the residents and businesses that were displaced. But they also provided better housing on the sites. The original tenants likely moved to worse housing, but the people who moved in likely moved from worse housing. Slum clearance created very little of the city's new housing, involved many unfortunate side effects, and, with the exception of Lincoln Center, did not improve the quality of life in New York.

THE ART OF GETTING THINGS DONE

The overall agenda for growing the New York metropolitan area was successful because, in general, it conformed to the economics and politics of the times. There was genuine demand for highways, bridges, and tunnels. Thus, the Port Authority, the Long Island State Park Commission, and the TBTA could charge tolls that paid for the arterial network they created. And while the federal PWA, CWA, and WPA subsidized the construction of facilities created by the New York City Parks Department, the staff that Commissioner Moses brought into the agency operated the

system in a cost-effective manner, which provided greatly expanded recreational opportunities to millions of people.

As long as the new governmental agencies provided services to the region's populations as a whole, they had no trouble implementing an extremely ambitious program. As dislocation resulting from highway construction and urban renewal increased, however, so did opposition. Eventually, the opposition triumphed and, as could have been expected, those components of the agenda that produced it had to be dropped.

Implementing agencies like the ones established in New York are now common throughout the United States. There are 425 redevelopment agencies in California alone.[113] Some agencies, like the Tennessee Valley Authority, engage in a variety of activities over a very large region. Others serve only one function and operate within a narrowly defined territory. But all of them are authorized to operate in a manner different from traditional government agencies.

The unique element in New York was the entrepreneurial activity of Robert Moses and his colleagues. He played the planning game so

Staten Island, Brooklyn, and the Verrazano Narrows Bridge (2005).

well that without him the New York metropolitan area would now be a very different place. Nevertheless, Moses, his supporters, and his critics have all exaggerated that role.

Moses persevered in the face of opposition, sometimes winning, sometimes losing, sometimes compromising, and sometimes accepting other people's agendas, often without acknowledgement. For more than three decades Robert Moses retained public support without significant opposition, except from obviously parochial interests and wealthy, powerful property owners. He kept public support by adopting generally agreed-upon agendas, which he advocated in countless newspaper articles, books, and speeches, and he developed close working relationships with public officials who shared his goals.

Moses began to falter when he was in his sixties and failed to grasp that the federally approved and financed agenda of highway construction and urban renewal was not a universally agreed-upon agenda, but instead faced growing local opposition. During his seventies, he often ignored the political rules that govern the planning game (so important to his early successes), started to lose too many battles to remain an effective player, and was forced from the field.

The region's air and water quality are better, the quantity and quality of recreational opportunities are greater, and the cost of producing and distributing goods and services is lower than they would have been without Robert Moses. So much was achieved in the New York metropolitan area, not because of Moses's often contentious and aggressive personality, but because implementation had been made an integral part of New York's agreed-upon investment strategy. The region created new agencies, such as the Port Authority, the Long Island Park Commission, the Triborough Bridge and Tunnel Authority, and the consolidated New York City Parks Department, that were specifically designed to implement the agenda. The new agencies always had legislative sanction for what they were implementing. They succeeded because they also had the ability, within the constraints of politics and economics, to raise money, hire staff and consultants, acquire property, enter into contracts, and manage facilities in a manner that ordinary government agencies could not match. After all, success at the planning game requires a generally accepted agenda and, in addition, the legal authority and the financial and human resources to achieve carry it out.

Philadelphia (2011).

SEVEN

REINVENTING DOWNTOWN PHILADELPHIA

In 1950, Philadelphia, with a population just under 2.1 million, was the country's third-largest city. Over the next sixty years it would lose half a million residents, dropping to the nation's sixth-largest city. Six of the cities that had been among the country's top ten at mid-century were no longer on the list. Yet, unlike those cities, Philadelphia in 2010 had significantly diversified its economic base, contained "the third largest residential downtown in the United States and [was] number one in the percent of residents who walk to work."[1] Its thriving downtown was the product of more than six decades of effective planning.

The changes that happened downtown were the product of a remarkable group of planners who identified desirable changes, combined them into a vision that others could see, accept, and make their own, and then did whatever is necessary to bring their vision into being. For most of that time they were led by Edmund Bacon, executive director of the City Planning Commission (1949–70). In 1990 that role was assumed by Paul Levy, founding president and still CEO of the Center City District business improvement district.

PHILADELPHIA AT MID-CENTURY

In 1950 the labor force of the Philadelphia metropolitan area had reached roughly 1.4 million, of which 54 percent worked in manufacturing, 18 percent worked in retail trade, and 8 percent were government employees.[2] Most retail shopping took place in downtown Philadelphia, largely along East Market Street, while the majority of offices were clustered along South Broad Street. Rail service entered the city on elevated tracks on West Market Street and terminated at the Broad Street Station. A second commuter railroad entered the downtown on elevated tracks that culminated in the Reading Railroad Headhouse on East Market Street, where most of the major retail stores were concentrated.

Those with enough money lived in exclusive northwestern suburbs, such as Chestnut Hill, within the city limits, and Merion or Bryn Mawr on the Main Line of the Pennsylvania Railroad, outside the city proper; or they lived in the vicinity of Rittenhouse Square in the southwestern quadrant of downtown. City Hall was located at the very heart of Philadelphia, where Broad and Market streets crossed. City Hall dominated everything, as the city's tallest building and the center of its decision-making.

Downtown Philadelphia (1945).

In 1950, Philadelphia was governed by the same Republican Party machine that had controlled the city for nearly a century.[3] Attempts by civic groups and philanthropic organizations to free the city from the machine and improve conditions throughout Philadelphia had been ongoing through the years of the machine's ascendancy. These efforts differed from similar activities in New York and Chicago only in that they were directed at a Republican rather than a Democratic machine, and one that was responsible for particularly egregious fiscal mismanagement. In 1940, when the city's debt had climbed to $500 million and its operating deficit stood at $33 million, the city's borrowing capacity hit bottom.[4] Yet despite such failure, Republicans continued to control Philadelphia for another decade.

Democrat Joseph Clark succeeded in winning the mayoralty in 1951. Most of his cabinet had spent years working to reform city government. With their help Clark began to repair the results of decades of deferred maintenance. Democrats Richardson Dilworth (1956–62) and James Tate (1962–72) won the next two mayoral elections and cemented control of the city by their Democratic Party machine.

THE PLANNERS WHO TRANSFORMED PHILADELPHIA

Not long before World War II a group of reformers that initially included Walter Phillips, Roy Larson, Oskar Stonorov, and Edmund Bacon came together to do something about what they thought was an intolerable state of affairs. These self-styled Young Turks were intent on improving government, solving urban problems, and defeating the Republican machine that had controlled the city for nearly a century. Naturally, when the Democrats won City Hall, the reformers allied themselves with Mayors Clark, Dilworth, and Tate and provided essential support for William Rafksy, who was in charge of the city's redevelopment program during their administrations.

Walter Phillips was a Harvard-educated lawyer from the Philadelphia establishment. He helped found the three private organizations that pushed for renewal of Philadelphia: the City Policy Committee, the Citizens' Council on City Planning, and the Greater Philadelphia Movement. The reform effort gained momentum when the City Policy Committee was created in 1940. At that time Phillips brought together a circle of friends who had been trying to reform the city charter. He became president of the committee and Bacon became vice president.[5] With Phillips's support, Bacon persuaded the group to make city planning a major part of its agenda.[6]

The group convinced Edward Hopkinson, Jr., one of the city's leading Republican investment bankers, of the importance of planning to the future of Philadelphia. A city planning commission had been included in the 1919 city charter but had never been formally estab-lished.[7] Hopkinson helped the reformers win the support of Mayor Bernard Samuel and the City Council for the creation of the City Plan-ning Commission, which was formally estab-lished in 1942. Phillips went on to manage Democrat Joseph Clark's successful campaign for mayor in 1951.

Stonorov was a German-American archi-tect of the modernist school, who collaborated with architects George Howe (1886–1955) and Louis Kahn (1901–1974) on a series of housing projects. Perhaps because of Bacon's training as an architect, these architects played cen-tral roles in his early work in Philadelphia. As a result, urban design became an integral part of the city's planning process. Vincent Kling, I. M. Pei, and John Bower were among the other architects whom he attracted to work on planning projects for the city. After Bacon retired, he continued to play the roles of pub-lic advocate and behind the scenes advisor. As time passed, however, that role diminished till Paul Levy came on the scene.

Unlike Bacon, Levy was not a native Phil-adelphian or a trained architect who focused much of his attention on urban design. He has guided the revival of downtown Philadel-phia for two decades largely as a public admin-istrator. Levy grew up in New York City and earned his Ph.D. at Columbia University. Levy taught in the New York City public school sys-tem and at Columbia, Temple, and the Uni-versity of Pennsylvania (where he still teaches) before spending five years working for the City of Philadelphia in the Office of Housing and Community Development and six years in the University of Pennsylvania Department of Real Estate.

All these planners took the change busi-ness very seriously. They believed their job was to identify desirable changes; combine them into a vision that others could see, accept, and make their own. Then they would do whatever was necessary to bring that vision into being. Edmund Bacon fused these tasks into a single, ongoing activity. That is the ultimate goal of the planner.

EDMUND BACON

Edmund Bacon was born in 1910 to a Quaker family in West Philadelphia. They lived in a house without electricity until they moved to the suburbs twelve years later. Graduating from Cornell in 1932 with a five-year professional degree in architecture, Bacon used a family bequest to travel around the world. During this time he worked in an architect's office in Shang-hai and eventually returned to a similar job in Philadelphia. In 1936 he received a fellow-ship to study with Eliel Saarinen at Cranbrook Academy, outside Detroit. After an unsuccess-ful stint as a city planner in Flint, Michigan, where he was accused of having "radical" ideas, he returned to Philadelphia in 1940.

Bacon became managing director of the Philadelphia Housing Association, a long-estab-lished nonprofit organization devoted to improv-ing housing. He held this position until he joined the Navy in 1942. Right after the war, in 1946, Bacon went to work on the staff of the Philadel-phia Planning Commission, and three years later he became its executive director. It was from

Edmund Bacon with model of Society Hill (1960).

this post that he worked to improve Philadelphia; he remained the commission's executive director until he retired in 1970.

During the last half of the twentieth century, most Philadelphians would have said that Ed Bacon was primarily responsible for the transformation of their downtown, and they would have been right. And yet it is difficult to give concrete examples of what Bacon actually did during his tenure as executive director of the City Planning Commission (1949–70). Like most planners, he had to accept the idea that while he was in the change game, it was others who made that change: civic leaders, interest groups, community organizations, property owners, developers, bankers, lawyers, architects, engineers, elected and appointed public officials—the list is endless. If one considers the city as a whole, however, one can identify Bacon's continuing and essential role in helping other players achieve objectives. He generously shared with them his

- profound understanding of the physical landscape of Philadelphia and of its population and diverse culture;
- ability to gauge the appropriateness of development projects, whether proposed by himself or others, and a capacity to fit together these disparate projects into an interdependent whole greater than the sum of its parts;
- facility for combining and synthesizing different ideas (many of which were conceived by others) to provide a vision that appealed to the city's residents;
- readiness to adjust and readjust proposals—to the physical demands of a site and the demands of construction, to the desires of people who would be affected, and to the requirements of the government programs that made them possible;
- stubborn willingness to persevere until his ideas and projects were accepted;
- facility for using publicity to gain general acceptance of his ideas, and (astonishingly for so self-motivated an individual); and

- gift for letting others adopt his visions and bring them to fruition.

These are the skills every planner must have.

As executive director of the City Planning Commission, Bacon was involved in the planning for North Philadelphia, Germantown, West Philadelphia, and all the housing and redevelopment projects in the city between 1940 and 1970. But above all, he is remembered for the transformation of downtown Philadelphia. Yet Bacon owned no land, developed no properties himself, and controlled no powerful government bureaucracies.

Bacon himself, and many others, believed he was responsible for creating Penn Center, Market East, and Society Hill. But Bacon did not own the Broad Street Station; the Pennsylvania Railroad owned it and transformed it into Penn Center. He did not develop Market East; the Southeastern Pennsylvania Transportation Authority (SEPTA) and the Rouse Company did that after Bacon left government. Nor did Bacon possess a single lot in Society Hill; the Philadelphia Redevelopment Authority (RDA) and individual property owners in the area accomplished its transformation. Nevertheless, Bacon was the key figure in the creation of all three: Penn Center, Market East, and Society Hill.

Bacon was central because he conceived the projects as an indissoluble combination that would spark revitalization of *all* of downtown Philadelphia. The Penn Center, Market East, and Society Hill projects removed major impediments to downtown investment, improved access and circulation by mass transit and on foot, and provided middle-class households with attractive downtown residential alternatives to suburban living.

He did not accept Daniel Burnham's dictum to "make no little plans." On the contrary, he believed that big recommendations lead to proposals that are "bigger than the electorate can swallow" and create "a very unfortunate dichotomy between planning and real life, leading to the rejection of planning and planners."[8] Consequently, he adopted an incremental approach to change.

Better Philadelphia Exhibition (1947). A model showing downtown Philadelphia that flipped over to show what the city might become.

At the same time, Bacon always knew where he was headed. He always fit the components of his plans into a coherent whole—something he referred to as a "total vision" of the city.[9] He identified public actions that would eliminate impediments to the city's growth, improve pedestrian and vehicular circulation, and trigger privately financed improvements to privately owned real estate. His proposals included something for everybody and thus were particularly appealing. But Bacon was able to get them implemented because he had an uncanny ability to connect with the public.

Bacon devoted considerable effort to securing the involvement and support of Philadelphia's business establishment, its mayors, City Council members, and municipal bureaucracy. Once he had tested his proposals with property owners, financial institutions, government officials, and ordinary city residents, he became a tenacious, even sometimes raucous, advocate for their implementation. Like Walter Moody, Bacon believed that planning "in all its practical essentials is a work of promotion—salesmanship."[10] The similarity in their thinking is striking, especially so because when Bacon

spoke or wrote about the *Plan of Chicago*, it was about Burnham, not Moody.[11] Yet, like both of them, Bacon believed that planning went beyond implementing a vision of the future to include continued stewardship of that vision and of those elements that had already been brought to fruition. One reason Bacon was so successful is that after he retired, his ideas asserted themselves with Burnham's famous "ever growing insistency."[12]

PLANNING A BETTER PHILADELPHIA

In 1945, as the Second World War was ending, Phillips and Stonorov decided to mount an exhibition to mark the three hundredth anniversary of Philadelphia's founding. To this end, they established a nonprofit corporation, the Philadelphia City Planning Exhibition, to raise the necessary money for the show, which Stonorov was to design and which was known as the Better Philadelphia Exhibition.[13] Major civic and business leaders became enthusiastic supporters, as did Mayor Bernard Samuel, who persuaded the City Council to appropriate $125,000.[14] The aims were to educate the public about urban planning and to offer a vision of what Philadelphia could be like in 1983.

Stonorov designed the show, and he made sure that Robert B. Mitchell, executive director of the City Planning Commission at that time, and commission staff were thoroughly involved in its planning. Stonorov wanted Bacon, who was still in the Navy, to work with him, and in 1946 Bacon agreed and was hired by the City Planning Commission specifically to work on the exhibition; he became its de facto co-designer. Louis Kahn, Stonorov's business partner and later the city's most famous architect, learned about the venture after it was already underway. As a result, Kahn played only a minor role in putting together the show, and his partnership with Stonorov ended after the exhibition closed.[15]

The exhibition's planners pointedly rejected a Beaux-Arts approach, one that would have proposed designs which, while often quite beautiful, did not address the problems of the city. There were major Beaux-Arts projects in Philadelphia at that time, either completed or under construction. Benjamin Franklin Parkway was typical of what the exhibition planners considered an old-fashioned approach. This diagonal boulevard, tree-lined, handsome, and extremely wide, was conceived in 1903 and completed in 1918. Its function was to connect City Hall to the Philadelphia Museum of Art.[16] But Benjamin Franklin Parkway never made sense as a roadway for people traveling between the museum and government offices, because people who go to an art show do not go next to an appointment at City Hall, or vice versa. It functioned from the beginning simply as an attractive way to get into and out of downtown Philadelphia.

A second Beaux-Arts project was about to begin construction as the exhibition was being prepared. This was Independence Mall. The idea for the Mall came from a 1932 scheme by architect Roy Larson.[17] By 1937 the proposal had grown into a 2,000-foot-long axial forecourt to Independence Hall, a design more appropriate for an imperial palace than for the birthplace of the American Revolution.[18] Nevertheless, it grabbed people's imagination and

was adopted by a group of civic leaders, who created the Independence Hall Association in 1942 to advocate federal acquisition and development of "a suitable approach to Independence Hall."

The Mall was promoted, beginning in 1943, at a series of public exhibitions. Congress approved its funding in 1948.[19] Property condemnation began in 1953.[20] By the time Independence Mall opened in 1965, the project had torn down all the businesses and dwellings on three downtown blocks, damaging the vitality and safety of street life in the area. Later efforts to remedy the damage included a contiguous urban renewal project, relandscaping of the Mall, and in 2001, construction of the Independence Visitors Center and of a new home for the Liberty Bell, as well as the establishment in 2003 of the National Constitution Center.

Stonorov, Bacon, and Phillips included the as-yet-unfunded Mall in the Better Philadelphia Exhibition, although they did not consider urban design to be the supreme consideration in a planning project. Unlike Beaux-Arts designers, they conceived of design as one of many components in planning, along with the movement of goods and people throughout the city and the revitalization of urban neighborhoods. It was this broader, multipurpose vision that attracted the city's attention when the Bet-

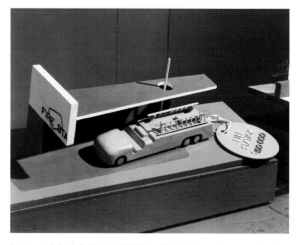

Better Philadelphia Exhibition (1947). Investments in the public realm are never cheap. The exhibition put price tags on possible projects so that people could make intelligent recommendations.

Broad Street Station, Philadelphia (pre-1950). No property owner was likely to develop anything near the noise and pollution caused by trains clattering into downtown Philadelphia.

Dock Street Market, Philadelphia (1951). People who could afford to live elsewhere could avoid the early morning traffic, constant noise, and vermin generated by the movement of produce into and out of downtown Philadelphia.

ter Philadelphia Exhibition opened in Gimbels Department Store in September 1947.

More than 6,500 people visited the exhibition each day, a total of 385,000 visitors during the two months it was open.[21] The exhibits were then moved to the Philadelphia Civic Center and remained on view until the 1970s.[22] The eleven displays led the viewer through the stages of the planning process, always focusing on Philadelphia and its neighborhoods. They served as a primer for the public, a public relations course on the benefits of planning, with titles such as, "To Get Things Done You Need to Plan for Them," "Progress Must Be Bought and Paid For," and "How City Planning Affects You and Your Family."

Visitors were treated to a bird's eye-view of the nineteenth-century city and a giant diorama of what Philadelphia might look like thirty-five years into the future. Among the other exhibits were cartoons by Robert Osborne illustrating how planning was part of daily life and a conveyor belt with scale models of twenty public works (a school, a fire house, etc.), each with a price tag. The most spectacular exhibit was a 30-by-14-foot representation of downtown Philadelphia, with scale models of 45,000 buildings, 25,000 cars, and 12,000 trees. At crucial moments large sections of the model flipped over to display what the area would be like in thirty years. By the time visitors had been through the exhi-

bition, as Bacon later explained, the organizers had "gained the confidence of a public made cynical by utopian futuramas and the inertia of local politicians."[23]

BACON'S VISION OF A REVITALIZED DOWNTOWN

Whether Bacon's "total vision" for the center of Philadelphia predated the Better Philadelphia Exhibition or grew out of it is immaterial; it became an agenda implemented by thousands of Philadelphians. Bacon's vision entailed removing impediments to private investment, improving access and circulation, establishing two major generators of economic activity, on either side of City Hall, and encouraging residential development downtown, especially in the eastern part of the city.

In the mid twentieth century there were two serious impediments to private investment in downtown Philadelphia. One was the so-called Chinese Wall on the west side of the business district, and the other was the Dock Street Market on the east. Their removal had been discussed long before Bacon advocated it. The Chinese Wall consisted of elevated railroad tracks that terminated immediately west of City Hall, at a station owned and operated by the Pennsylvania Railroad. Noise and soot from the 530 trains per day that used its 16 overhead

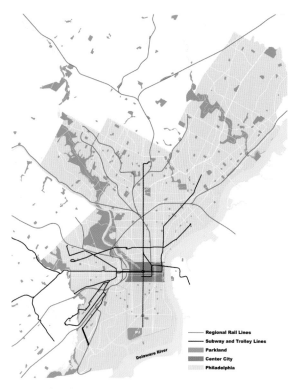

Regional rail and subway service leading to downtown Philadelphia (2010).

gestion generated by the Market. Bacon, like many other Philadelphians, understood that as long as the Pennsylvania Railroad and the Dock Street Market remained in the center of the city, real estate developers and property owners would be reluctant to invest in downtown Philadelphia.

Eliminating impediments to downtown investment was all well and good, but Bacon knew that more was required. The future of downtown business was also dependent on easy access for a labor force that had begun moving to the suburbs in the nineteenth century.[25] It was a fact that relatively few people lived downtown. People traveled to work by railroad, subway, and bus, and while the subway system covered much of the city, the suburban rail lines terminated at separate stations on either side of City Hall. A member of the Planning Commission staff suggested to Bacon that they connect the Reading and Pennsylvania railroad systems and relocate them where transferring to the subway would be easy.[26] This was brought to fruition in Market East, the mixed-use redevelopment project east of City Hall discussed later in this chapter.

tracks discouraged expansion of the business district west of City Hall.[24]

The Dock Street Market had been the city's major food distribution center for a century. Trucks arrived early each morning to supply wholesalers and retailers at sunrise; in the process, they jammed all the loading platforms and virtually blocked traffic. Residents and businesses tried to steer clear of the vermin and con-

Access by truck and automobile was also part of Bacon's vision for downtown. In determining highway location, he deferred to federal highway engineers, who proposed a rectilinear interstate highway loop around downtown. This idea had been promoted in 1926 in a Regional Planning Federation publication titled *A Picture of the*

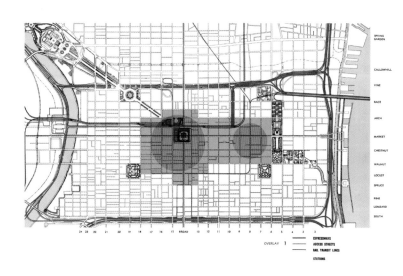

The Plan for Downtown Philadelphia (1960) proposed including a network of highways encircling downtown and major concentrations of commercial activity around railroad stations on the east and west side of City Hall.

Region.[27] Another version of the downtown loop had been on display at the Better Philadelphia Exhibition; this version was promoted by the Citizens' Council on City Planning in *Express Highways for Philadelphia*, published in 1947. It was supported by federal and state transportation officials and by Robert B. Mitchell, Bacon's predecessor as executive director of the Planning Commission. In 1953, Mitchell founded the Urban Traffic and Transportation Board (UTTB) to articulate regional highway policy and promote the highway loop.[28] The loop's first three parts opened in stages: the Schuylkill Expressway (I-76), across the Schuylkill River from downtown, on the west; the Vine Street Expressway (I-676) on the north; and the Delaware Expressway (I-95) along the Delaware River on the east. As described later in this chapter, the projected southern route along South Street generated opposition from the start and was eventually dropped.

In his effort to make downtown easier to navigate, Bacon placed great emphasis on making pedestrian movement easy and pleasant. Philadelphia is one of the most walkable cities in America. The distance from the Delaware River on the east to City Hall is a bit more than one mile, and the distance from there to the Schuylkill River on the west is a bit less than a mile. Philadelphia's two main streets, Mar-

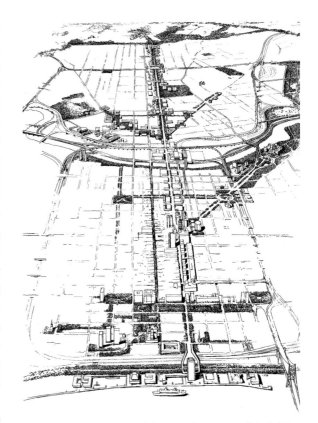

Edmund Bacon's vision of the new downtown Philadelphia (1967).

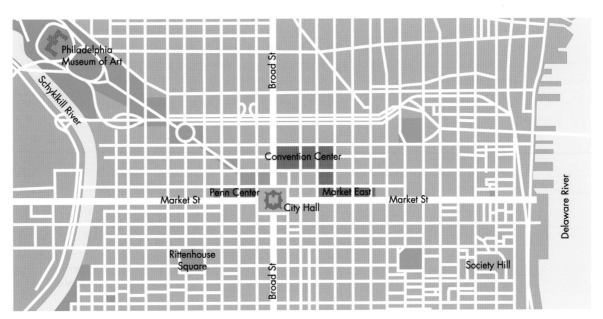

Major projects that triggered the reinvention of downtown Philadelphia.

Society Hill, Philadelphia (1999). St. Peter's Walk is one of the greenways Bacon proposed to create a pedestrian network tying together the entire neighborhood.

ket and Broad, are each 100 feet wide (property line to property line), like the north-south avenues in Manhattan. The others, however, are 50 feet across or less, compared to 60 feet in New York City. Deducting 12 feet on each side for sidewalks leaves only 26 feet for the roadways. The small streets and alleys that replaced the large backyards of the original 1682 William Penn–Thomas Holme plan added to the crowding. They were often insufficient even for easy pedestrian use.

Bacon therefore proposed to thread an additional pedestrian-only system of greenways through the projected residential district of Society Hill on the eastern side of downtown. Furthermore, every version of the Penn Center and Market East projects included carefully designed pedestrian concourses on different levels.

At the end of the twentieth century, pedestrianization was further developed by the Cen-

ter City District (CCD), Philadelphia's business improvement district, in the form of extensive landscaping, way-finding signs, and improved lighting throughout the business district. During the first decade of the twenty-first century, the CCD gave its encouragement to sidewalk cafés. Philadelphia today, as a result, benefits from an increase in social interaction, business transactions, and natural surveillance and safety.[29]

The third part of Bacon's strategy was to provide attractive residential opportunities on the eastern side of downtown, similar to the upscale Rittenhouse Square district on the western side. The trigger for private investment in residential real estate in this area was the Washington Square East Urban Renewal Project, which became better known as the Society Hill residential district, and replaced the Dock Street Market. Bacon envisioned the renovation of hundreds of deteriorated late-

Way-finding signs installed by Philadelphia's Center City District (2011).

middle-class returned to other older cities. The middle class provided the city with an alternative economic base, balancing the decline in industrial activity that followed World War II. Thus, downtown Philadelphia was spared the negative fates of Detroit, Cleveland, St. Louis, and other comparable large cities that had been economically dominant before the war.

Bacon's responsibility as a planner was for the whole city of Philadelphia. He developed plans and the necessary rezoning to develop the far northeast as a dense agglomeration of row houses.[30] He influenced the plans for the Southwest Temple, Northwest Temple, East Poplar, and West Poplar urban renewal projects that the Redevelopment Authority (RDA) was carrying out in the corridor between Temple University and downtown Philadelphia. He was also involved in planning one of the nation's largest residential redevelopment projects, Eastwick in Southwest Philadelphia.

At the same time, Bacon managed the City Planning Commission's staff in preparing master plans for west and northwest Philadelphia. These were traditional planning documents with visions of a future that may have been desirable, but they did not include either financing for the proposals or mechanisms to bring the recommendations of private property owners to fruition. The urban renewal projects were the responsibility of the RDA, under the supervision of William Rafsky. Rafsky was effectively the coordinator of the city's housing programs during the administrations of Mayors Clark and Dilworth, and he became director of the RDA and of the Old Philadelphia Development Corporation under Mayor Tate. Rafsky probably kept Bacon from having a major role in redevelopment outside Center City Philadelphia.[31] Whether that or something else explains Bacon's focus on downtown, he was primarily responsible for its revitalization, and it remains his greatest achievement.

eighteenth- and early nineteenth-century row houses. Once renovation of the Society Hill district was largely completed, new apartment buildings came to be erected on financially feasible sites all over downtown. They did much to maintain the vitality of the business district after hours. This three-pronged strategy was made necessary by the departure of middle-class white residents to the suburbs, the same trend that was then underway in so many American cities. As a result of Bacon's plans, Philadelphia attracted a downtown middle-class residential population decades before the

PENN CENTER

In 1923 a damaging fire in the train shed of the Broad Street Station ended daily service for sev-

Broad Street Station, Philadelphia (1923).

eral weeks. The Pennsylvania Railroad decided to relieve congestion by building the 30th Street Station across the Schuylkill River, to serve passengers from all over the United States, as well as an underground Suburban Station, beneath an office building, to serve commuters. The new Suburban Station was to be built one block north of the Broad Street Station, and in 1925 the Pennsylvania Railroad entered into an agreement with the city to demolish both the Broad Street Station and the Chinese Wall.[32]

Even before Ed Bacon joined the staff that was planning the Better Philadelphia Exhibition, he had decided what they must do. He already had in mind "the whole . . . system of organization of spaces and movement" that would reshape Market Street and the entire downtown business district west of City Hall.[33] The idea was to replace the Chinese Wall with a sunken pedestrian concourse, one level below the street. The concourse, three blocks long, would be open to the sky between the north-south streets that crossed the site. Lined with retail stores, this new pedestrian realm would connect the various components of downtown: the suburban commuter railroad station, City Hall, several high-rise office buildings, the east-west subway line under Market Street, the north-south subway line under Broad Street, and a new regional bus terminal. People traveling downtown by subway, rail, or bus would be able to see and reach their destinations uninterrupted by automobile and truck traffic.

In 1949, Bacon persuaded the Philadelphia

chapter of the American Institute of Architects (AIA) to create a committee to consider Penn Center within the context of the triangle between Market Street, Benjamin Franklin Parkway, and the Schuylkill River. The committee was chaired by Louis Kahn, who, although greatly respected, had not yet designed a single major building. Kahn produced a scheme consisting of an underground concourse covered by eleven identical slab office buildings extending from City Hall to the Schuylkill River.[34] Bacon would later explain that this "was a great test of the efficacy and viability of how the two men could work together."[35] They got along "with total joy until they reached the guts of the matter—expressing the structure of the organizing concept of the sunken concourse."[36] Kahn prepared drawings that illustrated separate and specific buildings, open spaces, and landscaping plans.[37]

This was not at all what Bacon had in mind; he needed general ideas—easily understandable and practical—to convince the Pennsylvania Railroad and the real estate developers, not a finished design. He also decided that he needed an architect who was not wedded to a specific plan, someone who would adjust the project to the requirements of the market. Therefore, Bacon terminated the relationship with Kahn and brought in Vincent Kling, one of Philadelphia's successful commercial architects. Although Bacon had never met Kling, he had seen a model for a hospital that Kling had designed, was "impressed by his ability to relate several buildings to each other . . . and decided [to get him to work on Penn Center] purely on the reaction to his work."[38]

From then on Bacon and Kling collaborated on every scheme that Bacon proposed for Penn Center, and they worked together on many of the other issues facing Philadelphia. While Kling did not design Penn Center, he was deeply involved and became the architect for many of the new buildings that were built around it. Most important, the two men used their network of relationships to discuss their ideas with James Symes, the Pennsylvania Railroad's executive vice president. Symes was already working with New York realtor Robert Dowling and the eminent industrial designer Raymond Loewy, one of the railroad's major consultants since the 1930s. Loewy prepared models and drawings that contemplated new, aboveground office buildings covering a basement level. This lower level would accommodate service vehicles, passenger cars, and pedestrians, all of which would have basement access to the office buildings, Suburban Station, and the subway.

Most Philadelphians thought that the site was not particularly valuable or appealing, surrounded as it was by vacant, run-down, or underutilized properties. Lenders, too, were skeptical and were unwilling to risk investing the large amount of money needed to develop this 22-acre property. But Symes and Bacon believed the site had substantial value, whether it was developed as a whole or in stages by a single developer, or subdivided and sold in individual parcels.

Joseph S. Clark was elected mayor in the fall of 1951, and Bacon, who had been executive director of the City Planning Commission for two years, presented him with his vision for Penn Center. He thought he would obtain Clark's support, explaining, "This is something I've saved for you as a present."[39] Clark, however, was not ready to embrace the proposal, probably because it had not yet been seen or accepted by many of the city's business community and civic leaders.

In early February 1952, Bacon convinced Symes to announce, at a joint luncheon of the Citizens' Council on City Planning and the Chamber of Commerce, that the Pennsylvania Railroad was about to start demolition of the Broad Street Station.[40] Symes agreed to let Bacon follow with a slide presentation of the Bacon-Kling vision for Penn Center.[41] Bacon worked with the railroad and citizen groups to maximize attendance at the event. There were 950 people in the audience when he announced that "this moment in the history of Philadelphia will not occur again" and presented the scheme he had shown to Mayor Clark, who sat, silent, in the audience.[42]

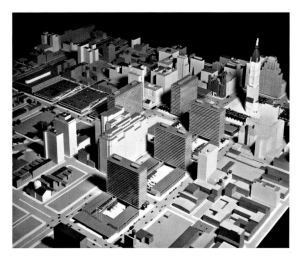

Penn Center, Philadelphia (1952). Edmund Bacon and Vincent Kling prepared a number of different versions of the commercial complex they hoped would replace the Broad Street Station.

Penn Center, Philadelphia (1953). The Pennsylvania Railroad, which needed to maximize the revenue generated by the site, proposed building much more floor area than Bacon had initially envisioned.

Bacon now began a determined campaign for his vision of West Market Street. He persuaded Wanamaker's Department Store to display Kling's model of the project in its Market Street store, just east of City Hall. The display included many of the elements of the Bacon-Kling plan: an open-air pedestrian concourse that extended from City Hall westward for three blocks over an underground service loop. The city's north-south streets continued at grade in the form of bridges over the concourse. The retail stores that flanked the concourse extended upward for two floors, but from the outside appeared to be single-story retailing along Market Street and Kennedy Boulevard. High-rise office slabs terminated the east end of each of the three blocks.

Thousands of shoppers liked what they saw and became supporters of this vision for Penn Center.[43] Week in, week out, Bacon advocated the project whenever and wherever he could. The support he generated helped create the constituency Mayor Clark wanted. Symes, however, was no longer so sure about Bacon's model. Whatever the Pennsylvania Railroad did with the site would require the approval of the City Council, and to gain its approval the plan would have to maximize revenues from what was potentially the most valuable real estate in the city. Consequently, Symes hired Kling to be the company's liaison with the City Planning Commission. Together, they considered a variety of proposals, including one from Albert Greenfield, one of Philadelphia's major realtors and later chairman of the City Planning Commission.

Working with Dowling, the New York realtor, Symes brought in Uris Brothers and Emery Roth & Sons. Uris was a developer and owner of New York office buildings, many of which were designed by Emery Roth, at that time New York's most successful office building architect. Symes felt this team had the credibility to negotiate with the city of Philadelphia on an ongoing basis. More important, Symes believed the team would devise a project that could be successfully marketed to businesses and law firms, who would have to pay top dollar for such modern space. The railroad, determined to minimize risk, proposed to develop the site in stages. This would enable the planners to react to changing market demand, reduce the amount of capital needed at any one time, and proceed with the next building only when significant office space had been rented in the previous one.

The team made its formal proposal in May 1953. Bacon was pleased that the new scheme rejected Loewy's inclusion of motor vehicles below grade, but he was very upset that the concourse was no longer open to the sky. Instead of three office buildings, the team proposed six; doubling the amount of office space would make the project financially feasible. The team's design also moved the pedestrian concourse to the level of existing city streets and transformed it into a relatively narrow, dim canyon between office slabs. The office buildings had been turned 90 degrees, so they would now have a major presence on Market Street and Kennedy Boulevard.

With Bacon's assistance, City Planning Commission staff devised a few rectangular openings at grade, which provided some natural light, views, and stairway access for people coming up from or going down to the concourse. Bacon wanted other changes as well. Mayor Clark, however, had not yet begun negotiations with the railroad executives. He appointed a Citizens' Advisory Commission (CAC) to negotiate on the city's behalf. The CAC was chaired by architect George Howe, who, in addition to being a co-designer of Philadelphia's most admired modern office building, the PSFS tower, was a former architectural

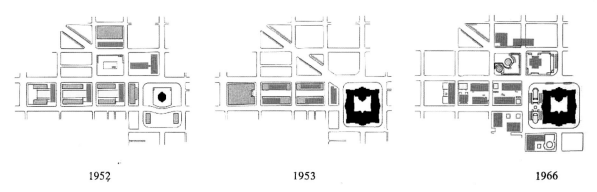

1952   1953   1966

Penn Center, Philadelphia. The plans discussed in 1952 and 1953 led to what was finally decided by 1966.

Philadelphia (2011). While Bacon achieved his planning objectives for Penn Center, he was not as pleased with true ultimate design.

associate of Kahn and Stonorov. In 1953 he was chairman of Yale University's Department of Architecture. The CAC wanted the overall design changed to include sub-basement truck loading and the rectangular openings to the sky for the pedestrian concourse that Bacon recommended.

While the developers agreed to some of the concourse openings, they balked at paying for underground truck access, which would increase development costs enough to render the Penn Center unfeasible. Finally, in Febru-

ary 1954, Mayor Clark negotiated a deal that Bacon and the development team could accept. The developers added rectangular openings from the street to the concourse and individual underground truck access ramps to each building's basement. In exchange, the city accepted the staged development sequence and agreed to pay for the truck ramps and the underground street, which it also agreed to maintain.

Within a few months of the agreement, the first building, designed by Vincent Kling, went into construction. This was an office slab on 17th Street, at the western end of the site. The basement and ground floor of what they called the Transportation Center housed a Greyhound bus terminal. The rest of the 18-story building contained the headquarters of the Pennsylvania Railroad, rental office space, and a 1,000-car garage.

Although some elements of Bacon's vision were executed, he remained unhappy. Uris, Dowling, and the railroad continued to ignore his objections until Clark's successor, Richardson Dilworth, took office in 1956. While the new mayor was more sympathetic to Bacon's urban design objectives, he wanted to eliminate the office slab at the eastern end of the site so that visitors and occupants of Penn Center would have a direct view of City Hall. Using his influence with the Philadelphia Art Commission, which had to approve any construction

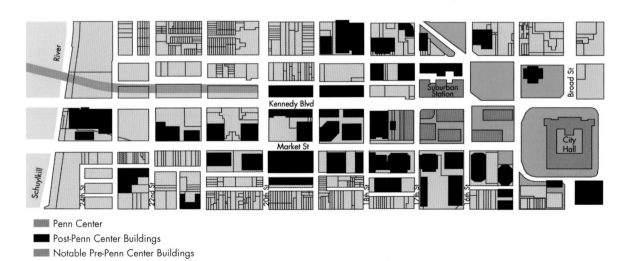

Penn Center
Post-Penn Center Buildings
Notable Pre-Penn Center Buildings

Penn Center, Philadelphia (2011). A widespread and sustained market reaction to the removal of the "Chinese Wall" and the erection of Penn Center resulted in rebuilding most of the western section of the city's downtown.

West Market Street, Philadelphia (2011). Redevelopment of Penn Center shifted the locus of commercial activity to the corridor along West Market Street.

within 200 feet of Franklin Parkway, he forced the developers to remove the building on 16th Street that blocked the view of City Hall.[44]

Bacon, like so many others, was deeply disappointed by the Penn Center that took shape. The pedestrian precinct between the office towers was barren, uninviting, and in shadow most of the time. Street-level retailing never materialized, nor did any real connection with the below-grade concourse. Bacon remarked that Penn Center was created by "a group of stockholders expecting dividends," rather than by someone trying to create a glorious addition to the city.[45]

Although Penn Center was not exactly what Bacon had in mind, it nevertheless included many of his ideas. Once the project was complete, an underground pedestrian precinct connected Suburban Station, the subway, City Hall, and Penn Center. More important, the project triggered a wave of new office and hotel con-

struction west of City Hall that has continued into the twenty-first century. During the early twentieth century, the business center of Philadelphia had been concentrated south of City Hall. Removal of the Chinese Wall eliminated the impediment to developing the cheaper, underdeveloped sites west of City Hall. The new offices at Penn Center offered up-to-date, air-conditioned space, wired for modern office equipment. They set the standard for developers attracted to available development sites all along west Market Street.

Gregory Heller, Bacon's biographer, has explained that "Penn Center was a turning point for Bacon's career." Although he had relatively little impact on its ultimate appearance, it allowed him to become a major player in Philadelphia's planning game, and it "greatly elevated his local and national profile."[46] Although Bacon felt that Penn Center could have been much better from a design perspective, he knew that from a planning perspective, he had been remarkably successful.[47]

Penn Center shifted the locus of office development to West Market Street, in much the same way that the Michigan Avenue Bridge shifted Chicago's prime commercial district from State Street in the Loop to North Michigan Avenue. Although Penn Center was a small project, compared with the building of the Michigan Avenue Bridge and the widening of North Michigan Avenue or the reconstruction of the central core of Paris, it had a similarly dramatic impact on the city. West Market Street became Philadelphia's new business center.

Like the redevelopment of the historic center of Paris, the redevelopment of central Philadelphia was appropriate to the economic and political context of its time. Bacon was the big winner in the planning game not just because he had advocated a project that met the requirements of that context or because he was one of the country's most skilled advocates of planning, but because he had done what was necessary to generate the investments that would provide Philadelphia with a modern office district.

INVOLVING THE BUSINESS COMMUNITY

The creation of Penn Center involved significant players in the civic, political, and business leadership of Philadelphia. Their interaction with Edmund Bacon provided a model for the next steps in the revitalization of downtown Philadelphia, in a manner quite similar to the planning process initiated by Daniel Burnham when he worked with the Commercial and Merchants clubs on the *Plan of Chicago*. The various participants in the Penn Center project, though dissatisfied with one or more aspects of what emerged, learned what Bacon had understood from the beginning: a compelling vision may inspire individuals, but to bring a project to completion, the players have to exercise cooperation and flexibility, a willingness to work together and to adjust their plans to the requirements of property owners and to the city's economic and political realities.

In Philadelphia the process had been chaotic, and the results were less than satisfying. One reason for this was that the participation of business was unfocused. Business leaders had founded the Greater Philadelphia Movement (GPM) in 1949 in order to effect the sort of public-private partnership they thought necessary to implement some of the ideas presented at the Better Philadelphia Exhibition. Personal rivalries and political conflicts kept the GPM from playing this sort of quasi-developer role with respect to Penn Center. Moreover, the business leadership of the city was skeptical about the need for large civic projects and their cost-effectiveness in stimulating economic development. Mayor Dilworth understood their skepticism and was determined to harness the energies of the city's civic and business leadership in executing the city's next redevelopment projects: Society Hill and Market East. With enthusiastic support from Bacon and Rafsky, he decided to spearhead a better-functioning planning process.

In July 1956, Dilworth brought together fifty-four of the city's leaders to see a film entitled *The Heart of the City*, which took the position that without a serious commitment to Center City revitalization, "the entire city would fall apart."[48] Within a few months, the leaders of the GPM incorporated the Old Philadelphia Development Corporation (OPDC) to "aid and assist in the redevelopment, renewal, replanning, and general improvement of the declining core of the historic city."[49] Its leadership included many of the city's major bank, insurance, real estate, and business executives. They proved to be crucial to the success of the downtown revitalization projects that followed Penn Center.

Once the urban renewal program had been completed, OPDC changed its name to the Central Philadelphia Development Corporation (CPDC) and in 1985 altered its mission, to focus on the development and stewardship of downtown Philadelphia as a whole. In 1990 it spun off the subsidiary Center City District (CCD) to provide sanitation, safety, and other services that were being provided by business improvement districts throughout the United States. In 1996 the CPDC eliminated its existing staff and entered into a management contract for the staff of the CCD-run CPDC, effectively establishing a strong link between the planning-and-advocacy function and the operating-and-implementing function. As the rest of this chapter explains, these three public-private partnerships, particularly the CCD, played essential roles in the revitalization of downtown Philadelphia.

SOCIETY HILL

The Better Philadelphia Exhibition had included a program to alter and improve the concentration of historic buildings on the eastern side of downtown. In addition to the plan for Independence Mall, it included a 1944 version of Roy Larson's proposal to create a National Historic Park, which would include all the historic structures immediately to the east and south of Independence Hall. (The plan for the park was later implemented by the National Park Service.) Bacon expanded this idea, adding "a series of meandering garden footpaths leading from the National Historic Park and connecting together parts" of the old residential neighborhood farther south and east, known as Society Hill, which contained 700 Georgian, Federal, and Greek Revival row houses. Bacon believed these row houses were excellent candidates for renovation.[50] The idea challenged conventional wisdom, which thought of Society Hill as a slum. Developers, public officials,

Dock Street Market, Philadelphia (1942).

architects, and planners assumed that the way to deal with slums was by replacing them, not preserving and rehabilitating them. In fact, the Housing Act of 1949 provided money only for clearance and new construction.

One of the models at the 1947 exhibition illustrated new residential development for the section of Society Hill occupied by the Dock Street wholesale produce market. Moving the market was something that many Philadelphians thought was a good idea. Bacon believed that few people would choose to live or work in this prime downtown location until the market was gone. Unless every part of downtown Philadelphia was welcoming to residents and businesses, there would be no way to avoid the inevitable decline of the Center City. Thus, the revitalization of Society Hill became one of his major objectives.

There was a second rationale for moving the market out of the neighborhood. It no longer provided efficient or economical distribution of fish, meat, and produce. Refrigeration and more efficient cargo-handling techniques had changed the economics of the food business. Further, highway construction would soon bring down shipping prices and squeeze out many local suppliers. The national firms that now supplied the market also required a different capital plant. For this reason a new food distribution center became one of the major projects of the Greater Philadelphia Movement. The GPM sponsored a series of feasibility studies and exhibited a model at its 1954 annual dinner, at which forty invited representatives of national food companies were in attendance.[51]

The following year, with support from Mayor Clark, the Greater Philadelphia Movement chartered the nonprofit Food Distribution Center Corporation (FDC) to implement the project. It persuaded forty businesses to contribute $250,000 and the Fels Foundation to donate $100,000; with this money it was able to begin development on a site in south Philadelphia. Some people objected that the GPM had too much control and the city too little. Albert Greenfield, one of the city's major real estate investors, raised questions about the reliability of the feasibility studies, maintaining that he had been kept out of its activities because he was Jewish, and that because of his religion the GPM did not believe he could represent Philadelphia's leadership. Soon after, Mayor Dilworth appointed Greenfield chairman of the Philadelphia Planning Commission.

The proposed 358-acre site in south Philadelphia was a largely city-owned swamp that was being used as a garbage dump. The project required condemnation of a few additional parcels (completed in 1956) by the city's Redevelopment Authority, plus an investment of $14 million for landfill, utilities, paving and road construction (completed in 1959). When this phase of development was completed, the FDC occupied the site and invested $100 million in stages, as leases were signed by the food merchants who would occupy the space. The move was good for the merchants; more business was transacted on the new site than at Dock Street. Because there was less spoilage, and cartage and loading costs were lower, the occupants could afford higher rents. FDC revenues exceeded expectations, as did its expenses. By 1969 the project was virtually complete, and tenants were employing 9,000 workers.[52]

A new container facility just below the Walt Whitman Bridge brought further change. Situated close to the new Food Distribution Center, it made the finger piers on the central waterfront obsolete. The waterfront had been hardhit by the city's decline in manufacturing; there were simply fewer items to export from the city. Furthermore, the Port of Philadelphia, 90 miles from the ocean, found it increasingly difficult to compete with New York, Baltimore, and New Orleans, all of which had easier access to shipping lanes. So the neighborhoods all along the Delaware that had been dependent on waterfront employment had declined steadily after World War II.

Bacon thought that elimination of the produce market would make Society Hill's historic assets far more attractive. However, he also believed it was necessary to remove incompatible structures and, particularly, dilapidated buildings. Many of the resulting sites were made available to

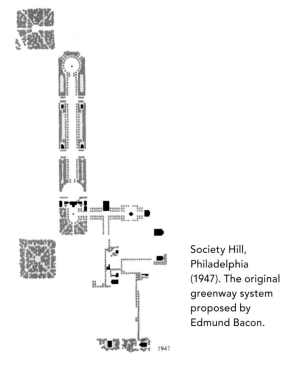

Society Hill, Philadelphia (1947). The original greenway system proposed by Edmund Bacon.

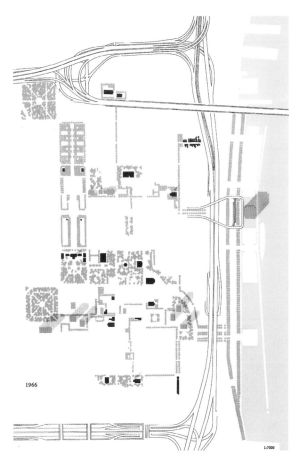

Society Hill, Philadelphia (1966). Property ownership and building conditions resulted in a greenway system that was more extensive than originally envisioned.

Society Hill, Philadelphia (pre-redevelopment). Run-down and abandoned buildings would be replaced by open space or new structures that would be compatible in character with their neighbors.

residential developers. But rather than leave gaps in the neighborhood fabric or fill all these spaces with new buildings, Bacon proposed to use some of them to provide greenway shortcuts that ran through whole blocks and tied the neighborhood together.

At the time of the 1947 Better Philadelphia Exhibition, there had been no way to pay for such a massive redevelopment project. Nevertheless, in 1948 the City Planning Commission certified Society Hill as one of nine areas of Philadelphia that would be suitable for action when Congress enacted the urban renewal program under Title I of the Housing Act of 1949. That program paid two-thirds of the cost of property acquisition, clearance, site preparation, and losses from the resale of development parcels.

Depressed prices made Society Hill row houses a bargain, provided that banks would lend the money to renovate them. But since banks refused to finance new construction or rehabilitation in an officially designated slum, Bacon's vision for a revitalized Society Hill was temporarily shelved. Then, in 1954, Congress amended the Housing Act to offer federally guaranteed mortgage insurance to banks that lent money for new or rehabilitated housing in urban renewal areas. This made Bacon's strategy feasible. Three years later the first section of Society Hill—officially known as

the Washington Square East Urban Renewal Project—was approved for federal Title I assistance. This urban renewal project, generally bounded by Walnut, Front, Pine, and 6th streets, was approved in three stages (a fourth was added later).[53]

Redevelopment of the former Dock Street Market site seemed the obvious place to begin. It would be big enough to highlight the area's transformation, to change market perceptions of the neighborhood, and to interest major developers. Bacon's 1947 plan had been a cluster of mid-rise slabs in a green superblock. In 1957 the City Planning Commission hired architects Vincent Kling, Roy Larson, and Oskar Stonorov to reexamine the scheme. They proposed to scatter buildings of different sizes and shapes throughout the neighborhood, but the Redevelopment Authority wanted something more dramatic. It commissioned yet another plan, from architect Preston Andrade, which placed high-rise residential buildings on the site of the former Dock Street Market.[54]

Everybody wanted better buildings than the ones that had emerged at Penn Center. One way to achieve a good result was to attract national developers to compete for the project; the second was to make clear that the city would select "the best design proposal." The appropriate entity to help seemed to be the Old Philadelphia Development Corporation, which had been created by business, labor, and civic leaders to aid in the development of Center City. After a meeting convened by Mayor Dilworth, the OPDC was given a major role in the development of Society Hill. This was significant, because while government bureaucracies usually relied on "the usual suspects" for public work, the OPDC was able to go about things differently.[55] It reached out to the real estate industry and induced four national firms and one local team to spend $260,000 on designs for the project.[56] OPDC had been designated as the redeveloper for construction on some of the vacant lots and for rehabilitation of some historic buildings. Its role was to find buyers for these sites and help individual owners satisfy RDA requirements. Its most important function, however, was as general promoter of the revival of Society Hill.

The winning design for the first and most important project in Society Hill came from the New York development firm of Webb & Knapp, which was active in urban renewal projects around the country. Its scheme, designed by I. M. Pei, called for the local streets to be lined with modern single-family row houses, while on the crest of the hill, on the axes of Locust and 2nd streets, where they would create dramatic vistas, he placed an asymmetrical cluster of three towers. The towers were intended to announce the revival of Society Hill to local residents, to visitors downtown, and to commuters as they approached the city.

The three towers offered good marketing for the neighborhood, but that alone was not enough to renew it. At Bacon's insistence the RDA and the OPDC made the decision to create a public realm framework that would

Society Hill, Philadelphia (2005). The three towers became a beacon announcing the area's redevelopment.

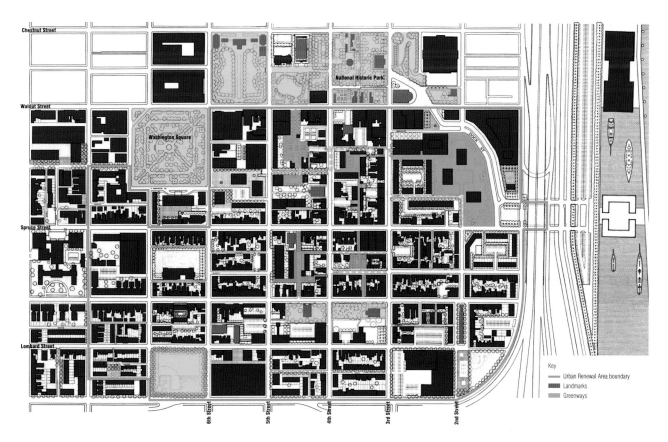

Final approved site plan, Society Hill, Philadelphia (c. 1967). Compatible combinations of old and new characterize the area's redevelopment.

induce property owners to invest in the area's decaying housing. Consequently, the RDA used federal urban renewal funds to pay for new granite curbs, brick sidewalks, reproductions of old gas lamps, street trees, small parks, and Bacon's greenways.

Creating the greenway system required the acquisition of vacant properties and parking lots but hardly any occupied buildings. When it was completed, residents and visitors could easily reach everything in the neighborhood on foot. As pedestrians came to the end of a greenway, they had only to turn 90 degrees to head for another landmark, continuing this way until they reached their destination. Bacon based the navigation of the greenways on an orientation system he had come across in China, where there is an ancient belief that by constantly changing direction people can shake off any evil spirits that may be following them.[57]

After the City Planning Commission had formally designated 127 acres of Society Hill as the Washington Square East Urban Renewal Area, and after the project had been approved for

urban renewal funding by HUD in 1957, Society Hill became the responsibility of the Redevelopment Authority. The authority divided the area into three sections. It began by condemning 66 acres, including the Dock Street Market and several other large development parcels. Property owners, including more than two hundred who went on to renovate their houses, were required to bring their property up to code standards. Those who were willing to comply with the redevelopment scheme were entitled to repurchase their sites from the RDA.

The RDA designated the Old Philadelphia Development Corporation as the redeveloper of the buildings that were not repurchased by their owners. Its obligation was to find people with "the desire, taste, and means to buy a historically certified house and restore it in accord with sensible but sound historic standards."[58] To accomplish this, OPDC took possession of property the RDA had taken by eminent domain (without ever actually playing the role of owner) and transferred it directly to owners who could and would renovate the buildings.

Society Hill, Philadelphia (2009). Historic Headhouse Market was retained as one of the neighborhood's significant landmarks. Federal urban renewal funds paid for two-thirds of the cost of restoring cobblestone streets and brick sidewalks, installing old-fashioned gas lamps, and planting street trees, all providing a much-appreciated public realm.

Society Hill, Philadelphia (2008). The greenways have become a beloved neighborhood asset.

The RDA adopted a simpler approach for the rest of the project. Many of the buildings, mostly row houses, were excluded from condemnation, provided that their owners renovated their buildings sufficiently to meet city code and urban renewal standards within three years of plan approval. The rest were acquired for greenways, small parks, and scattered new construction.

The third phase of the Society Hill project included Pennsylvania Hospital, the nation's first hospital, founded in 1751 by Benjamin Franklin and Dr. Thomas Bond. It was added to the Society Hill project in order to facilitate the hospital's expansion. Today the hospital and related medical facilities treat 25,000 patients a year and employ more than 2,500 doctors, nurses, and service people.[59]

The role of the federal government was critical to the renovation of Society Hill. The federal urban renewal designation entitled banks to FHA Section 220 mortgage insurance on loans to developers of apartment buildings that complied with the renewal plan. Owners of single-family and two-family houses were entitled to FHA Section 312 mortgages, which only charged 3 percent interest and were administered by the RDA. Residents used the mortgage money to finance the rehabilitation of existing row houses. In other places, developers filled in "missing teeth" with new residential buildings, which had to be built of brick at similar scale. Wherever development costs exceeded mortgage limits, the RDA willingly condemned the property and resold it at a price that made rehabilitation or new construction feasible. The difference between the acquisition cost and the resale price was subsidized with Title I funds, two-thirds of which were federal.

The redevelopment of Society Hill provided attractive urban housing for the upper-middle-class residents seeking an alternative to the suburbs. More than that, it became the most expensive neighborhood in Philadelphia, generating huge amounts of tax revenue from an area that had previously required major city expenditures on sanitation, safety, and traffic management. In 1950 approximately 3,600 people lived in its 1,700 housing units.[60] At that time the average price of a housing unit in Society Hill was $5,200, compared with $3,700 for Philadelphia as a whole and $15,000 for the Rittenhouse Square area. Half a century later, approximately 4,400 people lived in 2,900 housing units.[61] The average price of a housing unit in Society Hill had increased 78 times, rising to $407,000, compared with $60,000 for Philadelphia as a whole and $265,000 for Rittenhouse Square.

These economic benefits, however, came at a substantial social cost. Twenty-six manufacturing firms and at least 438 households (83 percent white) and 551 unrelated individuals (89 percent white) were forced to move.[62] The total cost of the Washington Square East Renewal Project was $36 million. The federal government covered $30.3 million, the State of Pennsylvania $3.4 million, and the City of Philadelphia $3.3 million.[63] Planners of the project had relied "on the natural processes of neighborhood growth and increasing land values for the desired improvement in buildings and lands not to be acquired."[64] The results demonstrated beyond any doubt that their reliance had been justified.

Bacon never intended Society Hill to be a self-contained island within the city. From the beginning the project had been conceived as an integral part of downtown Philadelphia, and the greenway system was intended to be a growing network of open space that would evolve as the city changed. As a result, Society Hill has continued to spread out gradually from its urban renewal boundaries and has become an integral component of Center City Philadelphia.

In 2001, Ed Bacon agreed to take some of my Yale students on a walk through Society Hill. Like so many bright students, they were skeptical of any unproven assertion, from Bacon or anyone else. But a chance encounter convinced them of the importance and meaning of Bacon's accomplishment. A middle-aged woman came up to Bacon, introduced herself, and explained that although she now lived in the suburbs, she and her family once lived along one of the greenways in Society Hill. "Those were the happiest of times," she said. "We loved the greenways. You made our lives so wonderful. I just had to say thank you, Mr. Bacon."

MARKET EAST

Once Society Hill was underway, there remained one unrealized component in Bacon's strategy for the revitalization of downtown Philadelphia. This was a program to reverse the decline of retailing and the deterioration of buildings between City Hall and Society Hill. He was convinced that this project, when combined with Society Hill, Penn Center, and improvements to the transit system, would provide the physical framework within which Center City Philadelphia would thrive.

Until World War II, most people did their shopping downtown, largely along East Market Street, which at that time had five department stores. After World War II, however, many people who worked downtown lived in outlying sections of the city or in the suburbs. An increasing number of them chose to do their shopping close to home in the shopping centers that were beginning to open up throughout the region.

Between the mid-1950s and the mid-1970s, sixteen regional shopping centers opened in the suburbs of Philadelphia.[65] By 1963, retail sales in downtown Philadelphia had sunk to 10 percent of sales in the metropolitan area, and to 6 percent in 1972.[66] Downtown business leaders, especially those in retailing, understood they had to do something to keep East Market Street economically healthy.

Bacon responded to this problem with Penn Center East—a multilevel, mixed-use complex similar to the one that he had hoped would emerge for Penn Center. He quickly dropped the name in favor of Market East because Penn Center was turning out to be so much less satisfying than he and others had hoped. Over the next two decades Bacon persisted in his advocacy of this mixed-used, retail-centered project until it finally emerged in 1977 as the Gallery at Market East.

Market East went through six main incarnations. The first was designed under Bacon's supervision in 1958.[67] It included the connection between the Reading and Pennsylvania railroads, a new bus terminal, a parking garage, three levels of open-air shopping, 1.3 million square feet of new office space, and an underground concourse connecting to Penn Center. Drawings were exhibited at Gimbels and on Reyburn Plaza.[68] While the transportation improvements captured the city's imagination, the real estate industry thought there was not enough market demand to attract developers. Bacon, on the other hand, was certain that the rail-subway connection would increase accessibility, enough to create the demand. He was eventually proven correct.

Bacon's 1960 version was largely the work of Willo von Moltke, a member of the City Planning Commission staff. This plan connected four department stores by glass-enclosed bridges.[69] But it, too, was doomed, since no public agency had money to finance such massive redevelopment, and no private developers were willing to take on any of the specific projects. So the commission hired Larry Smith & Company to do preliminary market studies and Louis Kahn to devise designs that might have greater appeal.[70] They, too, failed to alter the perception of the real estate industry.

Without the certainty of retail tenants, no developer would consider the project, and

Market East, Philadelphia (1958). Like Penn Center, proposals for rebuilding East Market Street kept changing.

Market East, Philadelphia (1964).

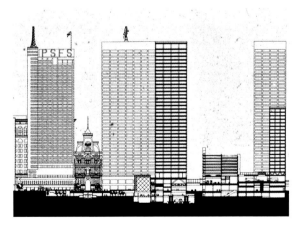

Market East, Philadelphia (1968).

without a developer, Market East could not go forward. In 1962, therefore, the Old Philadelphia Development Corporation adopted the project and commissioned version three. This included a more elaborate market study from Larry Smith & Company, a design from architect Victor Gruen, and a more realistic version of the project from shopping center developer James Rouse. The OPDC rejected Gruen's proposals, which would have transformed Market Street into a pedestrian shopping precinct along the lines of the one he had designed for Kalamazoo, Michigan, and would have relocated vehicular traffic to the second level.[71]

Meanwhile, Bacon asked architect Romaldo Giurgola to replace the open-air retailing with a linear, glass-enclosed, air-conditioned shopping complex. His 1963 version placed a six-story pedestrian concourse one level above the street so that people could use glass-enclosed bridges to get to the department stores. However, department store executives resisted the second-story entry idea, because it would allow shoppers to bypass the eye-catching merchandise—perfumes, jewelry, bags, and scarves—that was traditionally displayed on the ground floor.

Market East, Philadelphia (1998). The station at Market East provides both subway and rail service.

Market East, Philadelphia (1998). The interior, air-conditioned Gallery developed by the Rouse Company drew shoppers away from Market Street itself.

In 1964, HUD provided the city with initial funding for Market East.[72] The project was added to the city's agenda and became the responsibility of the RDA. Two years later the RDA retained Skidmore, Owings & Merrill (SOM) to design the project. Bacon, skeptical of the firm's understanding of Philadelphia, continued to work with Giurgola.[73] SOM went ahead, retaining the basic conception and developing a practical plan for staging demolition and construction. The project died, however, when HUD withdrew its funding. Funding was restored in 1969, after HUD designated Market East one of the nine Philadelphia projects approved for urban renewal assistance; the RDA selected the Philadelphia architectural firm of Bower & Fradley to design the project.

The turning point for Market East finally came in 1972, two years after Bacon had retired. The Southeastern Pennsylvania Transportation Authority (SEPTA) received federal Urban Mass Transportation Assistance funding for the renovation and extension of the transit hub, and the Rouse Company began to consider whether to become its primary developer. The following year HUD increased its grant to $18 million. By then the counterculture was flourishing,

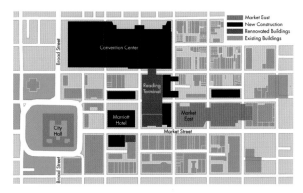

Market East, Philadelphia (2011). The area east of City Hall is turning into a major destination for hotels, restaurants, and conventioneers.

and East Market Street was "lined with noisy sound stores, class D discounters, purveyors of triple knit fashions, plastic shoes, and dog hair wigs."[74] Finally, in 1974, Gimbels Department Store and Rouse formally agreed to implement the RDA plan. The resulting project included the new 1.8-mile underground rail connection between the Penn Central (subsequently Conrail) and Reading railroads, a renovated SEPTA subway station, a four-level shopping mall accommodating 122 retailing and food service establishments, a new building for Gimbels, connections to a renovated Strawbridge & Clothier department store, an 850-car parking garage, and truck service behind and beneath the entire complex.[75]

Market East was successful in its goal of attracting shoppers back to downtown Philadelphia. In its first year of operation, sales at the Gallery at Market East reached $250 per square foot, double that of a typical suburban shopping mall.[76] Five percent of shoppers came from downtown Philadelphia, 71 percent from sections of the city outside downtown, and 23 percent from beyond the city limits. The project was initially responsible for providing more than 1,200 new jobs and $1.9 million in taxes.[77] The surrounding area grew as well; by 2010 the area between City Hall and Market East included office buildings, the 1-million-square-foot Convention Center, more than 20,000 new and renovated hotel rooms, and countless new restaurants.

For a long time, Bacon had been virtually alone in believing that Market East could be built in the foreseeable future. Over two decades market analysts issued reports showing that there would not be enough customers, retailers refused to consider relocating into such a project, and lenders were unwilling to finance anything like Market East. In fact, Bacon delighted in regaling people with the story of the student at Wharton who received a failing grade for believing in its feasibility. Finally, seven years after Bacon retired, and after more than half a dozen major designs, the first Gallery at Market East opened. Six years later Gallery II opened; in 1984 the combined railroad-subway station opened; and in 1993 the complex was linked via Reading Terminal to the huge new Pennsylvania Convention Center.

POLITICAL DEFEAT

As biographer Gregory Heller has observed, Bacon was a salesman of ideas, a force in meetings, a skilled orator, and a genius at figuring out how to convince his particular audience.[78] For nearly three decades he was able to depend on continuing public support. But by the late 1960s he began to face opposition. Bacon had worked diligently to adapt the federal highway system to the realities of his hometown. He tried to integrate the Vine Street section into the city by proposing links that fed directly into garages at Market East, but they were not built. The southern part of the loop was vehemently opposed by the many residents and businesses that faced relocation. Bacon examined the possibility of making it an at-grade boulevard but failed to convince anybody that this was an acceptable alternative. In 1968 the Planning Commission deleted the roadway from its comprehensive plan, but not before it had seriously eroded Bacon's reputation as a promoter of desirable public projects.

Bacon also faced increasingly vocal oppo-

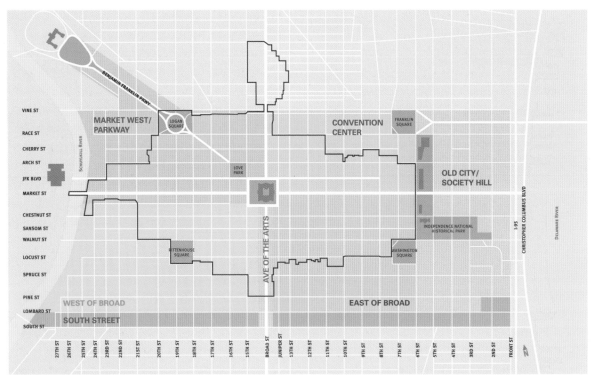

Center City Development, Philadelphia (2011). For more than two decades, the downtown business improvement district has been increasing the area's safety, improving its cleanliness, and generally upgrading the quality of life downtown.

sition from the people who had been relocated to clear the way for federal urban renewal areas. They identified both highways and urban renewal with Bacon, and for good reason. Although other agencies were in fact responsible for both programs, Bacon had done everything he could to be remembered as the man who changed Philadelphia. In the event, he came to be identified with all changes to the city, the ones he liked and the ones he did not.

Opposition to Bacon came from different quarters and focused on several complaints. The most virulent was the opposition to the proposed federal Crosstown Expressway. This highway would have mowed down everything on South Street in its path, and of all opposition, this did him the most harm. Although he was not responsible for highways, his identification with urban change gave his opponents a powerful weapon. Eventually, opposition to federal highways merged with the other grievances of Bacon's opponents.

One charge leveled against Bacon was elitism. Newcomers to the planning game believed that Penn Center, Society Hill, and Market East were conceived by and for an elite, and that they ignored the needs of the poor. Neither Bacon's early championing of low-income housing nor his days as managing director of the Philadelphia Housing Association seemed relevant to them. In fact, one of the reasons they opposed federal redevelopment projects in the 1960s was that those projects bulldozed the poor. Moreover, Title I did not require that low-rent public housing be provided within the renewal area, or even on a one-for-one basis somewhere in the city. The second criticism of the program was that there was inadequate citizen participation in the planning process. Bacon had spent the early 1940s fighting to create a City Planning Commission that held public hearings and could pressure the Republican Party machine for greater transparency in government. Those battles had been won and were long forgotten. Opponents identified Bacon with the current elite that ran Philadelphia, not with his long-ago championship of disenfranchised community residents.

Like Moses, Bacon was wrongly implicated in project scandals. The Republican district attorney of Philadelphia (later U.S. senator), Arlen Spector, began an investigation of the Tate administration, and this was, by implication, an investigation of the aging liberal establishment, which had been the backbone of Bacon's support. Bacon was called to appear before a grand jury, and his reputation was tarnished because his testimony was characterized in the press as "evasive."[79]

The reality was that Bacon had been unswervingly loyal to four mayors, often advocating things they wanted but he did not. By the late 1960s Bacon's loyalty was becoming a burden that he was less and less willing to carry.[80] He was managing two jobs: executive director of the Planning Commission, and development coordinator for the City of Philadelphia. He had been deeply hurt by the implied charges of corruption and was, in any case, about to reach the official retirement age of sixty. More important, because he could no longer depend on ongoing public support, he doubted that he could continue to play his usual assertive role. In 1968, *Philadelphia* magazine printed an article that claimed he had "outlived his usefulness" and was "ill-equipped to change with the times."[81] Two years later, when he reached retirement age, he resigned.

SUSTAINING THE NEW PHILADELPHIA

When Bacon described what he did to change Philadelphia, he made it sound easy: "Plan for the future since it doesn't affect anybody and minimizes opposition; discard the nonessential and concentrate on what is a genuine priority; give it a name (like Penn Center or Market East); and be clear in presenting it to the public."[82] But changes of any magnitude have to be sustainable over decades. In Philadelphia they have been sustained and elaborated.

Once its mid-twentieth-century redevelopment projects were in place, Philadelphia, like countless other cities, discovered that more than physical plant was needed to produce a thriving downtown. Philadelphia differed from other cities that invested in urban renewal, however, in that its redevelopment projects were not stand-alone islands of new construction. Bacon had induced property owners, businesses, civic leaders, and public officials to create a remarkable public realm framework in which redevelopment projects were embedded, and around which downtown continued to grow long after he retired in 1970. Pedestrian and transit systems were introduced that amplified both William Penn's seventeenth-century street grid, anchored by the axes of Market and Broad streets, and the nineteenth-century City Hall, which had been built where they crossed.

Private construction on West Market Street provided additional modern office space, essential for the region's primary employment center. Construction on East Market Street attracted the tenants that allowed the city to remain a major retail and tourist destination. The revival of Society Hill as a residential neighborhood coincided with the start of the movement of the middle class back into American cities. The revival of downtown Philadelphia itself was a success not only because of private and public realm construction; the strategy succeeded because it was supplemented by an ongoing program to provide personnel and services to keep all downtown clean, safe, attractive, and well managed.

Following World War II, governments everywhere felt pressure to expand their activities. The demand for increased social services had to be satisfied, but since they were financed by state and federal programs that often required a local contribution, local governments had to raise the necessary matching funds. Since no one wanted to pay more taxes, city governments reallocated their spending by moving services away from commercial areas (which had fewer residents) to residential neighborhoods with more voters. As a result, despite the success of Penn Center, Market East, and Society Hill, and like center cities across the country, downtown Philadelphia began to lose business to suburban shopping centers and office parks. But change was on the way. Starting with Bloor West Village in Toronto, Ontario, in 1970, cities began to create business improvement districts (BIDs) to provide services that were routinely provided by their suburban competition.[83] The money to pay for those services came from a real estate tax surcharge collected from properties within a specified business district by the city and transferred directly to its BID. In 1990 the Philadelphia City Council and the mayor voted to create a downtown BID: the 120-block Center City District (CCD), bounded by the Delaware River, the Vine Street Expressway, the Schuylkill River, and South Street.

The CCD "mission is to keep Center City Philadelphia clean, safe and attractive, an easy place to get around and a great place to do business, visit, and live."[84] The BID is governed by a twenty-three-member board of directors, which consists of major area property owners and businesses, realtors, and neighborhood civic leaders. In 2010 its annual budget was nearly $20 million. Revenues come primarily from a real estate tax surcharge of 7.5 percent on top of the annual real estate tax bill. In addition, the CCD has raised approximately $56 million in the last decade from foundations, local, state, and federal sources. It spends 29 percent of its annual revenues on cleaning and maintenance, 16 percent on safety and crime protection, 19 percent on services outside district boundaries and in the subway system (funded on a separate fee-for-service basis), 11 percent on marketing and communications, 7 percent on debt service on bonds used to finance capital improvements, and 18 percent on everything else.[85]

Paul Levy, CEO of the CCD, like Edmund Bacon, worked hard to gain a profound understanding of Philadelphia and developed an ability to gauge the reaction of the real estate industry to development projects. He has a similar facility for combining different ideas into a vision that is appealing to the city's leadership and to ordinary citizens, a willingness to adjust and readjust proposals till they are implementable and, like Bacon, a remarkable skill at promoting anything that he believes will benefit downtown Philadelphia. But, unlike Bacon, Levy runs an agency that spends $20 million per year delivering services. Thus, like Robert Moses, he manages the people and controls the

Center City Development, Philadelphia (2001). Street-sweeping equipment.

Center City Development, Philadelphia (2011). The Center City District keeps initiating new projects to improve the pedestrian character of the city.

money needed to make proposals happen, once they have been given legislative sanction.

The CCD started by providing basic services to make downtown clean and safe; it devoted money and personnel to marketing the

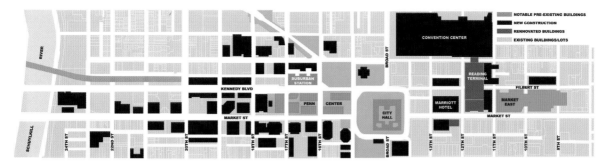

Center City, Philadelphia (2012). The replacement of the Chinese Wall with Penn Center paired with the creation of Market East has generated widespread development throughout downtown.

business district; and then made streetscape and public space improvements. Working with business, civic, foundation, institutional, and community leaders, it has promoted additional development along the Market Street corridor. Because so many white-collar businesses had moved to West Market Street, Mayor Edward Rendell made the transformation of South Broad Street into an Avenue of the Arts one of his priorities when he took office in 1992. The Avenue of the Arts today includes the Academy of Music (the old home of the Philadelphia Orchestra), the Kimmel Center (a new concert facility for the orchestra), the High School for Creative and Performing Arts, and numerous theaters and hotels. The CCD was part of the coalition that promoted the extension of Market East to a new Pennsylvania Convention Center in 1994 (and its further expansion to North Broad Street in 2011). In the first decade of the twenty-first century, the redevelopment of Philadelphia came full circle when the CCD helped to create a park along the Schuylkill River, which had been one of the components of the "new downtown" presented at the Better Philadelphia Exhibition in 1947.

An even more important extension of Bacon's legacy, however, has been Levy's emphasis on "the quality of the pedestrian experience and on civic spaces."[86] By 2010 the CCD had invested more than $55 million in streetscape, façade, and public area improvements.[87] Downtown Philadelphia today is "clean, safe, attractive, and well-managed."

Downtown Philadelphia is also economically more powerful today than it was in 1991, when the CCD began its work. Then, much of the Center City was empty after 5 P.M.; in 2010 it was alive with activity generated by the hospitality, convention, and tourist industries. These supported nearly 39,000 jobs, generated $804 million in taxes, and kept the city's sidewalks, restaurants, theaters, and hotel lobbies busy well into the evening.[88] The number of downtown hotel rooms has increased by 80 percent, and downtown Philadelphia receives more than 29 million tourists every year. By the end of the decade it boasted nearly 700 restaurants, takeout establishments, and other food-related businesses, 1,400 retail establishments, and, particularly significant, 12,250 apartments.[89] There is no better indication of the effectiveness of intelligent planning than the fact that Philadelphia was spared the fates of downtown Detroit, Cleveland, and St. Louis. Center-city Philadelphia had been reinvented. In 2010 it was one of the few older American downtowns that was busier and had an economy that was healthier than in 1950.

Paris (2010).

Chicago (2008).

New York (2009).

Philadelphia (2009).

EIGHT

PLAYING THE PLANNING GAME IN THE TWENTY-FIRST CENTURY

Paris, Chicago, New York, and Philadelphia won the planning game by devoting their efforts to the one thing over which they had control: the space shared by all residents of the city, its public realm. Paris engaged in a dramatic expansion of its public realm in the third quarter of the nineteenth century. Since then the city has more than doubled in population and is now the administrative center of a territory with 11.8 million people. Chicago has been making additional investments in the public realm since the publication of the *Plan of Chicago*. A century after its publication the city is "buzzing with life, humming with prosperity, sparkling with new buildings, new sculptures, new parks, and generally exuding vitality."[1] New York's mid-twentieth-century public realm investments have helped to accommodate a 60 percent increase in the city's population and a metropolitan population that has more than tripled. In Philadelphia, because of investments in the public realm and despite the loss of one-quarter of its population, "everything old [downtown is] new again: dense, diverse, and walkable . . . the regional hub for a multimodal transit network [that] provides employment opportunities for more than 160,000."[2]

All four of these cities won the planning game by adopting a public realm agenda.

Many Chicagoans and Philadelphians will tell you that an effective public realm approach to planning starts with a vision—a big idea that grabs people's imagination, something most people will want. As Daniel Burnham explained, "a noble logical diagram once recorded will never die; long after we are gone it will be a living thing, asserting itself with ever-growing intensity."[3] In the early twentieth century an effective plan, providing a compelling vision, was necessary to gain public acceptance for a program of investments in the public realm. But at the same time, cities throughout the nation adopted plans that were comprehensively ignored. By the latter part of the twentieth century even successful planners like Edmund Bacon had to worry about gaining the "confidence of a public made cynical by utopian futuramas and the inertia of local politicians."[4] As Burnham and Bacon both knew very well, vision alone is not enough. The planner has to convince the public that the vision can become reality—something they were both extremely skilled in doing.

Daniel Burnham died before much of his vision for the future of Chicago could be implemented. Implementation of the *Plan of Chicago* was largely the work of Walter Moody; Moody stressed the key role of marketing when he wrote that a successful city planner "must be a salesman—a salesman of civilization, convenience, health, and beauty . . . arousing interest, creating human desire, stirring the spirit for better things and inspiring human action."[5]

There are many ways to promote a vision. Robert Moses devoted two years to town meetings in Babylon, Oyster Bay, Hempstead, and the beachfront communities of Long Island, as well as to negotiations with political leaders in Nassau and Suffolk counties. That is what it took to obtain the approvals to create Jones Beach State Park. Once he had established a sufficiently impressive record of accomplishments, however, Moses, a genuine intellectual, preferred to promote his proposals by writing articles for the *New York Times* and other periodicals, making speeches, giving lectures, and publishing brochures and books. But whatever technique he employed at any particular moment, Moses, like anybody else who wishes to succeed at the planning game, was an accomplished marketer of his projects.

The displays at the 1947 Better Philadelphia Exhibition did the job of marketing a believable course of action better than any planning initiative before or since. Perhaps that is where Bacon became a master marketer. He used to say that he succeeded because whenever he said anything to a community group or civic organization he "always thought about what it would look like as a headline in the *Philadelphia Inquirer*."[6]

Vision and marketing, even in tandem, do not by themselves constitute planning. This is true even when the vision has been adopted by a government agency. Other aspects of execution are also essential: the timing must be appropriate; the financing must be in place; the implementing entity must be capable of taking the necessary actions; critical players must be able to provide entrepreneurial leadership; and a major effort must be made to insure ongoing public support.

Great patience is required of anyone who hopes to succeed in the planning game; good

planners know that there is a right moment for change. Those of us who work at it are usually impatient with the pace of change and eager to achieve what seems to us obvious and necessary. To win, however, we need the right opportunity, and we need to be ready to recognize and seize the right moment when it comes.

When is the time ripe for a proposal? There is no easy answer. Robert Moses exploited opportunities by combining constituencies. In the late 1930s, when a world's fair was proposed, Moses suggested locating it where he could create Flushing Meadows Corona Park, make improvements to the Grand Central Parkway, provide sewage treatment facilities for the surrounding neighborhoods, and use access to the fair as an additional reason to build the Bronx-Whitestone Bridge.

The important thing is to have the capacity to act effectively when it is time for a project to go forward. Edmund Bacon could be counted on to be around whenever his presence would make a difference. In the case of Penn Center he was ready with a reconstruction proposal when the Pennsylvania Railroad announced it would begin tearing down the Broad Street Station. He continued to be present wherever there was a chance to influence decisions, until Penn Center was completed.

There is no way to make anything happen without the necessary money and personnel. Haussmann was unusually effective at securing money and identifying talent. He knew he could not depend on annual tax revenues or legislative appropriations to pay for everything that he and Napoléon III had in mind. Consequently, he devised a variety of techniques for generating money. He issued bonds to pay for public improvements, confident that increased revenue from the improved properties would be sufficient to service the debt. He acquired more property than was necessary for a project and sold the surplus to private developers; the price they paid reflected the certainty that improvements to nearby public property would increase the value of their purchases. He had his contractors take out bank loans, and he paid

Whitestone and Throgs Neck bridges, New York (2007).

them back the amount of the debt when the project was satisfactorily completed. Finally, he persuaded Napoléon III to appropriate national funds when he was unable to pay for his projects using these other techniques.

Robert Moses was perhaps even more adept than Haussmann at financing his projects. Like Haussmann, he refused to depend on annual appropriations and avoided going to legislators for his highway, tunnel, and bridge projects. Instead, he convinced the bond market that toll revenues would cover future debt service on the bonds that paid their development costs. While he was dependent on New York City capital budget appropriations for park, beach, parkway, and playground development, he supplemented that money by attracting huge amounts of federal funding. Moses honed this ability during the Depression, when he pre-commissioned project plans and specifications so that he would be ready to take any federal funds that might be available for shovel-ready projects. He did the same in applying for Title I urban renewal subsidies.

Successful planners know they must attract the talent that will help them to produce great things. Haussmann's approach was to find and support capable executives, such as Alphand, Deschamps, and Belgrand, to run the agencies that executed projects. He earned and retained their personal loyalty, and he continually improved the working conditions of their staffs. Daniel Burnham's most eminent rival,

Louis Sullivan, wrote that Burnham helped his colleagues produce their best work by borrowing "heavily from the business and organizational principles of his capitalistic friends and clients."[7] While Edmund Bacon earned the loyalty of some of the brightest young planners at the Philadelphia Planning Commission, it was by collaborating with fine local architects that he was able to achieve his goals. George Howe, Louis Kahn, Oscar Stonorov, Vincent Kling, Romaldo Giurgola, and John Bower were among the architects who worked with him on a succession of projects. He was, however, always on the lookout for the best talent for a project. That is the reason that at the end of the competition for Society Hill Towers, he discarded previous designs by local architects and favored a team of New Yorkers built around developer William Zeckendorf and architect I. M. Pei.

Selecting a public agency to bring a vision to reality is quite different from making a deal with a private company. As Robert Moses observed:

> Government is not just another business with the profit motive left out—a business which, once divorced from politics, can readily be improved by itinerant experts armed with the lingo of efficiency. The electorate is not exactly like a group of stockholders who choose directors to run a corporation, and the Mayor is expected to have qualities, loyalties, and compulsions quite differ-

ent from those of a bank or business president."[8]

In one respect, government and business are very much alike: in both there is serious competition among the players. The major players we have examined here dealt with implementing entities differently—not only because they worked in different cities at different times, but because they adjusted their operations to political and economic conditions. Among the four, Haussmann probably best understood how to obtain approval from the various bureaucracies that had to be satisfied in order to proceed with his projects—even though he worked within a simpler governmental context, with fewer regulations than the other three. As the virtual CEO of Paris, he dealt with every aspect of running his city, and he had to balance the broadest set of interests and constituencies. It was perhaps to this end that he completely reorganized the government of Paris. And yet the public investments in Paris, as in the other three cities, eventually succumbed to political infighting.

Robert Moses began his adult life as a crusading reformer working to eliminate inefficient and corrupt government practices. It was this background that led him to use implementing agencies, such as the Long Island State Park Commission and the Triborough Bridge Authority, that were beyond interference from competing public officials. It is also the reason that he nurtured skilled civil service employees, who understood what he wanted to accomplish and who could implement his projects efficiently.

Moses operated in a manner very similar to Haussmann. As he enjoyed pointing out, "men, not charts and measures, make good government."[9] Over four decades, Moses developed a cadre of trusted colleagues, like Earle Andrews and Gilmore Clarke, who had administered large divisions within the agencies for which they later worked as professional consultants. They knew the nature of the work, and they knew what the agencies expected of them.

Entrepreneurial leadership is an intangible quality. In most cases entrepreneurial talent is combined with a strong personality. Robert Moses, certainly one of the most forceful personalities of the twentieth century, never relied on an ability to bully his way to victory. Throughout the Great Depression he remained dependent on funding from a national government whose president was his enemy. He knew that he would be forced from office if President Roosevelt had his way or if Mayor LaGuardia failed to be reelected. Consequently, he was acutely aware that he needed to amass visible accomplishments quickly. He could not wait for detailed studies to be done, nor consult all the people involved—he had to get things done. Thus, he announced the renovation of Bryant Park during his first year as parks commissioner and completed it the following year; he took only three years to complete the Triborough Bridge. During LaGuardia's first term, Moses built 265 playgrounds, 12 Olympic-size swimming pools, 8 golf courses, and 3 zoos.[10] Those projects contributed to the mayor's reelection and strengthened his continued support of Moses.

Bacon was a similarly astute government competitor. Like Burnham, but unlike Haussmann and Moses, he had no formal role in implementation. Therefore, when he proposed linking the two suburban rail lines at Market East and creating a commercial center above them, he owned none of the property, played no role in any of the businesses involved, and had no money to put into the deal. For years, nobody thought the project was feasible. Bacon persisted. Nineteen years later, it opened to the public. Bacon, in other words, had to devise projects that other entities would want to take on and that they would have the resources to bring to fruition.

Succeeding at the planning game requires still more than marketing, human and financial resources, and entrepreneurship. Because public investment strategies always face opposition, planning requires a continuous effort to maintain public support. The memory of opposition to most successful public works fades away, but the longer a public career endures, the more opponents a planner collects often until he is at last forced from the field. Burnham was the only one of the four legendary public entrepreneurs considered in this book who was not forced out. He had been dead for more than a decade when the *Chicago Tribune* revealed widespread graft, before the voters began to reject bond issues recommended by the Chicago Plan Commission.

Unlike Burnham, who held no public office, Haussmann, Moses, and Bacon in time succumbed to their accumulated opposition. The number and virulence of their opponents eventually grew to overcome the widespread (but often shallow) support for their investment programs. They became political liabilities and were forced from office. The rules apply even to the giants of the game.

It is, however, more difficult to determine whether the public investment strategies they advocated lost public support. Paris continued to extend broad new boulevards through the old city; many of them continued projects that Haussmann had initiated. Similarly, the lakeshore and regional parks of Chicago are still being enlarged and improved. But the federal urban renewal program, which both Moses and Bacon supported, was largely discarded by the mid-1970s. And as to highway construction, there remains both widespread support and heated opposition.

There is, as well, considerable debate about whether some of the things Haussmann, Moses, and Bacon accomplished were desirable, and even more debate about the appropriateness of what they did to accomplish their goals. There can be no debate, however, about whether they were winners in the planning game.

The neighborhood squares of nineteenth-century Paris, the lakeshore beaches of early-twentieth-century Chicago, the playgrounds of Depression-era New York City, and the greenways of later-twentieth-century Philadelphia continue to be remodeled to meet contemporary tastes, but they are used as actively today as they were when they were created. The boulevards of nineteenth-century Paris, the bridges across the Chicago River, the highways of the New York metropolitan region, and the

rail-transit connections in downtown Philadelphia continue to make it easier and cheaper for people to get to their jobs. The boulevards of Paris are still the framework that shapes private real estate development; so are Chicago's nearly twenty-four-mile-long string of lakeshore parks, the Long Island parkway network, and Philadelphia's redeveloped public realm along East and West Market Street.

Despite the successes, there is today a pervasive skepticism about the ability of planners, or anybody else, to improve a neighborhood, city, suburb, or region. This skepticism is the result of a belief that times have changed. The changes usually cited include: environmental protection legislation, designation of landmarks and historic districts, widespread citizen involvement in decision-making, the property-rights backlash, and the explosion of government regulation. With the possible exception of historic preservation, none of these factors would have prevented Paris, Chicago, New York, or Philadelphia from making the changes described in this book.

What environmentalist would try to stop Paris from creating a sewer system, Chicago from acquiring a park system, New York from preserving the wetlands in Jamaica Bay, or Philadelphia from eliminating the source of noise and soot that poured out from the elevated railroad coming into the center of the city? Haussmann, working in nineteenth-century France, had to obtain as many, if not more, permits and signatures to condemn a property as any government official in twenty-first-century America. The courts held up the creation of Chicago's North Michigan Avenue for several years while they dealt with suits filed by property owners. Jones Beach was built only because Robert Moses spent two years going to town meetings in his successful effort to obtain citizen approval. Edmund Bacon spent even longer making Market East possible.

Haussmann, Burnham, Moses, and Bacon would have told us that regulations and requirements are a fact of life in any planning process and that ignoring them guarantees failure; but they also would have been quick to point out that their successes were the product of intelligent public spending on public property, not the product of complying with regulations.

These planners succeeded when they did things that most people wanted. They failed when their projects threatened to cause excessive harm to any particular set of interests. Nevertheless, their prodigious talents—a compelling vision, powerful marketing and salesmanship, and effective implementation—went a long way toward achieving what people wanted. Contemporary planners get so little done in part because they devote too much time to obtaining and organizing data, surveying public opinion, and complying with proper procedure, and too little time getting right the substance of what they are proposing.

In the end, however, success at the planning game always necessitates doing things that people want. Parisians wanted a sewer system, a reliable supply of potable water, and convenient travel to employment, shopping, and recreation. Chicagoans wanted North and South Michigan Avenue to be connected, as well as a regional park system and the reclamation of Lake Michigan. New Yorkers wanted

Michigan Avenue at Grant Park, 1880s.

the beaches of Long Island, the Bronx, Brooklyn, Queens, and Staten Island to be open to the public; they wanted an easy-to-use system of bridges, tunnels, and highways; and they thought there should be recreational facilities in every neighborhood. Philadelphians wanted the Chinese Wall torn down, the Dock Street Market moved, and easy transit and pedestrian circulation downtown.

Successful planners must propose "the right thing," but they always adjust their proj-

Michigan Avenue at Grant Park, 2010.

ects to meet changing economic and political requirements. Gaining acceptance for planning proposals requires compromise; the players get or give up something they want. They identify and combine the requirements of various constituencies. The winners end up with a result different from their original proposal—something that serves additional purposes, augments the rationale for the project, and picks up additional, and sometimes unexpected, supporters.

Persistence is as important as flexibility. Edmund Bacon, probably the most relentless and determined of all planners, believed that the most important and difficult thing to do was deciding what to advocate, and that the trick in making that decision was selecting something that you could bring to fruition. He used to say that once you decided that something was the right thing to do, you had to devise "your own approach" to getting it done "without giving a damn about other people's ideas."[11] Planning isn't easy. It requires knowledge, skill, good judgment, obedience to the political and economic rules as they apply to planning, and a great deal of luck.

What, then, is the answer to the question posed at the beginning of this book? Are we really capable of establishing good government through reflection and choice, or are we destined to make decisions by accident and force? The answer is both, and in that answer lies the very essence of the planning game.

Society Hill, Philadelphia (2011).

NOTES

1. THE PLANNING GAME

1. Paul Davidoff, "Advocacy and Pluralism in Planning," *Journal of the American Institute of Planners* 21, no. 4 (November 1965). Later published in Richard T. LeGates and Frederic Stout, *The City Reader*, 2nd ed. (New York: Routledge, 1996), 423–33.
2. City of Charleston, *Zoning Ordinance* (Charleston: 1973), 24–25.
3. Alexander Garvin, *The American City: What Works, What Doesn't* (New York: McGraw-Hill, 2002), 290.
4. Walter Moody, *What of the City* (Chicago: A. C. McClurg & Co., 1919), 4, 9–10.
5. Ibid., 18.
6. Ibid., 32.
7. Alexander Garvin, "Philadelphia's Planner: A Conversation with Edmund Bacon," *Journal of Planning History* 1, no. 1 (February 2002), 72.
8. Jane Jacobs, *The Death and Life of Great American Cities* (New York: Random House, 1961), 23.
9. President Dwight D. Eisenhower, speech to the National Executive Reserve Conference (Washington, DC: November 14, 1957).

2. THE PLAYERS

1. Winston Churchill, speech in the House of Commons (London: November 11, 1947).
2. Alexander Garvin, *The American City: What Works, What Doesn't* (New York: McGraw-Hill, 2002), 299.
3. Historic District Development Corporation. https://sites.google.com/site/historicdistrictdevelopment/.
4. Roger Sale, *Seattle Past to Present* (Seattle: University of Washington Press, 1976), 223–27.
5. Sally B. Woodbridge and Roger Montgomery, *A Guide to the Architecture of Washington State* (Seattle: University of Washington Press, 1980), 134–36.
6. Alan J. Stein, "Essay 1244: Seattle City Council Votes for Urban Renewal of Pike Place Market on June 17, 1969," (June 4, 1999), http://historylink.org/index.cfm?DisplayPage=output.cfm&file_id=1244.
7. Thomas Veith, "Victor Steinbrueck," in *Shaping Seattle Architecture: A Historical Guide to the Architects*, ed. Jeffrey Karl Ochsner (Seattle: University of Washington Press, 1994), 276–281; Stein, "Seattle City Council."
8. Stein, "Seattle City Council."
9. http://www.squidoo.com/Seattle-Pike-Place -Market.
10. Dan McNichol, *The Incredible Story of the U.S. Interstate System* (New York: Sterling, 2006), 157.
11. 401 U.S. 402 (91 S. Ct. 814, 28 L.Ed.2d 136, 1971)
12. Charles Newman (one of the attorneys who represented Citizens to Preserve Overton Park), interview with the author, February 2, 2011.
13. Max Protetch, *A New World Trade Center: Design Proposals from Leading Architects Worldwide* (New York: ReganBooks, 2002), 1–147.
14. John Sergeant, *Frank Lloyd Wright's Usonian Houses* (New York: Whitney Library of Design, 1984), 121–36.
15. David Schuyler and Jane Turner Censer, eds., *The Papers of Frederick Law Olmsted*, vol. 6 (Baltimore: Johns Hopkins University Press, 1992), 279.
16. Ibid., 286.
17. Ebenezer Howard, *To-Morrow: A Peaceful Path to Real Reform* (1898; repr., London: Routledge, 2003).
18. Ray Thomas and Peter Cresswell, *The New Town Idea* (Milton Keynes, Buckinghamshire: Open University Press, 1973), 26.

19. Garvin, *The American City*, 409–11.

20. Richard Weston, *Modernism* (New York: Phaidon Press, 1996), 90–140.

21. Le Corbusier, *Le Corbusier, 1910–1929* (1929; repr., Basel: Birkhäuser, 1995), 38.

22. Ibid., 109–17.

23. Le Corbusier, *The Radiant City* (1933; repr., New York: Orion Press, 1967), 221.

24. Garvin, *The American City*, 256–59.

25. Alexander Alland, Sr., *Jacob Riis: Photographer and Citizen* (New York: Aperture, 1974), 5.

26. Jacob A. Riis, *How the Other Half Lives* (1890; repr., New York: Dover Publications, 1971).

27. Jacob A. Riis, *The Battle with the Slum* (1900; repr., as *Jacob Riis Revisited: Poverty and the Slum in Another Era*, Garden City, NY: Anchor Books, 1968), 301.

28. Garvin, *The American City*, 36–37.

29. Jacob A. Riis, *The Peril and the Preservation of the Home* (Philadelphia: George W. Jacobs & Co., 1903), 146.

30. Garvin, *The American City*, 233.

31. Robert W. DeForest and Lawrence Veiller, *The Tenement House Problem* (New York: Macmillan, 1903), 3; Citizens Housing & Planning Council of New York City, Marian Sameth and Ruth Dickler Archival Library.

32. Dr. Moon Wha Lee, *Housing New York City, 2005* (New York: New York City Department of Housing, Preservation, and Development, 2006); Citizens Housing & Planning Council of New York City, Marian Sameth and Ruth Dickler Archival Library.

33. Robert Wojtowicz, *Sidewalk Critic: Lewis Mumford's Writing on New York* (New York: Princeton Architectural Press, 1998), 12–29.

34. Garvin, *The American City*, 325–29.

35. *The City* © 1939, directed by Ralph Steiner and Willard van Dyke.

36. Howard Gillette, Jr., *Civitas by Design* (Philadelphia: University of Pennsylvania Press, 2010), 45–59.

37. Jane Jacobs, *The Death and Life of Great American Cities* (New York: Random House, 1961), 4.

38. Ibid., 19.

39. Ibid., 14.

40. Ibid., 150.

41. http://www.minneapolisparks.org.

42. Melvin G. Holli, *The American Mayor: The Best and the Worst Big-City Leaders* (University Park: Pennsylvania State University Press, 1999), 210.

43. Jacquelin Robertson, interview with the author, March 9, 2011.

44. http://www.miami21.org/Miami_Zoning_History.asp.

45. http://www.censusscope.org/us/m5960/chart_popl.html.

46. J. Joseph Huthmacher, *Senator Robert F. Wagner and the Rise of Urban Liberalism* (New York: Atheneum, 1971), 362.

47. Ibid., 3–11.

48. Ibid., 98–102, 163–71.

49. Nick Taylor, *American-Made: The Enduring Legacy of the WPA* (New York: Bantam Books, 2008), 135–36.

50. Ibid., 524–25.

51. Public Works Administration, *America Builds the Record of PWA* (Washington, DC: Government Printing Office, 1939), 8, 264.

52. Ibid.

53. Ibid., 213–16.

54. Garvin, *The American City*, 400–3.

55. New York City Department of City Planning, "Manhattan Office Space Market, 1960–1978" (unpublished, New York: 1979).

56. Robert A. M. Stern, Thomas Mellins, and David Fishman, *New York 1960* (New York: Monacelli Press, 1995), 167–70.

57. Ibid.

58. http://www.tpl.org/.

59. http://www.bridgehousing.com/.

60. William S. Worley, *J. C. Nichols and the Shaping of Kansas City* (Columbia: University of Missouri Press, 1990), 63.

61. Ibid., 112.

62. Garvin, *The American City*, 119–22.

63. http://www.allcountries.org/uscensus/1293_shopping_centers_number_gross_leasable_area.html.

64. Miles L. Berger, *They Built Chicago: Entrepreneurs Who Built A Great City's Architecture* (Chicago: Bonus Books, 1992), 232–44.

65. Ibid.

66. "Walls of Big Co-op Rising on S. Shore," *Chicago Daily Tribune*, July 11, 1948.

67. Berger, *They Built Chicago*, 233.

68. "Walls of Big Co-op Rising on S. Shore."

69. Robert J. Mowitz and Deil S. Wright, *Profile of a Metropolis* (Detroit: Wayne State University Press, 1962), 73.

3. THE RULES OF THE GAME

1. Alexander Garvin, *The American City: What Works, What Doesn't* (New York: McGraw-Hill, 2002), 418–91.

2. Walter Muir Whitehall, *Boston: A Topographical History* (Cambridge: Belknap Press, 1968), 41–43, 95–97.

3. Boston Redevelopment Authority, *1965–1975 General Plan for the City of Boston and the Regional Core* (Boston: 1965), 135.

4. Boston Redevelopment Authority, *Loan and Grant Application for Downtown Waterfront-Faneuil Hall*, submitted to HUD (Boston: 1964), 1.

5. Jane Thompson, interview with the author, May 27, 2010.

6. Joshua Olsen, *Better Places, Better Lives: A Biography of James Rouse* (Washington, DC: Urban Land Institute, 2003), 240. In an April 9, 2010, interview with

the author, Simon said he telephoned Rouse. Joshua Olsen refers to a letter dated March 2, 1972, from Simon to Rouse.

7. Olsen, *Better Places, Better Lives*, 243.
8. John Quincy, Jr., *Quincy Market: A Boston Landmark* (Boston: Northeastern University Press, 2003), 184.
9. Olsen, *Better Places, Better Lives*, 243–47.
10. Quincy, *Quincy Market*, 188.
11. Twenty percent of net operating income in excess of $3 million, 10 percent in excess of $4 million, and 11 percent above $5 million.
12. Quincy, *Quincy Market*, 193.
13. Ibid., 191.
14. Olsen, *Better Places, Better Lives*, 259–60.
15. Ibid., 90–93.
16. Martin Millspaugh, ed., *Baltimore's Charles Center: A Case Study of Downtown Renewal* (Washington, DC: Urban Land Institute, 1964), 13, 15, 31, 60.
17. Garvin, *The American City*, 161–64.
18. Michael Weiler Halle, "Baltimore's Inner Harbor" (unpublished manuscript, New Haven: 1997), 1–80; Howard F. Gillette, Jr., "The Inner Harbor, Baltimore, Maryland," *Land Forum*, no. 7 (December 2000).
19. Bruce Alexander, interview with the author, June 7, 2010.
20. Douglas M. Wrenn, *Urban Waterfront Development* (Washington DC: Urban Land Institute, 1983), 283–84.
21. Ibid.,152.
22. Howard Gillette, Jr., *Civitas by Design* (Philadelphia: University of Pennsylvania Press, 2010), 95–105.
23. Alexander, interview, June 7, 2010.
24. *Baltimore Sun*, October 8, 1977, A17.
25. C. Fraser Smith, "Harborplace Fight Pushes Politicians into Background as Year's Hottest Issue," *Baltimore Sun*, November 1, 1978, C1.
26. Ibid.
27. Ibid.
28. Olsen, *Better Places, Better Lives*, 286.
29. Wrenn, *Urban Waterfront Development*, 152.
30. Garvin, *The American City*, 178–88.
31. Roberto Brambilla and Gianni Longo, *For Pedestrians Only: Planning, Design, and Management of Traffic-Free Zones* (New York: Whitney Library of Design, 1977), 179.
32. Ibid.
33. Garvin, *The American City*, 133.
34. Olsen, *Better Places, Better Lives*, 252.
35. Ibid., 263.
36. Ibid., 266.
37. Garvin, *The American City*, 451–53.
38. Arthur M. Coppola (chairman and CEO of Macerich) and Randy Brant (executive CP of Macerich), interview with the author, January 20, 2011.
39. Ibid.
40. Walker Art Center, *The Architecture of Frank Gehry* (New York: Rizzoli, 1986), 84.

4. THE PUBLIC REALM APPROACH

1. Tertius Chandler and Gerald Fox, *3000 Years of Urban Growth* (New York: Academic Press, 1974), 373.
2. Société Historique et Archéologique des IVe et IIIe Arrondissements de Paris, *Les Inondations de Paris à travers les âges (Cité et Marais)* (Paris: H. Daragon, 1910), 30–31.
3. http://www.demographia.com.
4. Henri Lecouturier, *Paris incompatible avec la République* (Paris: 1848), 20.
5. Colin Jones, *Paris: The Biography of a City* (New York: Viking, 2002), 283.
6. Ibid., 19.
7. Georges-Eugene Haussmann, *Mémoires du Baron Haussmann: Tome III* (1890; repr., Boston: Elibron Classics, 2006), 457–58.
8. Karl Marx, *The 18th Brumaire of Louis Bonaparte* (New York: 1852; repr., New York: International Publishers, 2008), 43.
9. Alain Plessis, *The Rise and Fall of the Second Empire, 1852–1871*, trans. Jonathan Mandelbaum (Cambridge: Cambridge University Press, 1987), 25–57; Michel Carmona, *Haussmann: His Life and Times and the Making of Modern Paris*, trans. Patrick Camiller (Chicago: Ivan D. Dee, 2002), 200.
10. Willet Weeks, *The Man Who Made Paris Paris* (London: London House, 1999), 18–26, 37–45.
11. Carmona, *Haussmann*, 69, 108–10, 192–96.
12. Jean-Jacques Dudillieu, "Les Concessions à L'Époque d'Haussmann," in Jean Des Cars and Pierre Pinon, *Paris: Haussmann* (Paris: Éditions du Pavillon de l'Arsenal, 1991), 226.
13. Haussmann, *Mémoires: Tome III*, 2.
14. Carmona, *Haussmann*, 161.
15. Ibid., 219–21.
16. Haussmann, *Mémoires: Tome III*, 15.
17. Ibid., 9.
18. Ibid., 111–21.
19. Ibid., 496–97.
20. Ibid., 480.
21. Ibid., 481.
22. Carmona, *Haussmann*, 228.
23. Ibid., 274, 400.
24. David H. Pinkney, *Napoléon III and the Rebuilding of Paris* (Princeton: Princeton University Press, 1972), 115.
25. Haussmann, *Mémoires, Tome III*, 294–95.
26. Carmona, *Haussmann*, 345–47.
27. Pinkney, *Napoléon III*, 125–26.
28. Weeks, *The Man*, 63; Pinkney, *Napoléon III*, 10.
29. Pinkney, *Napoléon III*, 123, 126.
30. Ibid., 19–21.

31. Pierre Pinon, "Les Procédures et Les Services," in Jean Des Cars and Pierre Pinon, *Paris: Haussmann* (Paris: Éditions du Pavillion de l'Arsenal, 1991), 98.

32. Ibid., 94–95; Carmona, *Haussmann*, 210–11.

33. For a detailed discussion of expropriation practices, see Pinon, "Les Procédures," 72–79, and Carmona, *Hanssmann*, 158–61.

34. Haussmann, *Mémoires: Tome III*, 48.

35. Pierre Pinon, *Atlas du Paris Haussmannien* (Paris: Éditions Parigramme, 2002), 33–42.

36. Sigfried Giedion, *Space, Time, and Architecture* (Cambridge: Harvard University Press, 1956), 644.

37. Pinon, *Atlas du Paris*, 172–73.

38. Ibid., 13–27.

39. Anthony Sutcliffe, *Paris: An Architectural History* (New Haven: Yale University Press, 1993), 29, 53.

40. Ibid., 70.

41. Ibid., 86.

42. François Loyer, *Paris Nineteenth Century: Architecture and Urbanism* (New York: Abbeville Press, 1988), 234, 387, 390, 407–8.

43. Pinkney, *Napoléon III*, 70.

44. Patrice de Moncan, *Les Grands Boulevards de Paris de la Bastille à la Madeleine* (Paris: Les Editions du Mécène, 1997), 83–86.

45. Oscar Hammerstein II, "The Last Time I Saw Paris," from the film *Lady Be Good* (1941, music by Jerome Kern).

46. Adolphe Alphand, *Les Promenades de Paris* (1873; repr., as *Connaissance et Mémoires*, Paris: 2002), 3–5.

47. Alphand, *Les Promenades*, 6; Haussmann, *Mémoires: Tome III*, 312–13.

48. Alphand, *Les Promenades*, 6, 246.

49. Alexander Garvin, *Public Parks: The Key to Livable Communities* (New York: Norton, 2010), 138–39.

50. Alphand, *Les Promenades*, 246.

51. Ibid., 171–72.

52. Pinon, *Atlas Du Paris*, 168–69; Carmona, *Haussmann*, 288–91.

53. Alphand, *Les Promenades*, 191–98.

54. Haussmann, *Mémoires*, Tome III, 232–324.

55. Alphand, *Les Promenades*, 246.

56. Alain Frèrejean, "Preface" in Alphand, *Les Promenades*, 11.

57. Pinkney, *Napoléon III*, 72.

58. Carmona, *Haussmann*, 407–10; Pinon, *Atlas du Paris*, 129–32.

59. Haussmann, *Mémoires: Tome III*, 502.

60. Eugène Sue, *Les Mystères de Paris* (Paris: Robert Laffont, 1998), 31–33; Carmona, *Haussmann*, 295

61. Haussmann, *Mémoires: Tome III*, 87.

62. Pinkney, *Napoléon III*, 180–91.

63. Pinkney, *Napoléon III*, 58–60.

64. Carmona, *Haussmann*, 192–93.

65. Pinkney, *Napoléon III*, 193.

66. Carmona, *Haussmann*, 424.

67. Weeks, *The Man*, 132–33

68. Ibid., 132.

69. Quoted in Pierre Pinon, "Les Comptes Fantastiques d'Haussmann," in Jean des Cars and Pierre Pinon, *Paris: Haussmann* (Paris: Éditions du Pavillion de l'Arsenal, 1991), 167.

70. Weeks, *The Man*, 132–35.

71. Ibid., 168.

72. Ibid., 134.

73. *Paris Comique Journal Illustré*, January 15, 1870, cover.

74. F. Scott Fitzgerald, "Babylon Revisited," in *Taps at Reveille* (New York: Scribner, 1976; originally published in *Saturday Evening Post*, 1931), 322–23.

75. World Commission on Environment and Development, *Our Common Future* (Oxford: Oxford University Press, 1987), 8.

76. The Port of Paris Authority, http://www.paris-ports.fr/tourisme/tourisme-loisirs.

77. L'Office de Tourisme et des Congrès, *Le Tourisme à Paris: Chiffres clés* (2009), 25.

78. City of Paris, http://www.paris.fr/portail/english/Portal.lut?page_id=8125&document_type_id=5&document_id=29918&portlet_id=18748 (accessed on July 9, 2010).

5. THE PLANNING PROCESS THAT TRANSFORMED CHICAGO

1. Chicago Plan Commission, *Ten Years' Work of the Chicago Plan Commission: 1909–1919* (Chicago: 1920), 5, 1023.

2. Marion Clawson, *The Land System of the United States* (Lincoln: University of Nebraska Press, 1968), 37, 46–47.

3. Harold M. Mayer and Richard C. Wade, *Chicago: Growth of a Metropolis* (Chicago: University of Chicago Press, 1969), 98; Alice Sinkevitch, ed., *AIA Guide to Chicago* (Chicago: Chicago Architecture Joint Venture, 2004), 109–10.

4. James Grossman, Ann Durkin Keating, and Janice L. Rieff, eds., *The Encyclopedia of Chicago* (Chicago: University of Chicago Press, 2004), 146.

5. Lois Wille, *Forever Open, Clear, and Free: The Struggle for Chicago's Lakefront* (Chicago: University of Chicago Press, 1972), 71–81.

6. Dick Simpson, *Rogues, Rebels, and Rubber Stamps: The Politics of the Chicago City Council from 1863 to the Present* (Boulder, Colorado: Westview Press, 2001), 52–53.

7. Dwight H. Perkins, *The Metropolitan Park System: Report of the Special Commission to the City of Chicago, 1904* (Chicago: 1905), 63.

8. Daniel Burnham and Edward Bennett, *Plan of Chicago* (1909; repr., New York: Da Capo Press, 1970), 4.

9. Alexander Garvin, *Public Parks: The Key to Livable Communities* (New York: Norton, 2010), 124–26.

10. Frederick Law Olmsted, "The Landscape Architecture of the World's Columbian Exposition," *Inland Architect and News Record* (September 1893), 21.

11. Henry Van Brunt, "Architecture at the World's Columbian Exposition," pt. 1, *CIMM* 44 (May 1892), 94; and pt. 2 (September 1892), 726.

12. R. Reid Badger, *The Great American Fair: The World's Columbian Exposition and American Culture* (Chicago: Nelson Hall, 1979), 177.

13. Walter Moody, *What of the City?* (Chicago: A. C. McClurg & Co., 1919), 315.

14. Charles Edward Merriam, *Chicago: A More Intimate View of Urban Politics* (New York: Macmillan, 1929), 6.

15. Walter Moody, *Wacker's Manual of the Plan of Chicago*, 2nd ed. (Chicago: Chicago Plan Commission, 1916), 67.

16. Ibid., 11.

17. Charles Moore, *Daniel H. Burnham, Architect, Planner of Cities* (1921; repr., New York: Da Capo Press, 1968), 98–99.

18. Ibid., 99.

19. Thomas S. Hines, *Burnham of Chicago* (New York: Oxford University Press, 1974), 314; Carl Smith, *The Plan of Chicago: David Burnham and the Remaking of the American City* (Chicago: University of Chicago Press, 2006), 67.

20. James Mayo, *The American Country Club: Its Origins and Development* (New Brunswick, NJ: Rutgers University Press, 1998), 7–34.

21. Hines, *Burnham of Chicago*, 317.

22. Moore, *Daniel H. Burnham*, 203–8.

23. Ibid., 209–14.

24. Robert Bruegmann, *The Architects and the City: Holabird & Roche of Chicago, 1880–1918* (Chicago: University of Chicago Press, 1997), 285; Hines, *Burnham of Chicago*, 269–71.

25. Kristen Schaffer, *Daniel H. Burnham: Visionary Architect and Planner* (New York: Rizzoli, 2003), 13, 15.

26. Louis Sullivan, *The Autobiography of an Idea* (Mineola, NY: Dover Publications, 1956), 314.

27. John A. Peterson, *The Birth of City Planning in the United States, 1840–1917* (Baltimore: Johns Hopkins University Press, 2003), 80–93, 106–7, 157–58, 161–62, 171–72, 178–90, 186–87.

28. Moody, *What of the City?*, 25.

29. Peterson, *The Birth of City Planning*, 215.

30. Burnham and Bennett, *Plan of Chicago*, xv.

31. Charles Norton, in Walter Moody, *What of the City?*, 326.

32. Harvey A. Kantor, "Charles Dyer Norton," in *The American Planner: Biographies and Recollections*, ed. Donald A. Krueckeberg (New York: Methuen, 1983), 179–207.

33. Carl Smith, *The Plan of Chicago: Daniel Burnham and the Remaking of the American City* (Chicago: University of Chicago Press, 2006), 67; Burnham and Bennett, *Plan of Chicago*, xv; Moody, *What of the City?*, 320.

34. Alan Brinkley, "The National Resources Planning Board and the Reconstruction of Planning," in *The American Planning Tradition*, ed. Robert Fishman (Washington, DC: Woodrow Wilson Center Press, 2000), 174.

35. Moody, *What of the City?*, 26.

36. Kristen Schaffer, "Fabric of City Life: The Social Agenda in Burnham's Draft of the Plan of Chicago," in Daniel Burnham and Edward Bennett, *Plan of Chicago* (1909; repr., New York: Princeton Architectural Press, 1993), vii.

37. Burnham and Bennett, *Plan of Chicago*, 8.

38. There is no known source for this quotation, but it is always attributed to Daniel Burnham. It is quoted in a 1918 Christmas card from Willis Polk to Edward Bennett as a statement Burnham made in 1907.

39. Bruegmann, *The Architects and the City*, 390.

40. Moody, *Wacker's Manual of the Plan of Chicago*, xiv.

41. Moore, *Daniel H. Burnham*, 113.

42. Burnham and Bennett, *Plan of Chicago*, 7.

43. Thomas J. Schlereth, "Burnham's *Plan* and Moody's *Manual*: City Planning as Progressive Reform," in *The American Planner Biographies and Recollections*, ed. Donald A. Krueckeberg (New York: Methuen, 1983), 74; Chicago Plan Commission, *Chicago's Greatest Issue: An Official Plan* (Chicago: 1911), 7.

44. Moody, *What of the City?*, 1.

45. Ibid., 107–10.

46. Ibid., 97.

47. Chicago Plan Commission, *Ten Years' Work of the Chicago Plan Commission*, 11–13, 1029–31.

48. Moody, *Wacker's Manual*, xv.

49. Dennis McClendon, *The Plan of Chicago: A Regional Legacy* (Chicago: Burnham Plan Centennial Committee, 2008), 2.

50. Garvin, *Public Parks*, 129–30.

51. Smith, *The Plan of Chicago*, 136; Mayer and Wade, *Chicago*, 310–11.

52. Carl W. Condit, *Chicago 1930–1970: Building, Planning, and Urban Technology* (Chicago: University of Chicago Press, 1974), 233.

53. Garvin, *Public Parks*, 121–36.

54. John W. Stamper, *Chicago's North Michigan Avenue: Planning and Development 1900–1930* (Chicago: University of Chicago Press, 1991), 4.

55. Ibid., 4–6.

56. Ibid, 17.

57. Ibid., 12–18.

58. Chicago Plan Commisson, *Chicago Plan Progress* (Chicago: 1927), 21

59. Alexander Garvin, *The American City: What Works, What Doesn't* (New York: McGraw-Hill, 2002), 182–83.

60. See http://www.lccmr.leg.mn/.

61. Burnham and Bennett, *Plan of Chicago*, 132.

62. Ibid., 130.

63. Chicago Plan Commission, *Ten Years' Work*, 5, 1023.

64. See http://www.chicagoparkdistrict.com/index.cfm/fuseaction/parks.home.cfm.

65. Mayer and Wade, *Chicago*; Wille, *Forever Open, Clear, and Free.*

66. Moody, *Wacker's Manual*, 112.

67. Carl W. Condit, *Chicago 1910–1929: Building, Planning, and Urban Technology* (Chicago: University of Chicago Press, 1973), 195–97.

68. Ibid., 250–52.

69. Chicago Plan Commission, *The Outer Drive Chicago* (Chicago: 1929), 153.

70. Carl W. Condit, *Chicago 1930–1970*, 24.

71. Burnham and Bennett, *Plan of Chicago*, 2.

72. Chicago Plan Commission, *Ten Years' Work*, 60–62, 1078–80.

73. Chicago Plan Commission, *Chicago Plan Progress*, 24

74. Moody, *What of the City?*, 30.

75. Chicago Plan Committee, *Chicago Plan Progress.*

76. Smith, *The Plan of Chicago*, 133.

77. http://www.usinflationcalculator.com.

78. Daniel Burnham, "City of the Future Under a Democratic Government," *Transactions of the Town Planning Conference, Oct 10, 1910* (London: R.I.B.A, 1910), 369.

79. Moody, *What of the City?*,143–45.

80. William H. Stuart, *The Twenty Incredible Years* (Chicago: M. A. Donohue, 1935), 24.

81. Moody, *What of the City?*, 370.

82. Merriam, *Chicago*, 29.

83. Ibid., 30.

84. Simpson, *Rogues, Rebels, and Rubber Stamps*, 78–79.

85. Board of Local Improvements, *A Sixteen-Year Record of Achievement 1915–1931*, compiled by A. E. Burnett and Michael J. Faherty and Associates (Chicago: Buckley, Dement & Co., 1931), 41.

86. Chicago Plan Commission, *Facing the Future* (Chicago: 1941), 1.

6. GROWING METROPOLITAN NEW YORK

1. Robert C. Wood with Vladimir V. Almendinger, *1400 Governments: The Political Economy of the New York Metropolitan Region* (New York: Anchor Books, 1964), 297.

2. David C. Hammack, "Consolidation," in *The Encyclopedia of New York City*, ed. Kenneth T. Jackson (New Haven: Yale University Press, 1995), 277–78.

3. Gerald Benjamin and Edward T. O'Donnell, "Charter," in *The Encyclopedia of New York City*, ed. Kenneth T. Jackson, 202–8.

4. Walter Laidlaw, "When Will New York Overtake London in Population," *New York Times*, June 4, 1911, Magazine Section, SM3.

5. Jon C. Teaford, *Post-Suburbia Government and Politics in the Edge Cities* (Baltimore: Johns Hopkins University Press, 1997), 249.

6. Committee on the City Plan, *Development and Present Status of City Planning in New York City* (New York: Board of Estimate and Apportionment, 1914), 12.

7. Harvey A. Kantor, "Charles Dyer Norton," in *The American Planner: Biographies and Recollections*, ed. Donald A. Krueckeberg (New York: Methuen, 1983), 180–81

8. David A. Johnson, "Regional Planning for the Great American Metropolis: New York Between the World Wars," in *Two Centuries of American Planning*, ed. Daniel Schaffer (Baltimore: Johns Hopkins University Press, 1988), 176.

9. Thomas Adams, *The Building of the City: Regional Plan*, vol. 5 (New York: Regional Plan of New York and Its Environs, 1931), 486–86, 489–99, 542.

10. Daniel Burnham and Edward Bennett, *Plan of Chicago* (1909; repr., New York: Da Capo Press, 1970), 2.

11. Harvey A. Kantor, "Charles Dyer Norton," 192.

12. Julius Henry Cohen, "Developing the Port of New York: An Address," speech to the National Rivers and Harbors Congress (Washington, DC: December 6, 1922).

13. Ibid., 4.

14. Jameson W. Doig, *Empire on the Hudson: Entrepreneurial Vision and Political Power at the Port of New York Authority* (New York: Columbia University Press, 2001), 55, 81.

15. http://www.panynj.gov/press-room/.

16. Keith D. Revell, *Building Gotham: Civic Culture and Public Policy in New York City, 1898–1938* (Baltimore: Johns Hopkins University Press, 2003), 75–80.

17. Doig, *Empire on the Hudson*, 97–119.

18. There are two biographies of Moses: Cleveland Rodgers, *Robert Moses: Builder for Democracy* (New York: Henry Holt, 1952); and Robert A. Caro, *The Power Broker: Robert Caro and the Fall of New York* (New York: Knopf, 1974). A thorough compendium of his projects can be found in Hilary Ballon and Kenneth T. Jackson, *Robert Moses and the Modern City: The Transformation of New York* (New York: Norton, 2007), and a myriad of books discuss some aspect of his work. Rodgers, who worked with Moses, gives a very favorable account of what Moses wanted people to know about him up to the time of its publication. Caro's book is considered by many to be the definitive work on Moses. It is a marvelously written and exhaustively researched thriller that is difficult to put down

until one has finished all 1,246 pages. But the book contains errors of fact, sometimes provides an erroneous context for the events it describes, and includes opinions that ignore important, relevant information. Thus, despite my admiration of the author's achievement, I have avoided using any information from *The Power Broker* that is not corroborated by at least one other unbiased reference. Instead, wherever possible, I have relied on newspaper articles, primary sources, and Moses's published accounts of what took place and what he thought.

19. Hilary Ballon and Kenneth T. Jackson, *Robert Moses and the Modern City: The Transformation of New York* (New York: Norton, 2007), 158–60, 222–23.

20. Robert Moses, *26 Years of Parks Progress: 1934–1960* (New York: Department of Parks, 1960), 52–53.

21. Robert Moses, *Public Works: A Dangerous Trade* (New York: McGraw-Hill, 1970), 928–30.

22. Cleveland Rodgers, *Robert Moses: Builder for Democracy* (New York: Henry Holt and Company, 1952), 38–39.

23. Robert Moses, *La Guardia: A Salute and a Memoir* (New York: Simon and Schuster, 1957), 31–35.

24. In a conversation with the mayor's son, the late Robert F. "Bobby" Wagner, Jr. (my boss between 1978 and 1980 and a good friend), I learned that during the summer of 1956 his father summoned the chairmen of the City Planning Commission, the Housing Authority, and the commissioner of real estate to his summer house. There, on the porch, they plotted what eventually led to Moses's departure from city government.

25. Jeanne R. Lowe, *Cities in a Race with Time* (New York: Random House, 1967), 45–109.

26. Robert Moses, "New Highways for a Better New York," *New York Times*, November 11, 1945.

27. Robert Moses, "Comment on a New Yorker Profile and Biography," August 26, 1974.

28. Robert Moses, *Working for the People* (New York: Harper & Brothers, 1956), 1.

29. Robert Moses, "The Budget Must Go Up," an open letter to Lazarus Joseph, Comptroller of the City of New York, *The Atlantic*, November 1951.

30. Rodgers, *Robert Moses*, 83–84.

31. Moses, *Public Works*, 98.

32. Robert Moses, "The Building of Jones Beach," lecture to the Freeport Historical Society (February 26, 1974); transcript appears in *Robert Moses: Single-Minded Genius*, ed. Joann P. Krieg (Hempstead, NY: Long Island Studies Institute, 1989), 135.

33. Moses, *Public Works*, 78.

34. Ibid., 134.

35. Ibid., 3

36. Moses, *Working for the People*, 156

37. Rodgers, *Robert Moses*, 84; Moses, *Working for the People*, 136; http://www.usinflationcalculator.com.

38. Moses, *Public Works*, 686

39. Alexander Garvin, *Public Parks: The Key to Livable Communities* (New York: Norton, 2011), 29–31, 33–55

40. Moses, *Public Works*, 79.

41. John Hane, *Jones Beach: An Illustrated History* (Guilford, CT: Globe Pequot, 2007), 3.

42. Moses, *Public Works*, 85.

43. "To Add 2000 Acres to State's Parks," *New York Times*, November 30, 1925.

44. U.S. Bureau of the Census, *1920 Census of Population and Housing* (Washington, DC).

45. U.S. Bureau of the Census, *2000 Census of Population and Housing* (Washington, DC).

46. Hanes, *Jones Beach*, 14–17.

47. Ibid., 17.

48. Rodgers, *Robert Moses*, 51; Hane, *Jones Beach*, 6–14; Caro, *The Power Broker*, 204–5.

49. Hane, *Jones Beach*, 7.

50. Moses, *Public Works*, 97.

51. Hane, *Jones Beach*, 8; Caro, *The Power Broker*, 205.

52. *New York Herald Tribune*, November 14, 1925, quoted in Moses, *Public Works*, 99.

53. Moses, *Public Works*, 114.

54. Moses, *Working for the People*, 160–61

55. Ballon and Jackson, *Moses and the Modern City*, 142–43.

56. City of New York Department of Parks, *The Future of Jamaica Bay* (New York: City of New York Department of Parks, 1938).

57. Kenneth T. Jackson, "Robert Moses and the Planned Environment: A Re-Evaluation," in *Robert Moses: Single-Minded Genius*, ed. Joann P. Krieg (Hempstead, NY: Long Island Studies Institute, 1989), 21.

58. "Moses Gives Plan to End Bad Odors," *New York Times*, July 23, 1948.

59. http://www.nycgovparks.org/sub_about/parks_history/recreationcenters.html

60. City of New York Department of Parks, *26 Years of Progress: 1934–1960* (New York: 1960), 29.

61. Bruce E. Seely, *Building the American Highway System: Engineers as Policy Makers* (Philadelphia: Temple University Press, 1987), 25.

62. "New York's Motor Census," *New York Times*, January 8, 1922.

63. Ballon and Jackson, *Robert Moses and the Modern City*, 230–31.

64. Ibid.

65. Seely, *Building the American Highway System*, 151.

66. Moses, *Public Works*, 163.

67. Ibid., 162.

68. Ballon and Jackson, *Robert Moses and the Modern City*, 230.

69. Moses, *Public Works*, 163–64.

70. Ballon and Jackson, *Robert Moses and the Modern City*, 231.

71. Owen Gutfriend, "Rebuilding New York in the Auto Age," in Hilary Ballon and Kenneth T. Jackson, *Robert Moses and the Modern City: The Transformation of New*

York (New York: Norton, 2007), 89; Robert Moses, "New York Opens Bottlenecks," *New York Times*, October 13, 1940; Moses, *Public Works*, 197.

72. Christopher Tunnard and Boris Pushkarev, *Man-Made America: Chaos or Control* (New Haven: Yale University Press, 1963), 157–275.

73. Garvin, *Public Parks*, 137–42.

74. Gilmore D. Clarke, "The Parkway Ideal," in *The Highway and the Landscape*, ed. W. Brewster Snow (New Bruswick: Rutgers University Press, 1959), 38.

75. Robert Moses, *Six Years of Parks Progress* (New York: Department of Parks, 1940), 10.

76. "Moses Opens Fire on Regional Plan," *New York Times*, July 2, 1938.

77. Owen Gutfreund, "The Path of Prosperity: New York City's East River Drive, 1922–1990," *Journal of Urban History* 21 (Thousand Oaks, CA: Sage Publications, 1995), 147–83.

78. "$75,000,000 Highway Backed by Engineer," *New York Times*, April 25, 1931.

79. Henrik Krogius, *The Brooklyn Heights Promenade* (Charleston: History Press, 2011), 24–28.

80. Ibid., 12–13.

81. Ibid., 52.

82. City Planning Commission, transcript of public hearing (New York: March 10, 1943).

83. "Brooklyn To Get 46 New Play Areas," *New York Times*, November 3, 1949.

84. "Expressway Plan of City Cut in Half," *New York Times*, January 10, 1949.

85. "Moses Threatens to Halt Bronx Job," *New York Times*, March 12, 1953.

86. Charles C. Bennett, "Bronx Expressway Project Has Estimate Board Fuming," *New York Times*, April 24, 1953.

87. "Moses Threatens to Halt Bronx Job," *New York Times*, March 12, 1953.

88. Charles C. Bennett, "Bronx Expressway Route Approved to 'Demagogue,' 'Blackmail' Cries," *New York Times*, May 15, 1953.

89. Ballon and Jackson, *Robert Moses and the Modern City*, 212–14.

90. Richard P. Hunt, "Expressway Vote Delayed by City," *New York Times*, December 7, 1962.

91. Charles G. Bennett, "Expressway Plan Revived by Moses," *New York Times*, April 13, 1963.

92. "Expressway Goes Off City Map," *New York Times*, August 22, 1969.

93. Tunnard and Pushkarev, *Man-Made America*, 160–201.

94. Robert Moses, "New Highways for a Better New York," *New York Times*, November 11, 1945.

95. Alexander Garvin, *The American City: What Works, What Doesn't* (New York: McGraw-Hill, 2002), 230–33; 248–49.

96. http://www.nyc.gov/html/nycha/html/about/factsheet.shtml.

97. Robert Moses, "Housing or Riots," *Newsday*, January 27, 1968.

98. Nathan Sobel, *Community Development Program Progress Report, 1968* (New York: Housing and Development Administration, 1968), 320; Committee on Slum Clearance, "Title I Slum Clearance Progress," (New York: reports dated April 16, 1956, September 30, 1958, and April 1959).

99. Jeanne R. Lowe, *Cities in a Race With Time* (New York: Random House, 1967), 75–77.

100. Daniel Okrent, *Great Fortune: The Epic of Rockefeller Center* (New York: Viking, 2003), 27–28, 67–68; Victoria Newhouse, *Wallace K. Harrison: Architect* (New York: Rizzoli, 1989), 198–204.

101. Moses, *Public Works*, 516.

102. Samuel Zipp, *Manhattan Projects: The Rise and Fall of Urban Renewal in Cold War New York* (New York: Oxford University Press, 2010), 174.

103. Garvin, *The American City*, 93.

104. Zipp, 214–15.

105. Ibid., 197–249.

106. Sobel, *Progress Report, 1968*, 105–16.

107. J. Anthony Panuch, *Relocation in New York* (New York: Office of the Mayor, 1959), 52; J. Anthony Panuch, *Building A Better New York* (New York: Office of the Mayor, 1960), 112.

108. Zipp, *Manhattan Projects*, 164.

109. Committee on Slum Clearance, "New York City Title I Progress" (New York: 1959), 2.

110. Sobel, *Progress Report, 1968*, 19–249.

111. New York City Planning Commission, *Public and Publicly Aided Housing 1921–1972* (New York: 1973), 25; New York City Planning Commission, *New Dwelling Units Completed 1927–1973* (New York:1974), 128. These projects included buildings that were completed during the years after Moses had left city government.

112. Sobel, *Progress Report, 1968*, 320; New York City Planning Commission, *New Dwelling Units Completed 1921–1972* (New York: 1973), 25.

113. "On the Governor's Plan to Eliminate Redevelopment Agencies," *San Francisco Chronicle*, March 27, 2011, F-10.

7. REINVENTING DOWNTOWN PHILADELPHIA

1. Center City District & Central Philadelphia Development Corporation, "State of Center City Philadelphia 2010" (Philadelphia: 2011).

2. U.S. Bureau of Labor Statistics, "Occupational Wage Survey, Philadelphia, Pennsylvania, May 1950," *Bulletin No. 1008* (Washington, DC: Government Printing Office).

3. Peter McCaffery, *When Bosses Ruled Philadelphia: The Emergence of the Republican Machine, 1867–1933*

(University Park: Pennsylvania State University Press, 1993), 264.

4. "Philadelphia's Hole," *Time*, January 8, 1940.

5. John Guinther, *The Direction of Cities* (New York: Viking Penguin, 1996), 87.

6. Gregory L. Heller, "Biography of Edmund N. Bacon" (working title; unpublished manuscript, January 2010).

7. John Andrew Gallery, *The Planning of Center City Philadelphia from William Penn to the Present* (Philadelphia: Center for Architecture, 2007), 27.

8. Edmund Bacon, letter to Alexander Garvin, October 6, 1998.

9. Edmund Bacon, presentation at a conference sponsored by the Forum for Urban Design, then known as the Institute for Urban Design (New York: February 22, 1988).

10. Walter Moody, *What of the City?* (Chicago: A. C. McClurg & Co., 1919), 33.

11. Edmund Bacon, "New World Cities: Architecture and Townscape," in *American Civilization*, ed. Daniel J. Boorstin (New York: McGraw-Hill, 1972), 226, 231.

12. There is no known source for this quotation, but it is always attributed to Daniel Burnham. It is quoted in a 1918 Christmas card from Willis Polk to Edward Bennett as a statement made by Burnham in 1907.

13. Heller, "Biography of Edmund N. Bacon."

14. Ibid.

15. Ibid.

16. Gallery, *Planning of Center City*, 21–25.

17. Edmund Bacon, interview with the author, May 28, 2003.

18. Constance M. Greiff, *Independence: The Creation of a National Park* (Philadelphia: University of Pennsylvania Press, 1987), 48.

19. Ibid., 46–60.

20. Gallery, *Planning of Center City* , 37.

21. Ibid., 33; Gregory Heller, "Salesman of Ideas: The Life Experiences That Shaped Edmund Bacon," in *Imagining Philadelphia: Edmund Bacon and the Future of Philadelphia*, ed. Scott Gabriel Knowles (Philadelphia: University of Pennsylvania Press, 2009), 28–31.

22. David Clow, "The 1947 Better Philadelphia Exhibition: An Historic Turning Point," a paper presented at the Second National Conference on American Planning History (unpublished, September 25, 1987).

23. Edmund Bacon, interview with the author, September 26, 1998.

24. George Wilson, *Yesterday's Philadelphia* (Miami: E. A. Seemann, 1975), 86–87; H. W. Schotter, *History of the Pennsylvania Railroad* (Philadelphia: Allen, Lane & Scott, 1927), 200, 390.

25. Alexander Garvin, *The American City: What Works, What Doesn't*, 2nd ed. (New York: McGraw-Hill, 2002), 381–82.

26. Alexander Garvin, "Philadelphia's Planner: A Conversation with Edmund Bacon," *Journal of Planning History* 1, no. 1, (February 2002), 77.

27. Sam Ryerson, "Five Roads: Edmund Bacon's Philadelphia Highways," (unpublished manuscript, 2001).

28. Michelle Osborne, "The Crosstown Is Dead: Long Live the Crosstown?" *Architectural Forum* (October 1971), 40.

29. Center City District & Central Philadelphia Development Corporation, "Center City Reports: Sidewalk Cafés" (Philadelphia: July 2009), 4.

30. Gregory Heller, "Salesman of Ideas," 39–42.

31. Guian McKee, "A Utopian, a Utopianist, or Whatever the Heck It Is: Edmund Bacon and the Complexity of the City," in *Imagining Philadelphia: Edmund Bacon and the Future of Philadelphia*, ed. Scott Gabriel Knowles (Philadelphia: University of Pennsylvania Press, 2009), 53–66; Kirk R. Petshek, *The Challenge of Urban Reform: Policies and Programs in Philadelphia* (Philadelphia: Temple University Press, 1973), 91–99.

32. Edmund Bacon, "Philadelphia in the Year 2009," in *Imagining Philadelphia: Edmund Bacon and the Future of Philadelphia*, ed. Scott Gabriel Knowles (Philadelphia: University of Pennsylvania Press, 2009), 9.

33. Garvin, "Philadelphia's Planner," 69.

34. Heller, "Biography of Edmund N. Bacon."

35. Edmund Bacon, interview with the author, November 22, 1998.

36. Edmund Bacon and Gregory Heller, "Making the Future Real" (unpublished, c. 2004), 38.

37. Ibid.

38. Edmund Bacon, letter to Alexander Garvin, December 7, 1998.

39. Guinther, *The Direction of Cities*, 148.

40. Peter A. Evans, *Philadelphia Gets a Heart Transplant: The Evolution of Penn Center* (unpublished, 1977), 21.

41. Heller, "Biography of Edmund N. Bacon."

42. Bacon and Heller, "Making the Future Real," 43.

43. Guinther, *The Direction of Cities*, 152.

44. Bacon and Heller, "Making the Future Real," 46.

45. "Dream of Penn Center Being Realized, Planner Feels," *Philadelphia Evening Bulletin*, August 28, 1959.

46. Heller, "Biography of Edmund N. Bacon."

47. Edmund Bacon, interview with the author, November 22, 1998.

48. Petshek, *Challenge of Urban Reform*, 220–25.

49. Paul R. Levy, "Introduction: Establishing the Context," in *OPDC CPDC 50 Years Remaking Center City* (Philadelphia: Central Philadelphia Development Corporation, 2006), vii.

50. Edmund Bacon, "Philadelphia: Tradition or Progress," in Fairmount Park Art Association, *One-Hundred-and-Fourth Annual Report* (Philadelphia: 1976), 23.

51. Petshek, *Challenge of Urban Reform*, 185.

52. Ibid., 188–91.

53. I have excluded the fourth section, south of Pine

Street, that includes the Head House Market and retail stores, as well as some housing.

54. Edmund Bacon, "A Case Study in Urban Design," *Journal of the American Institute of Planners* XXVI, no. 3 (August 1960), 224–35.

55. Richardson Dilworth, in CPDC, *50 Years Remaking Center City*, 7.

56. Jeanne Lowe, *Cities in a Race with Time* (New York: Random House, 1967), 348.

57. Edmund Bacon, interview with author, September 26, 1998.

58. Jack Robin, in CPDC, *50 Years Remaking Center City*, 3.

59. Center City District, communication of February 11, 2011.

60. U.S. Bureau of the Census, *1950 Census of Population and Housing* (Washington, DC).

61. U.S. Bureau of the Census, *2000 Census of Population and Housing* (Washington, DC).

62. U.S. Department of Housing and Urban Development, "Relocation Estimates for Washington Square East," (unpublished, 1979); Armand LeGardeur, "The Washington Square East Renewal Project: Rehabilitation as an Alternative Form of Renewal," (unpublished, 1978), 16, 28; Philadelphia Redevelopment Authority, *Annual Report*, 1970; U.S. Department of Housing and Urban Development, *Report 666 on Relocation of Families and Individuals*, 1970.

63. Urban Land Institute, "Financial Background for Washington Square East (Society Hill) Renewal Project," (Washington, DC: July 1981).

64. Redevelopment Authority of the City of Philadelphia, Pennsylvania, *The Amended Urban Renewal Plan for Washington Square East Urban Renewal Area* (Philadelphia: June 13, 1958, revised July 1970), 10A.

65. Levy, "Introduction," vi.

66. Department of Commerce, *U.S. Census of Retail Trade*.

67. ULI Research Division with Gladstone Associates, *Joint Development: Making the Real Estate–Transit Connection* (Washington, DC: Urban Land Institute, 1979), 39.

68. Heller, "Biography of Edmund N. Bacon."

69. Edmund Bacon, *The Design of Cities* (New York: Viking Press, 1967), 253.

70. Heller, "Biography of Edmund N. Bacon."

71. Ibid.

72. ULI Research Division with Gladstone Associates, *Joint Development*, 39.

73. Heller, "Biography of Edmund N. Bacon."

74. Joshua Olsen, *Better Places, Better Lives: A Biography of James Rouse* (Washington, DC: Urban Land Institute, 2003), 250.

75. ULI Research Division with Gladstone Associates, *Joint Development*, 35, 46.

76. Olsen, *Better Places, Better Lives*, 262.

77. ULI Research Division with Gladstone Associates, *Joint Development*, 56.

78. Heller, "Biography of Edmund N. Bacon."

79. Ibid.

80. Ibid.

81. Nancy Love, "Paradise Lost," *Philadelphia*, July 1968, 99.

82. Edmund Bacon, interview with the author, November 22, 1998.

83. Howard Kozloff and James Schoder, "Business Improvement Districts (BIDS): Changing the Faces of Cities," *Next American City* 11 (Summer 2006), http://americancity.org/magazine/article/web-exclusive-kozloff/.

84. http://www.centercityphila.org/.

85. Ibid.

86. Center City District & Central Philadelphia Development Corporation, *Center City: Planning for Growth, 2007–2012* (Philadelphia: 2007), 22.

87. Central City District & Central Philadelphia Development Corporation, *State of Center City Philadelphia 2010* (Philadelphia: 2010), 1.

88. Ibid., 23.

89. Ibid., 1–66.

8. PLAYING THE PLANNING GAME IN THE TWENTY-FIRST CENTURY

1. "A Survey of Chicago: A Success Story," *The Economist*, March 16, 2006.

2. Central City District & Central Philadelphia Development Corporation, *State of Center City Philadelphia 2010* (Philadelphia: 2010), 3.

3. Daniel Burnham, "A City of the Future Under a Democratic Government," *Transactions of the Town Planning Conference* (London: Royal Institute of British Architects, October, 1910), 378.

4. Edmund Bacon, interview with the author, September 26, 1998.

5. Walter Moody, *What of the City?* (Chicago: A. C. McClurg & Co., 1919), 34.

6. Edmund Bacon, interview with the author, July 11, 2001.

7. Thomas S. Hines, *Burnham of Chicago* (New York: Oxford University Press, 1974), 269.

8. Robert Moses, "The Budget Must Go Up," an open letter to Lazarus Joseph, Comptroller of the City of New York, *The Atlantic*, November 1951.

9. Ibid.

10. Cleveland Rodgers, *Robert Moses: Builder for Democracy* (New York: Henry Holt, 1952), 83–84.

11. Edmund Bacon, interview with the author, November 22, 1998.

PHOTO CREDITS

All photographs and maps are by the author except on the the following pages:

12 (top to bottom) Walter Moody, *What of the City* (Chicago: A. C. McClurg & Co., 1919); Daniel Burnham and Edward Bennett, *Plan of Chicago* (1909; repr., New York: Da Capo Press, 1970)

22 Library of Congress, Prints & Photographs Division, Paul Rudolph Collection

23 (top) Courtesy of the National Park Service, Frederick Law Olmsted National Historic Site

25 (lower left) Ebenezer Howard, *Garden Cities of Tomorrow* (1898; repr., Cambridge, MA, MIT Press, 1965)

26 (top and bottom) *Artists Rights Society [ARS]/SPADEM, 1995, Paris*

28 The Museum of the City of New York, Jacob Riis Collection

35 Courtesy of Duany Plater-Zyberk & Co.

50 Boston Redevelopment Authority

67 Charles Marville, *Paris photographie au temps d'Haussmann* (Paris: Les Editions du Mecene, 2003)

69 Cham [Amédée de Noé], *Croquis Contemporains*, Paris, c. 1860.

75 (top) Marville, *Paris Photographie Au Temps d'Haussmann*

80 (bottom) Edmund Texier, *Tableau de Paris*, Paris, 1852

84 (top left) Adolphe Alphand, *Les Promenades de Paris* (1873; repr., Paris: Conaissance et Mémoires, 2002)

99 R. Reid Badger, *The Great American Fair* (Chicago: Nelson Hall, 1979)

101 Moody, *What of the City*

102 Moody, *What of the City*

104 Burnham and Bennett, *Plan of Chicago*

105 (left) Courtesy of Chicago Cartographics; (right) Burnham and Bennett, *Plan of Chicago*

106 (top) Moody, *What of the City*; (center) Burnham and Bennett, *Plan of Chicago*; (bottom) Moody, *What of the City*

107 (top) Moody, *What of the City* (bottom) Burnham and Bennett, *Plan of Chicago*

108 (top left) Chicago Historical Society; (bottom right) Chicago Historical Society; (top right) Chicago Historical Society

109 (top right) Burnham and Bennett, *Plan of Chicago*

112 (top and opposite) Burnham and Bennett, *Plan of Chicago*

114 Burnham and Bennett, *Plan of Chicago*

115 (bottom) Burnham and Bennett, *Plan of Chicago*

116 Burnham and Bennett, *Plan of Chicago*

117 (top) Moody, *What of the City*

125 Committee on the City Plan, *Development and Present Status of City Planning in New York City*, City of New York, Board of Estimate and Apportionment, Committee on the City Plan, New York, 1914

127 (top left and right) Regional Plan Association

133 City of New York/Parks and Recreation

159 (all) Committee on Slum Clearance Plans, *South Village*, New York, January 1951

167 Edmund N. Bacon Collection, The Architectural Arch-ives, University of Pennsylvania

169 Esto Photographics Inc.

170 Esto Photographics Inc.

171 (right) Used with permission of *Philadelphia Inquirer*, LLC Copyright© 2012. All rights reserved

172 (bottom) Philadelphia Planning Commission

INDEX